WITHDRAWN

CLIENT PARTICIPATION IN HUMAN SERVICES

CLIENT PARTICIPATION IN HUMAN SERVICES

The Prometheus Principle

Edited by

CONSTANCE T. FISCHER
and
STANLEY L. BRODSKY

Transaction Books
New Brunswick, New Jersey

Copyright © 1978 by Transaction, Inc.
New Brunswick, New Jersey 08903

All rights reserved under International and Pan-American Copyright
Conventions. No part of this book may be reproduced or transmitted in
any form or by any means, electronic or mechanical, including
photocopy, recording, or any information storage and retrieval system,
without prior permission in writing from the publisher. All inquiries
should be addressed to Transaction Books, Rutgers—The State
University, New Brunswick, New Jersey 08903.

Library of Congress Catalog Number: 76-1772
ISBN: 0-87855-131-X (cloth)
Printed in the United States of America.

Library of Congress Cataloging in Publication Data

Main entry under title:

Client participation in human services.

    Includes bibliographies and index.
    1. Social service—Citizen participation— Addresses, essays,
lectures. I. Fischer, Constance T., 1938- II. Brodsky, Stanley L., 1939-
HV41.C544   362   76-1772
ISBN 0-87855-131-X

215016

362
C636f

Contents

Preface

The Prometheus principle asserts that if a citizen is to make optimal use of the human service professions, he must be enfranchised to participate actively both in the gathering and evaluation of information, and then in subsequent decision making and reckoning. In the present volume, this "informed participation" or "client collaboration" is not regarded as cut-and-dry prescription; neither is it seen as some kind of ultimate panacea. Instead, it is offered as a challenging and guiding standard for the development of responsible practices.

The authors of the following chapters are all both workers and teachers in human service fields. While sharing a belief in the Prometheus principle, we differ among ourselves in professional areas, theoretical orientation, and personal style. Thus, although each chapter is self-contained, all of them complement, modify, and extend one another.

Every author presents a brief overview of the contemporary status of informed participation in his or her field (specifically: mental retardation, psychological assessment, industrial consultation, classroom teaching, psychiatry, prison management, psychotherapy, medical treatment, pupil records, psychological experimentation, and due process). Then he or she concentrates on concrete implementation of the Prometheus principle, including both actualized and proposed practices. Overall, we have attempted to be as practical as we are enthusiastic and idealistic.

We wrote this volume to share our goals and experiences with persons involved with the human service professions. It is designed to serve as a textbook for those preparing to enter, and as a resource for those with established practice in, psychology, casework, education, counseling, and their related specializations. These efforts will be equally of interest to the growing number of consumers who seek a voice in the nature and delivery of human services. Reform in these services calls for changes in expectations and goals by both professionals and clients; it is this objective toward which we reach.

Introduction

THE PROMETHEUS PRINCIPLE

Prometheus was a Titan (a half god) who, according to legend, defied Zeus by providing man with protective and creative power. Specifically, it was Prometheus (whose name signified forethought, or wisdom) who gave man upright posture, with its gifts of vision and perspective. Moreover, he stole for man the gods' secret of fire, thus furthering man's possibilities of knowledge, protection, and power.

Zeus condemned this treason by chaining Prometheus to a boulder, where eagles were to feast eternally upon his liver. This punishment was severe and prolonged, but Prometheus maintained his compassion for man above loyalty to Zeus, and eventually was freed by Hercules, the strongest of men and a son of Zeus.

The subject of this book is the sharing of knowledge and power. The Prometheus principle is: *knowledge, power, and responsibility should be shared by all parties engaged in offering human services with those receiving such services.*

The analogy to Olympus is deliberate. Those professionals who wield authority and decision-making power in medicine, psychology, education, industry, and other societal institutions often act in detached and isolated ways in regard to their clients. Events that vitally concern the lives of clients frequently are kept from them. Decisions with elements of risk and uncertainty are made unilaterally. Too often clients have inadequate knowledge about professional practices affecting their welfare; and they are seldom permitted fully informed ways of participating in decisions about the services to be rendered to them.

There is no malicious plot or insidious conspiracy by professionals and authorities to keep clients ignorant or dependent (although this is clearly one result). Rather, the present day Olympians are carrying out the tradition they were taught; they do what they know. The physician, the schoolteacher, and the administrator of an institution for the mentally retarded all typically exercise the role of benevolent ruler over their charges. Indeed, they do seek to be benevolent in their stated purposes, in programming, and to some extent, in their results. But they are rulers, too! They are the authorities, the sole judges of the appropriateness of their own actions in regard to clients. It is a rare citizen, patient, pupil, or institutionalized "retardate" who successfully challenges such rulers.

The Prometheus principle asserts that ruler-subject relationships are inappropriate in any offering of human services. The autocracy of professional power should be revised toward the democracy of full client partnership—sharing and working together. This goal is not easily achieved; indeed, collaboration is a *"laboring together"* (from the Latin, *collaborare*). Moreover, the route is hazardous, to professional and client alike. The current day equivalents of being pecked by eagles while chained to a rock, and of being burned by fire, are dangers all Litterans assume. Practice of the shared use of knowledge must be developed carefully and well.

PROMETHEUS ON THE ROAD

The legend of Prometheus never reported what happened after Hercules unchained him. It seems to us that Prometheus is alive and well and loose on the land. This book follows his tracks, in a dozen different fields, describing efforts by professionals to share knowledge and power. The relatively heavy representation here of psychology-related human services reflects the interests of the editors as well as current areas of successful social action. Prometheus has, however, also ventured into other human services and into government and business as well.

Our first chapter is an introductory one describing the role of technology in bringing America to its emerging awareness of the necessity for informed participation. Then Douglas Biklen's chapter vividly introduces the need for Promethean reform through a case study of an institutionalized "retardate," for whom records have been unintentionally but clearly and powerfully destructive. Suggestions for positive record keeping are specified. In the next chapter, Constance Fischer details practices through which the client collaborates in his own psychological assessment, from situating the referral to reading and amending the final report. Along the way, the client tries out alternative ways of being, brings in his Involved Others as consultants, and participates in formulating concrete plans for continued growth.

Consecutive chapters then address the "care-taking" professions of psychotherapy, institutional psychiatry, and medicine. Through detailed analyses of assumptions and practices of psychotherapy, Donald Bersoff strongly criticizes the coercive aspects of traditional therapy. He also challenges the newer behavioral therapies to dare to promote truly reciprocal influence. Finally, Bersoff reviews recent protections of the client's initiative in therapy, and makes some provocative proposals of his own. Ernest Keen's chapter provides an explicit theoretical framework for understanding how society, through its psychiatric institutions, violates the individuality and belongingness of its "losers." The chapter reviews recent innovations in psychiatric hospitals, community clinics, and underground psychiatry in terms of their successes and failures in reestablishing mutual obligation among all citizens. Rose Marie Parse then provides a straightforward review of proposals for protecting the rights of medical patients, particularly the "right to know." She supports in-hospital patient advocacy programs as well as formal development of nursing as the profession that must ensure that patients understand both what they are told and that they are entitled to ask about whatever else they must understand to carry out instructions or to make decisions.

The next three chapters deal with "captive clients"—prisoners and students. Stanley Brodsky advocates transformation of prisoners' role from that of passive recipients to participant managers of their programs. Existing steps in this direction are reported, and further innovations—such as prisoner access to files, consumer evaluation of treatment programs and grant applications, and offenders as paid treators of other offenders—are proposed. Rolf von Eckartsberg then provides an explicitly theoretical framework for Promethean practices in the classroom. The teacher provides for continuation of accumulated knowledge by addressing it to students' experiential biographies; from that ground conceptual articulation develops. In this process, students *and* teacher find a reciprocity of understandings: both learn. In her half of the chapter on classroom teaching, Mary Chisholm presents a case history of a college sociology course that embodies this reciprocity and mutuality. The chapter's halves may be read in either order. The third chapter in this trio is about the keeping of public school records. Leo Goldman overviews recent sources of criticism, and then identifies and directly questions such traditional assumptions as that schools know better than parents what is best for the child, that more information is better than less, that (public) school records are public property, and that the student becomes a client when addressed by counselors. Dr. Goldman's concluding recommendations are clear-cut, concrete, and practical.

The next two chapters find Prometheus traveling in areas that are typically bypassed by proponents of informed participation. Leslie Krieger succinctly describes three innovative programs actually conducted by a corporation of psychological consultants to industry. In the first, the job candidate participates in structuring test procedures and interpreting test data. The same practice is followed with groups of employees in a research project within an industrial firm. Third, an employee career counseling program supports employees' efforts to advance or travel within the company, while allowing them the option of whether to share the counseling report with the company. Robert Sardello's chapter documents experimental psychology's growing awareness that both the experimenter and research subject are persons rather than objects. Traditional psychology attempts to eliminate this *personal* influence, while a visionary psychology attempts to develop a foundation adequate to man's personhood. Dr. Sardello presents just such a human psychology. A sample of its contemporary research illustrates the principle that violation of the subjects' lived experience is a contamination of the research.

The concluding chapter attempts to address readers' questions by presenting our responses to the kinds of inquiries and reservations that have been posed to us at symposia, workshops, and various presentations.

All of us who have worked on this volume, as we look for possibilities of informed participation by clients with all manner of official authorities, have discovered it to be feasible everywhere. But sharing of power between citizen and expert takes varying forms in different areas, and there are many personal ways of collaborating. Knowing that tested procedures and concrete suggestions are more constructive than arguments alone, we hope that this book will effectively indicate to citizens the quality of services they could receive. To professionals we hope to indicate a range of alternative work styles, with accompanying rationale. Moreover, we trust that through our travels with Prometheus, fellow professionals will find courage to continue these journies in still other directions. The paths are rough but lead to the excitement and joy of important work well done.

1.

Informed Participation: Why Now?

CONSTANCE T. FISCHER and
STANLEY L. BRODSKY

Our authors hold theoretical orientations as diverse as behaviorism and existentialism. Some are interested primarily in philosophical foundations, others in everyday practices. Their professional identifications range from nursing and sociology through various education and psychology-related fields. Yet they all converge in the common cause of developing the Prometheus principle. Despite diverse backgrounds, interests, and styles, as well as client specialization, they univocally support the right of every individual to informed participation in the shaping of his future, both personal and societal. They all see this right as including access not only to professional interpretations of "data," but to that actual information and to the methods and rationales underlying its collection. Moreover, our authors all agree that informed participation includes the right to engage with one's would-be helpers in formulating and implementing decisions about one's life, whether these plans deal with oneself alone or with the environment shared with others.

How is it that this Promethean principle comes to be voiced at this particular juncture in the histories of our country and our professions?

1

WHY THE PROMETHEUS PRINCIPLE ARISES
AT THIS TIME

The necessary conditions for the emergence of the Prometheus principle can be viewed through the growth of modern technology. In partially releasing people from labor, this technology has afforded an ever-increasing number of citizens the occasion to reflect on the course of our society's history. Higher levels of basic formal education have provided skills for acquiring and examining information.

Contemporary media continue this education, but with special impact. Not only are we provided with "factual" information, we also begin to discover that all events occur in particular contexts. "Facts" are no longer isolable truths in themselves. Indeed, truth is composed of multiple perspectives. Not only political leaders but other professional experts are now understood as limited and as motivated in what they present as fact. We watch heads of state on "Face the Nation" as they misrepresent some information, misunderstand the intended implication of a question, contort to avoid offending allies. We see that they are just people, like you and me, not just potentially corruptible, but also restricted by personal style and by their own shortsightedness. We have watched medical doctors on the "David Susskind Show" and they too impress us more in terms of conflicting personalities and vested interests than in terms of their presumed expertise. They cannot even agree about whether low carbohydrate diets work. And then there are all those blithely earnest commercials each insisting that this brand of deodorant protects better than any other; indeed, the implied message is that this brand will promote financial success, charm, confidence, and sex appeal. So there are no immutable facts simply to be accepted; the citizen discovers that he must evaluate the "facts" and their presenters for himself.

We also watch instant satellite coverage of moon landings, Olympic competition, and summit meetings. Our homes are permeated with starving Biafran infants, American POWs marched through North Vietnam, a tarred Irish bride. Militants—black, woman, gay, poor—confront us on the livingroom television and the car radio with our part in perpetuating their grievances. On the happier side, Charles Kuralt brings us back to our heritage of small town hoedowns, solitary mountain dwellings, and cracker-barrel conversation. Travelogs, sports coverage, and human interest spots fill out our daily participation—wanted or not—in the larger community of man. Parochialism in the sense of constricted vision is on the wane.

The media—television, radio, movies, and print—tell us that we could all travel by air, live in expensive houses, and dress beautifully. The rich do not appear to have done anything spectacular to deserve their status. Their world does not seem foreign, distant, or unreachable. After all, everyone who has attended a high school senior prom has worn a tuxedo or formal gown. "Everyone" owns a car, eats out, refers to political and sports figures by first name. The driver of a basic Ford can envision driving a Lincoln or Cadillac. The issue is no longer whether wealth and opportunity are accessible, but how often and to what extent. At least on occasion each of us feels that he deserves as much as others, and has a right of some sort to demand it.

In addition, technology has done its work so well that each succeeding generation inhabits a different world. Slowly we begin to acknowledge that letting technological developments go their own way is not necessarily progress. We see that the world we build in turn forms society. We are sadly bemused at the impact of the 1950s Hollywood versions of success and happiness. We worry about the influence on our youth of current television violence and child-directed marketing. We know that we must take an active part in forming our schools, the shape of our government, the quality of our physical environment. We know now that we are responsible for making our world.

Even contemporary philosophers of science, including the positivists, acknowledge that our would-be sciences *man*ufacture the "laws" of nature; order is not discovered, it is constructed (cf. Heisenberg 1960, Kuhn 1962, Toulmin 1953). While constructions like test scores, hypothetical dynamics, reductive causes, and other such scientistic esoterica can be helpful in achieving conceptual distance from human affairs, they are *not* more real, and certainly they are not more consensually objective than the everyday-life events from which they were originally derived. Further, conceptual nicety not withstanding, the crucial proving ground of academic constructions is precisely that ordinary daily life. Converging with this challenge to build human sciences that are adequate to the new realities is the McLuhan-type (1964) comprehension that electronic media have opened up a nonlinear consciousness. We are learning to trust the flow of our own impressions, no longer giving greater credence to textbooks, no longer accepting the authority of exclusive labels, classifications and categories, no longer feeling submissive in the face of belabored step-by-step syllogistic deductions. We are sensing that truth is found in multiple perspectives rather than in any one privileged viewpoint of self-proclaimed experts. Now we find ourselves obliged not only to create our own society, but to do so through consultation not so much with the old "objective" authorities as with participants in everyday life.

In the earlier days of industrialization, Freud identified the otherwise unspeakable rumblings of desire awakened by material possibility and by new juxtapositions of the privileged with the productive masses. Anger and fear, related to their (differing) repressed states, were indeed bodily (if not sexual) and difficult to conceptualize for both classes. Through his own application of mechanistic technology, Freud could be said to have collaborated with industrial evolution to bring about recognition and open actualization of our "sexuality and aggression." Popularizations of this Freudian unconscious participated in freeing us to struggle now with a new "unconscious"—our vague, troubled glimmering that we must as individuals find our own meanings and purposes. Currently this search is conducted in the realms of spirituality, interpersonal relations, and community. Some representative surface phenomena here are the human potential therapies such as sensitivity training, the Jesus people, the following of Eastern religions, the commune movement, decentralization of government, indeed the *Greening of America* in general. Conceptual versions of today's frustrated strivings include Maslow's (1967), metamotivations, Buber's (1958) I-Thou, Frankl's (1972) noögenic neurosis, Erikson's (1950) eighth stage of development, and Van den Berg's (1971) spiritual unconscious. Scientism, whose "subject" matter is objects, has no expertise to offer this search for human relevance, for individual and societal values. Modern technology has had its glorious day; it has now brought us to the point of having to construct a science that also takes account of man's inevitable engagement in the meanings of his environment. Freud and technology have participated in freeing us from hidden and absolute determinism.

The following themes, then, are among those that are becoming part of public as well as academic consciousness: the perspectival constitution of truth, the fallibility of professional experts, the status of daily affairs as the ultimate reality, the existence of a nonparochial community of man, the essential commonalities with the privileged—and the concomitant rights to those privileges, our world as largely manmade, and the search for personal values consonant with communal relevance. It happens that these themes are emerging more clearly just when technology's very success has placed us in crisis. We are acutely aware of the possibility of nuclear holocaust, as well as of destruction of environmental life-support via pollution, waste, the greed of "progress," and shortsightedness. We see now that wars too are manmade, and that they demand conscience as much as loyalty. We have classified drug abuse as a national problem, as members of all ages choose to "drop out" and self-destruct via Cope, Sleep-eez, amphetamines, and heroin. We face the possibility of revolution in some new version of Watts, campus rebellion, and assassination. Corporate and street crime escalate in tandem. Concomitantly, we face the possibility of repression in the form of government secrecy and new versions of the Chicago convention, Kent State, and the trials of the Seven, the Nine, and so on.

It is in this crisis that we have cast about for escape routes, for new directions. In crisis we recognize that we must dare now to be Promethean, to take from the old gods of preexisting truth and of clear and distinct categories, their power of unilateral judgment. In public hands that power is not as restrictive and divisive. No longer can the constructions of specialists take on the power of quasi forces (Habermas 1971) such as IQ, mental illness, personality traits, and even actuarial classifications, all of which have indeed divided and repressed our clientele. As new experts our task is to be aware of our own assumptions and involvements while we construct a more comprehensive science. We should utilize our power of understanding the situated and perspectival human coconstitution of reality in order to coordinate further understanding among differing parties; that is, the ultimate task of the new experts is to enhance individual expansion within a true but diversified community. Our Promethean torch is our willingness to serve as consultants to and with particular individuals or groups, rather than as objectively disinterested authorities on how clients fit our preestablished reductions and dispositional options.

THE NECESSITY OF THE PROMETHEUS PRINCIPLE

The principle of informed participation is already emerging and will continue to evolve on its own with or without such efforts as this book. But the prospect of increasingly chaotic and pained clamorings to be heard, to have a voice, requires that we make history advisedly rather than let it "happen."

The larger context of the Prometheus principle's emergence is our democratic tradition. That tradition includes self-determination, individual accountability, and respect for differences. It is precisely in countries like ours that the expectations of even greater personal opportunity sensitizes us to the danger of the fragmenting, mechanizing, dehumanizing processes of our other tradition—unilateral management of efficient production.

This danger is present not only in the assembly lines of factories, but in multiple choice examinations and in the conduct of rat-maze models of psychological research (Kvale 1973). The old experts on factory production, education, and psychological research all have shared an interest in prediction and control. Essential humanness has been seen as a problematic source of error whether for production of automobiles, classroom motivation, or the data of psychology experiments. The "object-ifying" attitude of all three interrelated groups has, in effect, maintained a strict division between manipulator and manipulated, teacher and taught, observer and observed. Society in general as well as its particular members is constricted by adherence to privileged unilateral perspectives, whether expressed as profit margin equations or laboratory-derived learning axioms. Where this occurs, democracy gives way to technology as our actual form of government.

There is, however, another option—that of informed participation between professionals and workers, clients, students, and subjects. Both democracy *and* efficient production would be jointly served by transforming unilateral management to that of *discourse* and *consent*. Through the Prometheus principle, then, we can "make history advisedly," raising the hope and fostering the cooperation that are necessary for relatively smooth transition into common practice of informed participation.

Societal Readiness

The Prometheus principle's time seems to have come, not only in the sense of a need for it, but in society's readiness to embrace it. By giving the name "Prometheus principle" to the ideal of informed participation, we encourage a focused, planned, constructive coordination of current developments.

Already manpower problems in education and mental health have led to the utilization of everyday citizens as "paraprofessional" workers. The success of these groups has given additional confidence to antiintellectualism and antielitism trends. All across the country everyday people are taking community matters into their own hands—establishing open schools, free clinics, contract education, folk masses, televised coverage of local government meetings, open hearings, community ecology centers, sit-ins and demonstrations, increased strikes. Similarly, both the tax-paying middle class and pride-paying welfare recipients are eager to transform welfare's bureaucratic paternalism into self-help opportunities.

Governments and foundations are now reluctant to support scientist interest groups and their "pure research." Scientists and other "intellectuals" isolated from lower-class existence must now demonstrate that their underwritten livelihood makes a difference to public life. Expertise in esoterica no longer counts so much more than direct service. Competence is increasingly judged by effectiveness in dealing with diverse individuals, rather than by the old credentials of academic degree, licensing, publication, family connections, and so on.

Another notable example of societal readiness to embrace the Prometheus principle is the demise of the medical model of "mental illness." Granted, that demise is more apparent in the literature of "mental health" professionals than in their practice. Nevertheless, there is growing public recognition of the inevitable political aspects of institutions that are empowered to direct the course of lives. Halleck's work, *The Politics of Therapy* (1971); Laing's *Sanity, Madness, and the Family* (with Esterson 1964) and *The Politics of Experience* (1967); and Szasz's *The Myth of Mental Illness* (1961) and *The Manufacture of Madness* (1970), for example, are now popular paperback literature. Likewise, the wide distribution of *The Teachings of Don Juan* (Castaneda 1968) reflects contemporary fascination not only with transformations of consciousness but also with the human constitution of individual reality and values. Resigned acceptance of *presumably necessary conditions* of life is giving way to hopeful *involvement in building new possibilities*.

Protection of Professional Interests

The principle of informed participation does not obviate a need for systematic researchers and helpers; some groups still must gather and perpetuate accumulated knowledge of practices, information, theories, controversies. They also must revise systems of understanding as well as promote constructive planning. The new experts, however, can no longer carry out these responsibilities in a unilateral manner. In the end, the practitioner and researcher bear responsibility for their profession's impact on the public. We must be more than mere technicians. We must live with life's ambiguity and complexity, foregoing the clarity, simplicity, and security of mechanistic reductions. Test scores and productions, diagnoses and traits do not "tell us" what should be done with a client. They are not more real than the daily life-events and perceptions that must be the ultimate level of discussion and collaboration with clients.

Even for those professionals who do not agree with the above formulation, or who are not particularly concerned with its vision of the community of man, current social and philosophy of science developments demand reforms in the interest of professional self-preservation. Thus far it has been the courts and legislatures that have finally initiated informed participation rights for juvenile delinquents, mental retardates, and college applicants. Community and consumer groups have given impetus to the current public health movement. The free clinics, hot lines, suicide centers, and Synanons are manned largely by volunteers and paraprofessionals. Professional helpers thus far are lagging behind.

The new public consciousness is quite capable of criticizing human service professionals for the discrepancy between their unilateral judgments and their codes of ethics—whose preambles generally honor the integrity and dignity of the individual client. In our reflective moments we recognize that without the ideal of individual autonomy, personhood is lost in the industrialized mass society. All the codes of ethics explicitly or implicitly affirm that personal growth requires the right to know. They also affirm that scientific organizations are not value-free in their orientation. And most literature, if not codes, documents that growth and well-being are comprised of and facilitated by openness, tolerance for ambiguity, and effort toward self-determination. Our mandate now is for *individualized service and consensual decisions.*

The human service professions are vulnerable to the immanent criticism that their theories and practices are based on physical sciences that were surpassed several decades ago by both physics and the philosophy of science. The latter recognize that rigor does not restrict investigators to material operationalism, and that even sciences rest on certain value systems and interests (cf. Habermas 1971, Radnitzky 1970). Up-to-date scholars thus can criticize the classifiers, categorizers, and other unilateral decision makers for being unaware that they coconstitute their data. More important, vociferous minority groups already are attacking the social divisiveness and discrimination that allows the reduction of differences into absolute distinctions, especially when these are presented as though being actual defects, disease, or deficiencies. Here the mandate is to forsake the myth of objective, externally evident truth, and in its place struggle with individual variations of human commonalities.

If for no higher reasons, the principle of informed participation must be followed by the service professions if they are to avoid public condemnation and subsequent obsolescence. Public interest groups now rightfully hold us accountable for our practices and effects. Competence with everyday life is beginning to count more than academic credentials and scientistic trappings. We must dare to be ordinary even while we take on the more complex task of dealing with consensual reality. In that effort effectiveness at anticipating and guiding should increase as clients and their consultants collaborate without paying obeisance to bureaucratic or scientific constructs.

The Need for Naming the Prometheus Principle

Crisis and change are the occasion of new language, and our society *is* critically located between freedom and increasing chaos and repression. A partial resolution to this critical situation is the practice of informed participation. The term "Prometheus principle" is calculated to provide an explicit alternative to reactionary language, that is, to point constructively into the future as it brings diverse parties into joint pursuit.

Naming the principle renders practices more visible, thus encouraging a joining of public and professional efforts. Perhaps too the reference to mythology and to Prometheus in particular may encourage higher ideals and expectations. The principle is indeed intended as a guide, an ideal to be approximated no matter how difficult the actual circumstances. In addition, the phrase may serve as a concrete and realizable goal for various action groups, thus raising hope and trust in the real change that a working democracy can afford.

If informed participation does become incorporated into the regular practices of the human services, then the Prometheus principle will have done its work and will no longer require a name. Like Prometheus, it would undergo only the fate of occasionally being mentioned in discussions of past adventures and misadventures.

REFERENCES

Buber, M. 1958. *I and thou*. New York: Scribner's.
Castaneda, C. 1968. *The teachings of Don Juan: a Yaqui way of knowledge*. New York: Ballantine.
Erikson, E. H. 1950. *Childhood and society*. New York: Norton.
Frankl, V. E. 1972. *Man's search for meaning: an introduction to logotherapy*. New York: Pocket Book Editions.
Habermas, J. 1971. *Knowledge and human interests*. Boston: Beacon Press.

Halleck, S. L. 1971. *The politics of therapy*. New York: Harper and Row.

Heisenberg, W. 1960. The representation of nature in contemporary physics. In *Symbolism in religion and literature*, ed. R. May. New York: George Braziller.

Kuhn, T. S. 1962. *The structure of scientific revolution*. Chicago: University of Chicago Press.

Kvale, S. 1973. The technological paradigm of psychological research. *J. Phenomenol. Psychol.* 3:143–60.

Laing, R. D. 1967. *The politics of experience*. New York: Pantheon.

Laing, R. D. and Esterson, A. 1964. *Sanity, madness, and the family: families of schizophrenics*. London: Tavistock.

Maslow, A. H. 1967. A theory of metamotivation: the biological rooting of the value-life. *J. Humanis. Psychol.* 7:2, 93–127.

McLuhan, M. 1964. *Understanding media*. New York: McGraw-Hill.

Radnitzky, G. 1970. *Contemporary schools of metascience*. Oslo: Scandinavian University Books.

Reich, C. A. 1970. *The greening of America*. New York: Random House.

Szasz, T. S. 1961. *The myth of mental illness: foundations of a theory of personal conduct*. New York: Hoeber-Harper.

———. 1970. *The manufacture of madness: a comparative study of the inquisition and the mental health movement*. New York: Harper & Row.

Toulmin, S. T. 1953. *The philosophy of science*. New York: Harper and Row.

Van den Berg, J. H. 1971. What is psychotherapy? *Humanitas* 7:321–70.

2.

Mental Retardation and the Power of Records

DOUGLAS BIKLEN

Whose interests do records serve? Do they serve the "client's" needs or do they serve social workers, educators, institutional staff?[1] In the field of mental retardation, where records abound as hallmarks of the individualized case approach to service, one might assume that case records would serve the client and, yet, as will become apparent throughout this chapter, the effect of records may not reflect the assumed intent. The purpose of this chapter is to examine the impact of records on people's lives and to articulate whatever prescriptions seem to emerge from this analysis.

First, the chapter examines the role of record keeping as it is practiced in mental retardation programs (especially state schools) in hopes of answering the question: "Whose interests do records serve?" A case study, presented in some detail, of one young man currently institutionalized serves to reveal the broad social and professional attitudes that so often permeate service settings for the "mentally retarded." This case study concerns the fate of a single person and one service facility, yet my own experience as an observer in several state schools, public schools, and other mental retardation programs leads me to the conclusion that the context described here is, if not representative of every experience, at least

11

indicative of forces that commonly comprise the atmosphere in which the so-called mentally retarded are treated. An emphasis has been placed on institutional records rather than public school or vocational program records, mostly because, in light of repeated exposés, institutional life seems a more crucial issue in the field of mental retardation today.

The second section of this chapter, based upon observations in several state and public schools, categorizes the impact of records on people's lives. The data is not "representative" in the traditional sense of that word. No attempt was made to compare records of clients placed in different categories of "retardation" (mild, moderate, severe, and profound), though the individual records presented considerable variety. Rather, the issue of representativeness has been turned around so that instead of focusing on the many and varied conditions of clients, we have sought to portray, in representative fashion, the social and professional attitudes toward them.

Out of this description and analysis of records and their impact on people's lives can then emerge the construction of remedial proposals. The final section of this chapter is devoted to these proposals and the means for their implementation.

A LOOK AT INSTITUTIONAL LIFE

During a recent public discussion of dehumanization in institutions, a man approached me to ask assistance in securing the release of his son from a state prison. He said that, on the advice of a physician, he had placed his son in a state school when he was only five years old and that the state school had recently transferred his son, now seventeen years old, to a prison. Mr. Edwards explained that the state school had persistently discouraged the parents' visits, had not allowed them to view their son's living quarters, and never provided them with reports about their child's progress.[2] The parents ignored these barriers by their continued insistence on visiting their son. They also brought him home on many weekends and holidays. Before one long holiday, however, the institutional director notified the parents that their son was being detained in isolation following an "incident" between him and a staff member. The parents demanded to see their son. After several hours of waiting they were permitted to see him, only to find that he was badly bruised on the head and back. Other inmates of the state school informed the parents that he was being held in the isolation building, known as the "jailhouse," after a guard had beaten him. The institution's director, on the other hand, complained that their son, Dennis, had been responsible for beating a guard.

Mr. and Mrs. Edwards were unable to take Dennis home during that holiday, but they quickly notified a local "civil rights" lawyer who initiated a suit for damages against the state and against the director of the institution. Unfortunately, the attendant who had allegedly beaten or been beaten by Dennis was never identified by institutional staff and, after several months of legal hearings, the Edwards's case fell apart for lack of evidence. Just two weeks after the case deteriorated, the state school administration began proceedings to transfer Dennis from the state school to a state prison. He was then seventeen years old.

Mr. Edwards told me that they received a letter in the mail one Monday informing them that Dennis would be transferred to "another institution" which would have a fence around it and would, therefore, be better able to contain Dennis. No mention was made about a prison, though the state school staff were in fact planning to move Dennis to a prison for so-called criminal mental defectives operated by the state Department of Correction. The state school obtained a court commitment on the grounds that Dennis was a "dangerous male in a state school." On the Wednesday after the letter arrived, Dennis was transferred.

Mr. Edwards told me that he drove four and one-half hours to reach Eastern Institution. Though he arrived in the morning, he was unable to visit Dennis until afternoon; since Dennis's records had not accompanied him on the transfer, the staff had difficulty in locating him, and he took several hours to find. When Mr. Edwards asked a guard why the boy had been imprisoned, the guard replied that he thought it was because Dennis was taking drugs "in the streets" like so many of the other inmates. Mr. Edwards explained that Dennis had been heavily tranquilized at the state school, but that he had never been "in the streets."

In the ensuing months, after my first conversation with Mr. Edwards, I and several colleagues began to seek Dennis's release to another facility where he would receive educational and recreational service and where he would be allowed to go home on weekends. Before exploring an alternative placement, however, we secured a court order allowing us to meet with Dennis, to question guards at the institution, and to peruse his case records.

The following account confirms what we have learned from previous observations in other state institutions; namely, that staff often utilize "patients'" records to describe their inadequacies and, therefore, to justify institutional treatment and incarceration, as well as to control and discredit patients.

As we drove through an entranceway marked by two brick pillars, we noticed a group of khaki-clothed inmates raking brush and grass along the road leading to the state hospital for the "criminally insane." We passed several small brick cottages which served as staff housing and stopped next to a fifteen foot high wire fence which had a sliding gate operated electronically from a guard house. A guard instructed us to continue driving around a group of buildings in order to reach Eastern Institution, a large, four or five story yellow brick building on the grounds of Creighton State Hospital.

Eastern, like the state hospital, is surrounded by a high wire fence with a v-shaped expense of barbed wire at the top, presumably to discourage escapes. We parked in the visitors' lot and walked toward a sliding metal fence gate in front of the building. The gate opened electronically as we approached. A guard inside the building then buzzed the steel entrance door so that we could enter the building.

Once inside we asked a blue-uniformed guard if we could see the director, Dr. Yaro, who it turned out was just behind us. She smiled and nodded at us, as if to say hello. We proceeded to her office and were invited to sit down. Dr. Yaro, who is about fifty years old, sat down at her desk which was covered with papers and folders. I immediately began the conversation by introducing myself and the psychologist with me and explaining that we were interested in learning about, and visiting with, Dennis Edwards so that we could assess the possibility of having him transferred to a new state school near to his parents' home. I explained that we had obtained a court order for our visit because the judge had indicated we would, otherwise, be unable to meet Dennis. Dr. Yaro said, "Yes that's right. Well you're welcome to meet with him and to look at the records. I have the records ready in the other room, in the supervisor's room."

"Fine," I said. "Maybe we could start just by asking you a few questions."

"Fine," Dr. Yaro said as she sat with her hands folded on her desk, a slight smile on her face.

"Could you give us a general picture of Dennis' condition or situation now. Neither of us has ever met him, but we do know his parents."

· "Well he gets in many fights, and he is assaultive to other inmates and guards. He provokes fights. The reason why he is here is that he was very uncontrollable in the other institution. That's why they sent him here."

"Could you describe this misbehavior?" the psychologist asked.

Dr. Yaro replied, "Yes, he kicks, he hits, he throws chairs at the ceilings and ruins them, any number of things like that."

We nodded and then asked about his living quarters. "What kind of living quarters does he have?" I asked.

"Well, we have two kinds of arrangements here. We have the dormitories and the private rooms. We prefer the dormitories of course for the socialization it affords. But then, of course, if they are not able to live in the dormitories, we have to have them in the locked rooms."

"Which kind does he have?" I asked.

"He has his own room," she explained. We later observed Dennis's living quarters. Dennis lived in a cellblock of thirty cells. Each cell is a small cubicle with a bed, wash basin, and toilet. The steel cell door, which has only a peep hole in it, is locked nearly all of the time.

I then asked, "Does he have an educational program?"

Dr. Yaro answered, "We have education. He has a teacher."

"Would it be possible for us to meet with the teacher?" I queried.

"I don't know," Dr. Yaro responded, "the teacher's very busy. Perhaps this afternoon."

"Does he get any recreation?" I asked.

"We have basketball and baseball. The boys go out every day."

"Can he play these games?" I asked.

"Oh yes, he plays," Dr. Yaro assured me.

"Does he do any work here?" I asked.

"We give him little chores like mopping floors, but he can't do much. He causes these fights and disturbances because he's so retarded. It's not his fault. He can't control himself. It's because of his severe retardation."

We were startled to hear her argue that "He causes these fights and disturbances because he's so retarded." As far as this author knows, there is no experimental evidence or theory of mental retardation which links violent behavior with "levels" of mental retardation.[3] I asked Dr. Yaro what she thought about the possibility of Dennis benefiting from placement at a new state school near his parents' home.

She responded, "They couldn't control him there. They have no way of controlling him. He's too violent." She encouraged us to look at his records and to speak with Dennis. We expressed an interest in also speaking with a guard, a teacher, or some other person who knew him. She said, "Oh well you can meet a guard later." She then asked if we would prefer to see the records before meeting Dennis. The psychologist with me suggested that we meet Dennis first.

Dr. Yaro directed us to the prison waiting room where a guard told us we could wait. After about fifteen minutes we were told that Dennis was ready to meet us. We proceeded into the hall where we saw Dennis, a young man of average height, weighing about 160 pounds, and dressed in the khaki uniform of inmates. He was standing in the hallway next to the barred barrier through which he had been led. A guard spoke softly to me and said critically, "Good luck trying to understand him." The same guard entered the small visiting room with us, but we asked that we be left alone with Dennis. He agreed and said that he would be right outside the door if we needed him. He also said that he would have to keep the inmate's records since he was not allowed to let them out of his sight.

We sat down with Dennis in a barren visiting room that had only three chairs and a formica topped table. We spoke with Dennis, telling him why we were visiting him and that we were friends of his parents. Dennis has very limited language ability and was unable to say full sentences; however, he was able to enunciate words. When I asked him if he enjoyed listening to the radio, for example, he answered by saying, "Hi Fi, radio, tape recorder, television." When I asked him if he ever gets any presents, he said, "Cake, pie, candy, Mommy." Dennis smiled at both of us. "Do you enjoy this institution?" I asked. "Yes," he answered.

As I sat next to Dennis, I noticed that his gums nearly covered his teeth, a condition which is commonly found among institutionalized people who are given the medication Dilantin to treat epileptic fits. As Dennis sat there, saliva formed at the front of his mouth, but he periodically drew in his lips to avoid drooling.

Dennis was wearing a key on a piece of torn white cloth tied around his neck. I asked him what it was for and he said, "Locker. Locker." "Oh you have a locker," I said, and he nodded. "Where were you before this?" the psychologist asked. "Acropolis" he said, referring to the name of the state school where he had allegedly been beaten. We asked if he had friends at this prison, and he pointed to us and said, "Friends." We said "Yes," and laughed. "How about upstairs. Do you have any friends upstairs?" Dennis responded, "Bobby." We later learned that Bobby was the name of a guard who works in Dennis's cell block.

After about thirty minutes we finished our meeting with Dennis by going with him to a candy machine and giving him money to buy crackers. When I could not find the change, Dennis pointed to the coin return. A guard nodded and said, "He knows that machine."

As the guards prepared to take Dennis back upstairs to his cell block, we asked if we could visit with one of the guards who knew him. A man in his early thirties said that he would be glad to speak with us about Dennis. He introduced himself as Bob Bellows. We sat down in the large waiting room that is apparently used by visitors such as family members and relatives. Mr. Bellows seemed considerably more relaxed than Dr. Yaro.

"How is he on the ward?" I asked.

"He's really good," he explained, "but he's childish and he has trouble with the other inmates. They taunt him and provoke him and they fight."

As I nodded, the psychologist said, "Would you describe this?"

"Well they call him names and heap verbal abuse on him. They call him stupid. Then he yells at them since he can't really talk very well, and they hit him, then he kicks them. They call him dummy and things like that. They're higher level and they don't understand him. He's different than all the others. He's the only one like that. He's very childish."

"But he seems very gentle," my colleague remarked.

"He is gentle," the guard said. "But the others don't understand him. So they fight."

"Then it's with provocation that he fights," the psychologist said.

"Yes," Mr. Bellows agreed, "But never on his part. He's always provoked by them. He never does the provoking."

My colleague and I looked at each other and I said, "Well that fits with our impression of him." After a short pause, I asked, "What does he do during the day?"

Mr. Bellows held out his hands and shrugged his shoulders as he said, "Well to tell you the truth, most of the time, nearly all of the time, he's locked up in his room, because of the fighting. He likes to listen to the radio and to watch the television, but he gets in fights about it."

"Does Dennis get outside?" I asked.

"I make sure that I get [the inmates] out for a half hour each day. And the shift after mine, I think, in fact I know they get them out for a half hour too."

"So he gets out about a hour a day?" I asked.

"Yes."

"Does he get any education?" I asked.

"No. He doesn't get any education, at least during my shift. (Mr. Bellows' shift lasts from morning to mid afternoon.) No, there's no education for him."

Much of what Mr. Bellows told us seemed in direct contradiction to what Dr. Yaro had explained.

Before ending our discussion with Mr. Bellows, we asked him about the medications that Dennis receives. He explained to us that Dennis receives only Mellaril now, but had previously received Thorazine and Dilantin. He explained that the Dilantin was discontinued when it was found that he never had an epileptic seizure. He had apparently been given Dilantin for at least eight years while at Acropolis State School.

After meeting with Bob Bellows, we spent forty-five minutes looking over the institutional records on Dennis in the presence of a supervising guard.

Dennis's Records

As we finished our discussion with Mr. Bellows we had an opportunity to reflect on the day's proceedings. We were impressed with Dennis's gentleness and his interest in us; obviously we did not find him to be the violent inmate that the director described.

Our review of the written records on Dennis merely confirmed this finding. As we examined Dennis's records from the state school and the prison for "mental defectives" we realized that the director's comments to us about Dennis were based entirely on written reports which had been prepared by the director of the state school where he had been incarcerated for fifteen years. After meeting Dennis and the guard that serves on his cell block, and then after reviewing his records, we realized that the director seemed to be more concerned with justifying than describing Dennis's incarceration.

Aside from this insight into the director's behavior, what else can this experience tell us? First, it can be seen that records justify incarceration and promote control of the so-called mentally retarded. Second, it was readily apparent that the records, though quite voluminous, completely ignored any mention of the environment in which Dennis is situated, a context that plays an important role in his life. And finally, that the negative emphasis of records reveals a discrediting process where the record keeper searches for pathologies, syndromes, and deficits in the individual, while virtually ignoring the person's potential, creativity, interest, and hopes.

Professionals' remarks in Dennis's records alleging "very

dangerous, assaultive, violent" behavior convey a rather unmistakable image of an antisocial person who might justifiably, at least under state law, be incarcerated. It seems noteworthy, however, that neither at the time of imprisonment nor at any subsequent time was Dennis provided with an opportunity for a trial by jury or with a means of calling into question those professional allegations of violent and dangerous behavior. In other words, Dennis and his parents were powerless to challenge criticisms and charges entered into his records, despite the fact that some of these charges were utilized as justifications for his continued incarceration. Accusations that he was confused and disoriented or dangerous and assaultive appear in the records as if they were undisputed facts, substantiated by the rank and backgrounds of their authors.

One is hard-pressed to find a basis for saying that the record serves Dennis. Not only were the majority of statements about him condemning, but also there was no information about habilitative programs for Dennis. Where one might assume to find information concerning Dennis's progress, one finds a complete void.

What is the significance of this void in light of whatever else we know about Dennis and his history of institutionalization? Simply this, that in the context of state schools, and presumably other institutions as well, records serve primarily to justify policies of incarceration and control. The fact that there are (1) no mention of habilitative programming and (2) no positive remarks about Dennis, reflects more on the custodial and controlling functions of institutions than on Dennis's capacity to benefit from programming. The institutional preoccupation with control precluded habilitative programs.

Given that records reveal the custodial bias of institutions, it is not surprising that they avoid any mention of institutional conditions or public policies that might contribute to a person's difficulties. In short, records present a rather limited view of the person's situation. One would not expect to find in the records, for example, any descriptions of the processes of humiliation which Goffman (1961) describes as inherent aspects of institutional life. Similarly, records would not include discussions of school exclusion policies or any mention of societal prejudices toward the "mentally retarded." In Dennis' case, one finds (1) no mention of the harm caused to a child who receives no educational services and recreational programs; (2) no reference to the effect that living in a prison cell has upon an inmate; and (3) no mention of what it means to grow up as an outcast in a world of other outcasts. Records too often ignore the whole picture.

Dennis's records focused entirely on deficits, failures and "bad" points. It is as if the record keeping were intended to find faults rather than to find potential and hope in the "client." As Charles Dailey has noted in *Assessment of Lives* most assessment systems, especially those used to institutionalize or otherwise segregate people, as is the case in many instances for the mentally retarded, are preoccupied with pathology. Dailey explained that it takes a complex accounting of features and qualities to evaluate a person positively, but only a single negative mark to identify a person as one who is "sick," "schizophrenic," "emotionally disordered," "mentally retarded," "hyperactive," or "alcoholic." Dennis's records provide a fine example of this negative approach. The records include an accounting of faults ranging from flat feet to possible epileptic seizures (though he never had one seizure in his entire life) and severe mental retardation. Even his ability to smile was criticized by the institutional director as a "silly, childish smile." His style of walking, which appeared quite unremarkable to us, was characterized as an "awkward gait."

The fact that such negative evaluations appear in Dennis's records may seem inconsequential when compared to the realization that Dennis encounters such remarks and attitudes daily, undoubtedly with considerable personal suffering; the records simply confirm what Dennis experiences first hand. Even more inconsequential, one might argue, is that analysis of record keeping. Why look at records when one can see the nature of institutional life and human suffering as it occurs? Because records are a part of institutional life. One cannot understand the entirety of institutional life without understanding its many aspects.

Similarly, one cannot understand a single segment of institutional practice such as records without examining the overall institutional environment. Just as it is easier to understand Dennis's situation if one understands many aspects of his environment, including the records, one can best understand the records if one is versed in the human environment that they reflect. The next three sections of this chapter further elaborate on the nature of records and their relationship to people and environments.

RECORDS AS INSTRUMENTS OF CONTROL

A bit of seventeenth-century Quaker advice that has been relevant to past and contemporary Friends alike offers prudent warning concerning the possible impact of the written word:

Dearly beloved Friends, these things we do not lay upon you as a rule or form to walk by, but that all, with the measure of light which is pure and holy, may be guided: and so in the light walking and abiding, these may be fulfilled in the Spirit, not from the letter, for the letter killeth, but the Spirit giveth life [Religious Society of Friends, p. 4].

In considering the impact of records on people's lives, I suddenly recalled the phrase "the letter killeth" as one which bears considerable relevance to the subject at hand. The word is our creation, a vehicle for achieving immortality even, but also a confining force, a means of objectifying people as less than human, as caricatures or symbols rather than as changing, developing human beings. Through words, people are sometimes seen not as multifaceted beings but as unidimensional: "retards," "hyperactive," "passive-aggressive," "mongoloids," "blind," "deaf," "low grade," "high grade," "subnormal," "defective." Our propensity to locate people within cultural roles becomes a sanction for characterizing people according to IQ scores or by disability labels such as those just mentioned. When these labels and categories become our vision of people, "the letter killeth"; the person is lost in the overwhelming simplification and force of a constricting caricature.

How often in public schools does a committee for the placement of "mentally retarded" children seize upon certain "key" phrases and labels such as "trainable" and "educable" as a basis for placement? I recently saw school district officials refuse to offer public education to a seven-year-old child whom none of them had met, simply on the basis of one psychologist's written report that the "hyperactive" and "borderline retarded" child could not benefit from public education. This child has been illegally and, I think, unjustifiably excluded from school for five months, all because the written word has been attributed more importance than the child himself.

The effect of categorization, if it objectifies, is to transform human beings who have many qualities, including perhaps a disability, into objects with but one identifying feature—that disability. The record may objectify a person as "retarded" or "hyperactive," labels that in turn conjure up images of "slowness" and "dependency." No mention is made of the person's desire to learn, of a sense of humor, of the person's possible frustration with social prejudice. Rather, records are usually unidimensional.

Once a person has been categorized as "low grade" or "slow," it comes as a shock to institutionalizers that the person is indeed multifaceted—that is to say, in many ways normal. Staff reactions to patients' sex lives reveals this problem. It is not uncommon for institutional records to include, for example, remarks about inmates' sexual lives, especially if inmates have displayed repeated interest in sex or perhaps deviant sexual behavior. If we ourselves lived in institutions we might think it rather normal to use deviant sexual outlets since those are the only ones available. Yet, the "mentally retarded" are considered more deviant or inadequate for showing such normal behavior as interest in sex. The point here is that institutions cannot deal with the "mentally retarded" as normal people for they have been stereotyped as abnormal, to the point where any unacceptable behavior (such as public masturbation), even if it is a result of abnormal environmental conditions such as institutionalization and sexual deprivation, becomes further proof of deviance.

One man who is labeled "crippled" discussed this process of stereotyping in an article which examines what it means to live as a deviant. He described what he felt when a man said to him, "Why don't you plan to get yourself a nice store? . . . Where you don't have to work so hard but you could earn your own living. That's what you should do." The man knew nothing of Mr. Kriegel's emotional and intellectual capabilities and dealt only with his physical condition: crippled from the waist down. He dealt with Mr. Kriegel as a deviant, as an abstraction. Leonard Kriegel responded in his article:

> And so I learned that I existed for him as an abstraction, that he saw through me as if I, too were smoke he was blowing through his nostrils. The cripple had been liked to the Negro. A new they had been born. As a man of the world, who did not need to move beyond abstraction, he assumed that he had every right in the world to decide what the cripple or the Negro wanted. He knew what I "should do" because he possessed two good legs and I didn't. Not being crippled makes one an expert on the Negro. It was another example of the normal deciding how that which dared not to be normal should live [Kriegel 1969, p. 430].

In as much as records tend to stereotype people, they create role expectations of the kind Kriegel criticizes. Thus, as one reads through the records of institutionalized "mentally retarded" persons, one finds indications of stereotypic attitudes. In one instance a boy was criticized for his failure to follow orders: "He must learn to follow orders better." He was stereotyped as a patient and, therefore, one who should know how to follow orders. In another case, a social worker criticized a young man for quitting a job. The young man had quit the job because of low pay and had demanded at least $50.00 per week for full-time employment. The social worker wrote that he was well motivated toward working but that he was naive concerning the duties and responsibilities that accompany employment. Was it naive to request pay that would more closely approach minimum wage standards which the rest of us consider our right?

In some instances, records on the "mentally retarded" serve as charts of the person's conformity or lack of conformity. This is especially true of records maintained in token economy systems or other behavior modification programs operated within the institutional context where clients receive rewards for fulfilling prescribed behavior patterns that reflect institutional norms. I have observed record keeping procedures where it was noted whether or not an institutional resident was "talking sensibly," "working on the ward," "helpful with other patients," "participating in ward activities," and so forth. This kind of recording would appear to represent the most extreme, though not at all uncommon, form of what Kriegel called "another example of the normal deciding how [those who] dared not to be normal should live."

Nearly every institutional record on a "mentally retarded" person implies expectations about how the "client" should behave. Yet apart from an institution-based behavior modification program where the expected or prescribed behaviors are systematically presented as a habilitative plan, there is virtually no mention of habilitative programming, of services offered to the client. This should tell us something about the focus of institutions and of record keeping. Both are more concerned with other issues, such as control and custodial care, than with habilitation and human growth.

Recent court cases concerning institutionalized "mentally retarded" persons' rights to receive adequate treatment have shed light on this problem. Aside from the usual legal complaints (common in this type of suit) about the administration of toxic drugs by attendants, forced isolation and use of restraining devices, practices of institutional peonage and other conditions and policies that so commonly pervade state schools, the plaintiffs in an Alabama case (*Wyatt v. Stickney and the Partlow State School*, 1972) emphasized the complete lack of habilitative programming:

Even the most profoundly retarded residents could benefit from an active habilitation program. The absence of an overall philosophy of habilitation has had an adverse effect on the attitudes of the resident care staff. Staff members do not expect residents to develop skills and perceive themselves as "caretakers." . . . This becomes a self-fulfilling prophecy. . . . Most residents at Partlow have no habilitation program whatsoever. Indeed, they have been deprived of any stimulation or activity. . . . Most of the stereotyped behavior in which residents engage, such as rocking, is due to neglect and the lack of stimulation; it is not a consequence of mental retardation.

At present there is no established procedure for periodic evaluations of residents which are necessary to develop an individualized habilitation plan. Fifty per cent of the resident population of Partlow has been institutionalized there for 10 or more years and 274 of the residents for more than 30 years.

Given the near complete absence of habilitative programming in Partlow and other state schools throughout the country, including Willowbrook and Belchertown to name only two, we should not be surprised that institutional records reflect the custodial emphasis.

The meaning of the word "record" in the context of a state school then, is often that of keeping "tabs" on the "client." If we were to keep records on our own children, in the same manner that institutions keep records on "mentally retarded" children and adults, we would fill out a "ward report" (or living room report) everytime there was a squabble or outburst. We would virtually ignore positive remarks and observations, with the exception perhaps of noting when a child was quiet and manageable, but we would pay considerable attention to swearing, failure to follow orders, and lack of respect to elders. At no point would our children have an opportunity to look at what we wrote; neither would they be afforded opportunities to make their own entries with, for example, their own version of an incident. Just as the ward personnel in an institution are entitled to describe their perspective of a fight among inmates or even a fight between themselves and an inmate, with no other side of the story offered, so too would we be free to act as legislators, enforcers, judges, and jury if we chose to duplicate the role of institutional record keeper. In short, institutional records tend to provide a one-sided, control- and, implicitly, conformity-oriented perspective.

PERSPECTIVE OF THE RECORD KEEPER

What do records tell us about "clients" and service providers? A quick perusal of several state school records provides one with the impression that the evaluative processes involved in record keeping reflects as much on the record keeper as on the client. It is surprising to note, for example, the seeming inconsistency in the manner that institutional staff members evaluate clients. It would appear that the eyes of the beholder determine the content of reports. Thus one staff member may describe a child in the terms, "Eats well, weight normal, noisy at times—neat, clean, quiet most of the time, likes recreation, friendly," while another staff member can present a wholly different report on the same child a month later: "Appetite good—a trouble maker but blames it on other patients—very dirty and lazy—hates to do any work. Continues to pick fights inside and outside. Refuses to do what's told. Noisy, untidy, slovenly, lazy, sly, careless." Similarly, another child can be described in one breath as "affectionate, responsive, and trustworthy," and in the next as "forgetful . . . untrustworthy, immature. . . ."

If records lose their meaning for us when we note the vast discrepancies they present, they become even more questionable, and we become even more cynical, when we look beyond the records into the conditions of institutional life. It seems strangely ironic that staff should express a concern for cleanliness, trustworthiness, neatness, quiet, and affection while living amidst alarming filth and degradation. I am struck by the irony, for example, of a doctor's concern for neatness and clean dress in an institution where clothes serve as currency in an institutional status system, and where showers, toilet paper, and soap, which we might consider prerequisites to cleanliness, are rationed out meagerly. On a recent visit to a much talked about state school, I noted a complete absence of toilet paper.

Institutions may publicly expound laudable values such as cleanliness and trustworthiness, yet those values appear as a veil draped over conditions such as the following, which were observed in several state institutions:

On Dining:

On Thursday, I purposely hung around building B to watch the lunchtime activities. At 11:28 A.M., one attendant ordered

38 residents to line up. They all wore pants and some had shirts, but one man had no shirt, and his pants were ripped all the way up the seams. After some commotion the attendant led the residents to a dining room. Two more attendants followed up the rear. Thirty-seven of the men sat down quickly at the yellow formica-topped tables. The men sat on stools. One man sat on the floor along the wall. The attendants brought out yellow-sectioned trays with chopped up food. It was egg omelet, watermelon, relish, a cup of milk, buttered bread, and something white which I couldn't identify. The residents were each given a spoon. Three workerboys (two of whom were on this ward as punishment) were handed trays. They seemed to know whom to feed. All of the men stuffed their mouths with spoons, food, and hands. Many grabbed food off the trays of others who sat across from them. No one talked, but many moaned, groaned, and grunted.

As soon as the workerboys had finished feeding three of the men (this took two minutes), they sat down with their own trays. They each had an extra piece of watermelon that was not ground up.

The three attendants walked around the room and tried to keep the men from eating each other's food. One attendant passed out extra pieces of buttered bread. Everyone wanted one. The attendant literally threw the bread at the men. He threw one piece at least 15 feet to the man seated on the floor, against the wall. The bread landed on the floor, but the man grabbed it and ate it.

As the men finished, they lined up to leave. One of the workerboys was eating slowly and seemed to be enjoying his food. He was the only one I saw eat like this.

Except for the three workerboys, the dining room was empty. It was now 11:35 A.M., seven minutes since the attendant first told the men to line up in the ward [Biklen in Blatt, ed. 1973, pp. 74–75].

Who can pinpoint the cause of such conditions? There are so many, including: routinization of life patterns, objectification of inmates as subhumans, denial of dinnerware, food presented in unappealing form, and so forth. One attendant in a report of state schools characterizes the institutional environment as zoolike:

See that boy over there. He's been here for two weeks. He came right from home and they put him right on the ward. Christ, the place is like a zoo to him. He sits down to eat and he doesn't know what to do. He's used to eating at a table with his family. He's learning how to fend for himself. You have to be tough to survive here. These kids know all the tricks of the game; they know how to survive in a place like this [Biklen 1971, p. 123].

Within the framework of institutional life, even clothing becomes a source of inmate competition. The following passage, drawn from the same study of children's services in state institutions, reveals the importance that clothing plays in the life patterns of institutionalized children:

Those who are most well dressed are usually those who have proven to the staff that they are useful or else they are among that group of residents that has endeavored to obtain nice clothes as a way of setting itself off from others. We found that if a child was dressed better than most in the institution, it was usually because he or she was favored by the staff. If a child had nice clothes, he or she was often considered to be one of the "brighter" residents and was given more freedom than others.

A group of observers made a point of reviewing the method of dispensing clothes in one state school and found that the "brighter" children received different clothes than the "lower grades;" they also found that the institution had special sets of clothing for when a child received a visitor. Thus clothing was not only a means of differentiating status levels within the institution, it was a way of maintaining the institution's status image with the outside community [Biklen 1971, p. 137].

Obviously, no such descriptions of institutional conditions, practices and policies ever enter an inmate's records, at least not intentionally. Institutions continue to judge by standards that they do not live by. Evaluations of the individual's cleanliness, neatness, willingness to follow orders, and trustworthiness appear repeatedly, almost as if inmates were encouraged by their environment to display these qualities or as if the institutional environment were at least a neutral force in their lives. To expect cleanliness and neatness amid such environmental conditions is surely ironic.

School records for children with disabilities often reflect the same narrow approach, with little or no emphasis on the social and political forces which affect the "mentally retarded." There is no mention of the social prejudices regarding intelligence, policies of exclusion and segregation, discriminatory budget allocations, name-calling by a child's peers, and the stigmata that labels perpetuate. Rather, the same data appear over and over again—IQ scores, medical conditions, learning deficits, and personal habits. Somehow, the records invariably define a child's situation in terms of such personal qualities rather than in social or policy terms. When a child is out of school (excluded), for example, the records usually indicate that the cause is centered in the child; it is either character disorder, severe retardation, multiple handicap, or some other disability. I have yet to observe a student record that says the primary reason why a child is excluded from school is that the school system has failed to provide adequate services to include the child.

Even research in the field of mental retardation reflects the same narrowness. One is likely to find numerous articles on the ability of the "retarded" to perform certain tasks, but little research on the attitudes and prejudices of the society which affect policies toward the "mentally retarded." The field has spawned more than a few studies on the potential of institutional populations but relatively few on human degradation in institutions. Not surprisingly, records on the "mentally retarded" reflect this professional and, I think, societal, bias of examining the problems and needs of "clients" at a personal or individual level—for example, labeling each person served—and of avoiding the broader social and political forces such as exclusion policies or job discrimination which often create or exacerbate the person's needs and difficulties.

What records take account of the paternalism in our society toward the so-called "mentally retarded" or of the prejudice that is implicit in a society which systematically segregates and isolates the "retarded"? C. Wright Mills warned against examining people's lives as self-contained units apart from social and historical circumstances and forces:

> We have come to know that every individual lives, from one generation to the next, in some society; that he lives out a biography, and that he lives it out within some historical sequence [Mills 1959, p. 6].

Mental retardation records would seem to contradict Mills's view, in as much as they deal only with the individual's personal history and not with the social and political history of treatment for the "mentally retarded." Simple comparisons of mental retardation services in this country with those in Scandinavia would indicate the important effect of historical forces on individuals' lives. One would find in such comparisons that personal behavior such as hyperactivity, physical self-abuse, or even intellectual performance may not be understood entirely by looking only at the individual client; it may be equally—if not more—important to examine the situation in which the person is located. We cannot assume, therefore, that policies of segregation and exclusion play a neutral role in the life of a "mentally retarded" person, just as it would be foolish to ignore the import that the slave system and systemic racism have had on black Americans.

RECORDS AS A DISCREDITING PROCESS

In the field of mental retardation, records invariably utilize an evaluative approach, often a medical model, that emphasizes negative personal qualities. Goffman spoke to this issue in his seminal work, *Asylums:*

> This dossier (case record) is apparently not regularly used . . . to record occasions when the patient showed capacity to cope honorably and effectively with difficult life situations. Nor is the case record typically used to provide a rough average or sampling of his past conduct [Goffman 1961, p. 155].

Rather, the diagnostic mode of evaluation focuses on incompetence and weakness. Out of a person's entire life and a range of qualities, the diagnostic charts of state schools and special education school programs often enable diagnosticians to identify a few negative factors. As was noted earlier, the process is one of objectification.

The categories of state school evaluative forms necessarily reflect the need to justify policies of incarceration and therefore tend to emphasize "symptoms." One checklist that I recently found in a state school record included negative categorizations and positive ones in a ratio of almost two to one:

Negative	*Positive*
aggressive	ambitious
argumentative	courteous

boastful
egotistical
incorrigible
irritable
jealous
lazy
moody
narcissistic
nervous
potential troublemaker
quarrelsome
stubborn
superficial
timid

gregarious
obedient
responsible
socially adequate
superior
tidy
truthful

Even the positive categories, however, seem rather dubious. "Socially adequate," for example, is a rather negative characterization of a positive quality, and "obedience" reflects the institutional preoccupation with control and submission.

In a recent visit to a public school resource classroom for children who present behavior and learning problems, a teacher handed me an evaluative chart of "maladaptive behaviors" which he said he uses to evaluate each student.[3] The special education department of the school district apparently distributes the form to evaluate all "handicapped" children who receive specialized supplementary instruction. The form analyzes children's behavior in the following manner:

When faced with a challenge or problem becomes disruptive (e.g. calling out, acting up, clownishness, getting out of seat).

Wants his own way; seems to have difficulty with sharing, give-and-take, in relating to classmates.

Seems caught up in his own thoughts (e.g. daydreams, or seems preoccupied, or feels around by himself).

Seems to withdraw too readily from competition; tends to react as if he is not as good as the others (in competing).

Often instigates fights or behaves like a bully.

When faced with problems or challenges becomes over conscientious and puts in undue effort.

Seems bored with or not interested in the material itself which is to be learned.

A teacher can judge each of thirty-one such categories "significant" or "nonsignificant" for a particular child and may rate the degree of significance on a scale of one to five. Obviously, the form promotes a highly negative evaluation since any child might receive a check in one of several of the categories. On this scale, the best that a child can expect or hope for is a neutral score of nonsignificant in all categories.

As has been noted repeatedly throughout this chapter, the need for service agencies to justify their treatment of an individual can prejudice the evaluative or diagnostic process, even to the point where treatment in a mental retardation program in itself becomes a kind of significant symptom that proves the person is "mentally retarded." Goffman (1961), Szasz (1970), and others have argued that programs for deviant groups such as the "mentally ill" can have the effect of creating "mental illness," simply because every person who enters such a program takes on the mantle of "mental illness." Similarly, anyone who enters a state school, special education class, sheltered workshop, or other program for the "mentally retarded" will, despite all protestations, be viewed by others as "retarded." Children may attempt to avoid this categorization by refusing to accept the label of "mentally retarded," as was the case recently when a group of elementary school children refused to be seen publicly with their teacher for fear they would be identified as the "retarded" kids. But it is unmistakable that mental retardation programs cause their clients to be seen as "mentally retarded."

It would seem self-evident that there is a certain amount of circular thinking involved when people are judged "mentally retarded" because they are clients in "mental retardation" programs. Yet, records often incorporate such circular thinking by referring to an individual's past history of involvement in mental retardation programs as evidence of "mental retardation."

Perhaps this careless and unscientific practice indicates the importance of the evaluation. Institutional records tend to pay more attention to personal assessment than to descriptions of habilitative programs, in part because of the absence of habilitative programming but primarily because institutions, like other mental retardation programs, spend a great deal of time justifying the appropriateness of their existence, even if that involves claiming the incompetence of "clients."

Unfortunately, voluminous diagnostic records can have the effect of justifying inaction on the part of human service systems, since the more symptoms one identifies, and the more deficits one finds or imagines having found, the more plausible it is to write off a client as "incorrigible," "ineducable," or "custodial." Records therefore may play an important role in providing justifications for the denial of services. By the same token, however, records may reveal to a critical observer the enormous failure of many so-called treatment or service facilities such as state schools and other residential institutions.

Implicit in professional record keeping, however, is the practice of confidentiality which insures that clients' records remain solely in the hands of the diagnosticians and program personnel. Thus while records might reveal much to clients and their advocates about the "nonservices" received or about the overly negative evaluations, the professionals who control what appears in records also control their use.

PRESCRIPTION

Our discussion of record keeping for the so-called retarded speaks to many of the issues raised in other chapters of this book. Though one might assume that the field of mental retardation would present unique problems vis-à-vis record keeping and informed participation, we found that parents, guardians, and, indeed, many "mentally retarded" persons were profoundly aware of the impact that records can have on the client.

The mentally retarded are, more often than not, keenly aware of the manner in which they are treated. This finding is substantiated by Bengt Nirje (1971) who reported that one of the demands of the "retarded" in Scandinavia was to be provided with equal pay, adequate living quarters, and freedom from demeaning activities; such demands bear striking resemblance to the demands of prisoners, unions, and other sometimes disfranchised groups. This is not to say that many people who are labeled "retarded" would not have difficulty comprehending their case records, but that one should not assume them to be incompetent. Unfortunately, case records have been used to place "retarded" persons and their families or guardians in a position similar to that experienced by all human service clients, an essentially outsider role. They are denied access to records and, more importantly, they are victimized by the pejorative nature of record keeping that we have described. The purpose of this final section to our chapter is to provide suggestions on how to remedy the situation that the "retarded" and, to a great extent, all clients face with respect to records.

We have shown how records in the field of mental retardation have a potential, and sometimes a seemingly irreversible mandate (1) to justify given service patterns, whether they serve or dehumanize clients; (2) to control clients; and (3) to discredit clients. In none of our examples, however, was there any indication that records bore primary responsibility for program justification, control, or human invalidation. The works of Goffman (1961), the Braginskys (1971), Szasz (1970), Scheff (1966), and Blatt (1970), as well as our own previous studies (Biklen, 1972a & b) indicate that many forces, policies, and practices combine to create the three phenomena discussed above.

We cannot, therefore, pretend that our prescriptions about the future use of records will nullify the many other forces at work to discredit, control, and dehumanize the "mentally retarded." Nor do records represent a force in service organizations, such that our efforts to change record keeping would necessarily lead to transformations of other aspects of the service systems. Certainly inadequate services, control of clients, and discrediting of clients could continue without the benefit of records. Records simply formalize and dignify these processes.

We are left consequently with a rather difficult and perhaps less than central issue of what to recommend vis-à-vis records. Assuming that records contribute to the above cited ends—namely of justifying questionable programs, of controlling clients, and of discrediting clients—we might ask how we can alter the use of records so that they no longer promote these ends, so that instead they promote accountability of programming, independence for clients, and affirmation rather than invalidation of clients.

We might like to construct a blueprint of prescriptive steps toward these ends; however, a blueprint is precisely what we should not propose. That is not to say that we should not or cannot act on the discouraging information provided so far but, simply, that a blueprint assumes greater confidence about the outcomes of our actions than we should perhaps grant ourselves. Instead, what I suggest is an approach to record keeping that is linked to a larger movement toward program accountability, independence for clients, and affirmation of the clients' worth.

As part of the growing social movement to create program options and to open society to those who have been traditionally viewed as deviants, several changes have already occurred relevant to the uses of records. Recent court cases involving inmates of state schools in Alabama, New York, and Massachusetts have highlighted the failures of state schools (*Wyatt* v. *Stickney*, 1972; *Ricci* v. *Greenblatt*, 1972; *Parisi* v. *Miller*, 1972). At the Partlow, Willowbrook, and Belchertown state schools, attorneys for inmates have combed records to prove the absence of habilitative programming and the monolithic concern of institutions for control and obedience. What these cases represent, among other things, is an attempt by inmates and their relatives and friends to establish accountability of institutions to their clients. Records, which traditionally have served as controlling mechanisms for staff and administrators, have suddenly become useful evidence to the clients' attorneys as they seek to establish the rights of inmates to adequate care and treatment.

In each of these institutions (Partlow, Willowbrook, and Belchertown) the records typify other state school records and are similar to those described in this chapter. It is not the records which have changed, but the use that a group of professionals and consumers has made of these records. A few attorneys and experts in the field of mental retardation have joined forces with clients to attack certain patterns of service and "nonservice" in institutions. Similar action has been brought in the field of special education (*Pennsylvania Association for Retarded Children* v. *Commonwealth of Pennsylvania*, 1971). In all of these court actions, the experts who have represented the clients or plaintiffs have used client records as well as testimony from employees, relatives of inmates, and other data to show that certain institutions and service organizations have failed to provide adequate services and, in fact, have in some instances provided punitive treatment. In a sense, these experts have utilized the records as evidence in their efforts to make the services more accountable.

As these court actions against providers of (both educational and residential) services proliferate throughout the nation, one can liken the activity to a huge consumer protection movement, with a few lawyers and experts in the field of mental retardation serving as consumer advocates. This concept raises the *possibility of formulating a new notion of record keeping, one which evaluates and records the performance of service organizations rather than of those served.* Efforts in this direction have been suggested in the form of ombudsman systems, a regulatory agency of the type proposed by the Center on Human Policy (where state funds for mental retardation services would be contracted out to public and private service organization by consumer-controlled regulatory boards), and legal advocacy of the sort described above (Biklen, 1972b).

These and similar proposals for monitoring services will undoubtedly spawn a much greater amount of literature on the performance of service agencies than has ever before been available. Within the framework of legal advocacy, or consumer protection, professionals can begin to examine service systems in a manner that has been sadly lacking in the past. Instead of studying the failures of the so-called "retarded," we can look at our own failures as a society to respond to the needs of disabled people. Instead of producing self-justifying records and controling records, we will begin to produce records of societal and service performance that may produce more uneasiness than complacency.

It is difficult to predict how service agencies will respond to this increasing challenge, although there are several steps that concerned agencies might take in order to promote the accountability movement. The following is by no means a complete list; rather, it outlines the current thrust that institutions, schools, sheltered workshops, group homes, and other service organizations might join:

1. Records should be open to the person being served. The main obstacle to policies of open records is not so much professional confidentiality as professional mystique. Once one opens records and begins interpreting what has traditionally been privileged information, part of the mystique of the doctor or professional gives way to a more open and therefore more candid—less intimidating (for the client)—relationship. Of course for the openness to have any meaning, it must be an active policy where the client is not forced to feel he or she is encroaching on professional territory by requesting to view the records. It might be reasonable for agencies to regularly provide clients with each additional entry into the records.

2. There is a considerable need for records to incorporate more information about administrative policies and social attitudes and practices that affect the client's life. It may be more important, for example, to describe the total lack of habilitative programming in institutions (which may well be the cause of the prevalence of nervous energy, head banging, biting, and other bizarre behaviors in institutions), rather than to describe such behaviors as symptoms or deficits that are a child's fault. In short, it is recommended that service organizations cultivate an ability to be self-critical (Bogdan 1972).

3. One technique that has been experimented with in a graduate school of education is the policy that the client may make contributions to the record, so that the record ceases to be the domain solely of the service provider. Records for the "mentally retarded" might achieve a broader dimension if clients and par-

ents or other relatives were to contribute information. The purpose of such entries might be to respond to professional comments or to add new remarks.

4. The recommendations presented so far might easily lead to a power struggle between professionals and consumers over the nature of data collected in records. Obviously, the prestige and expertise of the professional puts him or her in a much stronger, more powerful position than the client or a client's relatives. One remedy would be to institute a program of advocacy, where individuals with some knowledge of mental retardation and human rights (who would by necessity have no stake in the maintenance of particular service systems and would not be employees of the service organization) would serve as ombudsmen and advocates by independently observing and evaluating service programs and conditions. Such an advocacy service might be instituted within service organizations as a legal aid service or an ombudsman system; but it could only achieve its purpose if it were independent financially from the service organization.

5. Hopefully, the discrediting nature of many evaluative systems could be ameliorated by a conscious effort on the part of service groups to find ways of describing positive development both in program offerings and in the responses of those served.

In making each of these points it is wise to caution ourselves against excessive optimism about the transformation of records, since past experience would indicate that record keeping inevitably reflects the nature of the organizational setting. Thus it would be difficult, even if one utilized all of the above mentioned techniques, to avoid having institutional records degrade or control inmates; the controlling nature of institutional life so powerfully defines individual actions and inaction in the setting that it would be difficult to transform records into more open documents. Consequently we must combine the above recommendations with the broader objective of changing the nature of certain service systems and social attitudes which promote control, objectification, and dehumanization.

The model of consumer advocacy and legal advocacy is essentially a power model, where consumers, attorneys, and specialists in mental retardation are combining to challenge certain historical practices of exclusion, control, nonservice, and dehumanization. It is a movement linked closely to the concept of normalization, a commitment to the principle that the so-called "retarded" can participate as full citizens in our society, with the same constitutional and human rights enjoyed by others.

Inevitably, this consumer rights movement will lead to an establishment of the right of consumers to know what service providers write in the case records and to a formulation of a new relationship between consumers and providers of service. Human service personnel will certainly find that facile criticisms of individual clients in the form of case records will no longer be possible, since lawyers, experts, and consumers themselves will demand to know the basis upon which decisions about the individual lives are being made. School personnel, institutional staff, diagnosticians, vocational trainers, and medical professionals will find it easier to move on to new relationships with their clients that are vastly more candid and where the professionals are directly accountable to the consumer.

As professionals in the field of mental retardation take more seriously the social implications of retardation and as a few in the field begin to offer their services to parents and clients as advocates, a process of demystification will ensue. The consumer movement will become more informed about the mental retardation profession, more aware of the impact of institutional life, more aware of the questionable effects of special classes as shown in the numerous efficacy studies, and more aware of the societal and cultural origins of the difficulties of the mentally retarded. As this movement develops increased consciousness, professionals will be less able to retreat into the negativisms of a solely medical or diagnostic model and to the myths about ineducability and incompetence. If the courts do not require the opening up of individual case records to clients and their relatives, professionals and service organizations will still be under considerable pressure to do so voluntarily, for the whole thrust of the movement that is developing throughout this country bespeaks a rejection of over-protection of the "retarded" and guilt about retardation; the movement afoot points toward militancy among the consumers of service to know about care and treatment and to seek human rights in the same manner that all self-respecting people seek to understand their development and future. To the extent that providers of service respond to this movement, the relationship of clients to professionals will become one of more equal participation wherein the clients' records would be open documents, rather than closed dossiers, for common use by clients and service providers.

We are suggesting, then, that the use of records as mechanisms for control has reflected modes of "service" where the helpers controlled those "helped." Once that controlling power relationship has been transformed into a more equal, sharing relationship, records will more likely reflect assessments of the helpers as well as the helped.

NOTES

1. The word "client" serves not as a descriptive term but as a label commonly applied to the so-called "mentally retarded" and other in our society who are voluntary and involuntary consumers of services and treatment. Throughout the text, the words "inmate" and "resident" are used interchangeably with "client" to refer to those who are incarcerated in state schools.

2. All names of people, institutions, and places have been changed.

3. This issue has been discussed by Klaber who concluded that behavior of institutionalized people often reflects institutional conditions; in addition Sarason and Doris discuss the tendency to assume a relationship between behavior and IQ (see Sarason et al. 1969, pp. 19, 60–61).

REFERENCES

Biklen, D. 1971. Children in institutions. In New York State Commission on the Quality, Cost and Financing of Elementary and Secondary Education, *Report on children with special needs in New York state*, ed. B. Blatt and H. D. Blatt. Mimeographed (Syracuse: Cornell University, Center on Human Policy.)

———. 1972a. Human development model: one alternative. In *Notes from the center, #1*, ed. D. Biklen, B. Shenkar, R. Buchnor. Syracuse: Cornell University, Center on Human Policy.

———. 1972b. The problem of change and closed institutions. *Maxwell Rev.* 8:31–39.

———. 1972. Human report. In *Souls in extremis*, ed. B. Blatt. Boston: Allyn and Bacon, 1973.

Blatt, B. 1970. *Exodus from pandemonium*. Boston: Allyn and Bacon, 1970.

Bogdan, R. 1972. Observing in institutions. In *Notes from the center, #2*. ed. E. Biklen, B. Shenkar, R. Buchnor, Syracuse: Cornell University, Center on Human Policy.

Braginsky, B. and Braginsky, D. 1971. *Hansels and Gretels*. New York: Holt, Rinehardt and Winston.

Daily, C. A. 1971. *Assessment of lives*. Washington: Jossey-Bass.

Goffman, E. 1961. *Asylums*. Garden City, N.Y.: Anchor, Doubleday.

Kriegel, L. 1969. Uncle Tom and Tiny Tim: some reflections on the cripple as Negro. *Am. Scholar* 38:430.

Mills, C. W. 1959. *Sociological imagination*. New York: Oxford University Press.

Nirge, B. 1971. Report of an international conference on mental retardation presented at Syracuse University.

Patricia Parisi et al. v. Alan Miller, M.D. et al., N.Y. E.D. (1972).

Pennsylvania Association of Retarded Children v. Commonwealth of Pennsylvania, David H. Kirtzman et al., Pa.D. 1972 (Civil Action No. 71-42).

Ricci et al. v. Milton Breenblatt, M.D. et al., Mass.D., 1972 (Civil Action No. 72-469 f).

Ricky Wyatt v. Dr. Stonewall B. Stickney, Ala. Mid.D., N.Div., 1972 (Civil Action No. 3195-N), pp. 10-11.

Religious Society of Friends n.d. *Faith and practice*. New York: New York Yearly Meeting.

Sarason, S. B. et al. 1969. *Psychological problems in mental deficiency.* New York: Harper and Row.

Scheff, T. J. 1966. *Being mentally ill*. Chicago: Aldine-Ahterton.

Szasz, T. 1970. *The manufacture of madness*. New York: Harper and Row.

3.
Collaborative Psychological Assessment

CONSTANCE T. FISCHER

Psychological assessment has traditionally been an evaluation of a client by the psychologist. It has been the clinician's responsibility to establish rapport, administer and score tests, analyze the results, draw conclusions, and write a report. If the psychologist is the one to discuss the assessment with the client, he interprets those portions of the report for which he thinks the person is ready. That all sounds reasonable enough, especially since those practices reflect the tenor of our technological times in general as well as psychology's particular efforts to model itself after the physical sciences.

More specifically, in its efforts to be scientific, psychology has assumed that people should be treated as *objects* amenable to measurement, prediction, and control. But in fact psychologists do not have to limit themselves to the restricted view of object-psychology. Instead, they can rediscover, promote, and work with those characteristics of being human that render strict physical-science approaches inadequate. A proper science of humans should take into account that humans are also purposive *subjects* who behave in accordance with their experience of situations.

41

DEFINITION OF COLLABORATIVE ASSESSMENT

Collaborative assessment recognizes that the professional's understandings are not more real, valid, or influential within the client's life than are the client's. Collaborative assessment, then, is one in which client and professional *labor together* (from the Latin, *collaborare*) toward mutually set goals, sharing their respective background information and emerging impressions. They develop and try out alternative approaches for the client as they explore the particular circumstances and ways in which he or she has wound up in some sort of difficulty. Insofar as the client is able, he also collaborates on the formulation of any written report, adds his commentary and signature to the actual document, and advises concerning who may and may not have access to the report. In short, in collaborative assessment, client and professional are mutually informed and both are active participants.

Before going on to elaborate the practices and then the guiding principles of collaborative assessment, I will briefly overview the current assessment scene and the restrictive nature of psychology's traditional way of being scientific.

THE CURRENT SCENE: "YES, BUT" AND "NEVER MIND"

Increasing numbers of professionals currently agree that a client ought to have greater access to the information about himself that is gathered by others. This agreement arises at a time of professional consciousness-raising in the face of public antielitism and demands for civil rights, accountability, and protection of consumer interests. Further impetus is provided by the recent state and federal legislation and court decisions that diminish obstacles to students' and clients' access to their files. Dissidents against the dehumanizing aspects of traditional physicalistic psychology call ever more strongly for "humanistic" reform.

Nevertheless, these "increasing numbers" are still decidedly a minority. In one study, 88 percent of the responding psychologists rarely or never gave written reports to their clients; half said that even upon direct request they would not consider giving the client a verbal account of the information (Vane 1972). "The Testee as Co-evaluator" (Fischer 1970) was apparently the first article to call for inclusion of the client as a full participant, including his or her reading and adding commentary to the report and designating who may receive it. Until then, and sometimes after that, my manuscripts (and presumably those of other authors) that were related to collaborative practices were rejected as being "too controversial," "irresponsible," and "unprofessional." Craddick (1975), Dana and Leech (1974), and Riscalla (1972) have authored three of the few publications with views similar to some of the themes in this chapter.

In the past five years or so, however, our legal system has challenged the tradition of professional secrecy. In Maine a superior court ruled that a rejected applicant to Bates College had a right to examine the records on which the decision was based. The youngster's parents then sued the high school counselor who had written an unsubstantiated derogatory letter. The United States Supreme Court has ruled (in *Gault* v. *Arizona*) that juveniles accused of delinquency should have access to their psychological reports prior to their hearings. In Pennsylavnia a right to education act for mental retardates assures parents of their right for a hearing considering whether their children are receiving the education they require; as part of this right, they also are assured access to psychological tests and records. On the federal level, the "Buckley amendment" assures parents of right of access to their children's school records; this right of access passes to the students when they become eighteen years old.

"Yes, but"

Here, we find the first "Yes, but"—that of "Yes, I know it's the law, *but* it's against professional interests." Some school systems, rather than open their files to parents and pupils, have considered dispensing with all evaluative records other than achievement test scores and final grades. A professional journal for college admissions counselors has carried an article advising colleges to devise an application form that would require the applicant to waive right of access to his files. The article admitted that such a waiver would not stand up in court, but that it might dissuade unknowledgable students. This article has been abstracted in two newsletters for advisors of preprofessional undergraduates. More openly, many college career planning offices require students to check a box on their requests for letters of recommendation indicating to the prospective writer whether they have waived right of access to the letter.

Counseling centers and psychology services across the country are devising a system of dual files: the institutional file that is subject to the law, and the individual practitioner's private notes, which are not. This gambit keeps scores, diagnoses, undocumented suspicions and hunches, and other negative comments in the personal file to which the client cannot gain access. The personal file is bequeathed as personal property to one's replacement upon transfer to another job. And so on.

When one inquires of colleagues and assorted officials as to whether this means they do not believe that clients should participate actively in evaluating their own situations, the second "Yes, but" emerges:

> "Of course, I believe in client participation, but as the expert, it is my responsibility to determine how much the client can understand or is otherwise ready for. Much of what is here in the records concerns unconscious or conditioned processes, which by definition the client cannot understand at his present stage. Besides, much of my report is just too technical for a layman to understand, even if I try to interpret it to him."

Sometimes one can cut through part of this argument by making a case for not underestimating the client's strength. The next challenge to colleagues is that if they cannot say what they know in layman's terms, then they are not particularly clear themselves about what their esoterica mean. Here the third "Yes, but" emerges:

> "Yes, I've felt that way myself, *but* surely all this technical know-how and information must be critical—what else is there that sets my work apart as professional? What would be 'expert' about talking in everyday language about things clients could already understand?"

Variations:

> "When I try to explain what I actually do with clients . . . like ask them to copy geometric designs or draw houses, trees, and persons . . . it seems embarrassingly simple"; "I do share my actual report with my private patients, but I don't think my clinic would stand for it"; "Our technology is not just a shorthand; it identifies the actual causes that underlie behavior. To refer to a client's obsessive-compulsive orderliness in any other way would dilute the precision of truth."

In short, we professionals have not been trained to notice, explore, and work with everyday events in their own right. Instead we have been trained to see those everyday behaviors as signs or symptoms of something (for example, IQ, defense mechanisms, traits) presumably more fundamental or real.

We continue to utilize these reductive notions despite our own widespread criticism of the circularity of attributing explanatory powers to the name we give to behaviors (for example, "Roger's high achievement reflects his Superior IQ."). The precision and objectivity of our measurements and constructs belie the actual state of human affairs—their necessarily fluid and intersubjective nature. Put differently, we want to be relevant, humane, and genuinely helpful, but our traditional model of laboratory object science confounds our efforts. We are caught in the "Yes, but." We don't know how to be professional and yet deal with the everyday in its own right.

"Never mind"

The second movement on the current scene in effect says, "Never mind doing individual assessments; let's get right on with treatment." The first variation of the movement is a culmination of our longstanding efforts to emulate the technological efficiency of the physical sciences. This first thrust is now dominant in psychology doctoral programs, less than half of which still require Ph.D. candidates to take courses in individual assessment. The assumption is that lower level technicians will accumulate scores which the Ph.D. *consultant* or *supervisor* will interpret. Together with the research psychologist, he or she continues to develop categories and to accumulate scores and actuarial data. Computers can then predict behavior and assign treatment modalities even more accurately and efficiently than their human counterparts. There are, of course, many clinicians who protest that statistics should serve the professional rather than supplant him; but because they too have argued largely within the traditional *object*ivistic (scientistic) notion of how psychology is to be scientific, they have not been persuasive.

The second variation of bypassing individual assessment in favor of immediate treatment is more directly related to recent awareness of the destructiveness of the "medical model of mental illness" (Szasz 1961). That is, we are now aware that although our bodies are of course always involved, "mental health" problems most often are ones of getting along in life rather than ones that are primarily either "mental" or medical. "Mental health" professionals (now more appropriately coming to be called human services professionals) historically have reified their diagnostic creations through jargon, discrete categories, professional distance, tests, and social status.

In reaction, the humanistic psychologists in particular have opted for instant therapy, usually along the lines of self-help opportunities for expressing feelings, asserting oneself, and exploring one's ways of relating to other people (for example, sensitivity training, gestalt therapy, transactional analysis). Many of the persons who conduct these sessions are B.A.'s and M.A.'s or M.Ed.'s whose training has not emphasized pathology patterns, personality theory, or research. Their jobs are an answer to a dual call: the antielitist spirit in which the community mental health movement was founded, and citizens' growing awareness of their problems and of hopes for their quick resolution. Personally, I welcome much of this trend and its emphasis on self-help and on positive growth. But I worry that the individual client's particular situation, goals, and style are not adequately taken into account, and that relevant, sometimes critical, professional knowledge is ignored to the client's detriment. Antitradition and proclient enthusiasm are not enough.

Finally, there is a third variation of the movement to bypass traditional assessment. It has arisen from a dissatisfaction with the limited usefulness of both object science assessment on one hand and subjectivistic (nonempirical) assessment on the other. In their place it has evolved practical, atheroretical means of addressing clients' problems in living. For example, "problem-oriented" psychiatric and general hospital charting spells out concrete problems and then lists specific explorations and actions, as well as points of reformulation, to be taken until resolution is attained. In some settings, the client or his family has access to these relatively self-explanatory charts, particularly where choices involving risk and personal values are called for. These charts serve the interests of general informed participation as well as those of professional accountability.

Psychologists and counselors in private practice similarly are finding that their clients now demand understandable accounts of what the professional has to offer. Many of these practitioners have discovered that, free from the constraints of institutional tradition, they can in fact meet these requests. Several have argued that all of us should draw up contracts with our clients specifying what the professional must provide or forego payment. Contracting also has arisen within clinical behavior modification, where (its contradictory deterministic theory notwithstanding) clients help to work out a set of goals and contingent rewards or penalties. Note that not only does the client participate in setting goals, but these goals are more closely related to his everyday life than were the older diagnostically oriented recommendations. The newest development within clinical behavior modification is that of "self-control behavior modification" wherein the client manages his own program, which the professional has helped him to develop.

Government insistence on program evaluation has led to the recording of clients' expectations and degrees of satisfaction, which in turn has required informed participation by clients in evaluating their own circumstances and progress. Thus far, such clients have expressed marked satisfaction.

The client involvement in this emergent thrust is promising. But it is still restricted by insufficient acknowledgment of the power and importance of the client's experience. Objectified units of client behavior are still plotted against actual or assumed time/space grids, whether on hospital progress notes, program evaluation sheets, or behavior modification charts. These records give priority to the professional's perspective as more objective and useful than the client's. Full client participation in assessing his circumstances and in shaping, trying out, and reevaluating new plans requires a transformation not only of human services practices but of theoretical assumptions.

COLLABORATIVE ASSESSMENT PRACTICES

This chapter now will address collaborative practices, each of which is grounded in the belief that the client (although always constrained by context) behaves in accordance with his or her own experience of situations, as do the assessor and reader. To be fully effective, the assessor must grapple directly with the client's realities, letting his or her scientific abstractions serve only as searchlights into these powerful realities. Moreover, each of the assessment practices is intended to assist the client himself to develop alternative ways of reaching his goals. These "ways" are not merely decision-making strategies or socially conditioned patterns. They are a person's styles of experiencing and forming his own unity with the milieu through which he travels enroute to his destination. No matter what or where, styles both limit access to some futures and open the way to others. Collaborative practices acknowledge this process and assist the client in developing alternative routes that provide greater latitude and probability of successful arrival.

Practices

Situating the referral. When I receive a formal referral from another professional, I note the wording so that I can later speak into
that frame of reference, since it is meaningful to the referring person. For example, "Distinguish between paranoid personality and
schizophrenia"; "Assess for emotional disorder"; "Test for IQ."
But I do not accept such abstractions as the focus of the assessment.
Instead, I speak personally with the referring person, and ask him
what decisions he is faced with that he requires a psychological
assessment. Typical responses: "Well, I don't know whether he is
dangerous and should be placed on a locked ward"; "I'm trying to
decide whether her problems are primarily situational or personal. . . . Should I suggest a change in job placement"?; "Timothy just
isn't keeping up with the other children. . . . Maybe he belongs in a
special education class."

Then I go a step further and ask for examples of the events that
heve led to these questions. During this conversation, I ask for
more detailed descriptions of the broader *situation* or *context*.

For example, upon reflection Timothy's teacher told me that he
falls behind his classmates in new "one shot" projects like making a
calendar or answering questions about how to give directions for
getting to the hospital. These activities required that the student
work or think by himself while only one teacher was available to
give instructions to an entire class. As a final step in situating or
contextualizing the referral, I encourage additional reflection on
the "when nots" of the problematic events. In Timothy's case, it
turned out that he caught on to new requirements readily enough
when they grew out of familiar routines and when classmates and
teachers could provide repeated examples. It is from such "when
nots" that Timothy could expand his effectiveness into previously
problematic areas.

This situating of the referral is already an assessment. Frequently, the referring person finds that this opportunity has already
answered his questions, and no further services from the assessor
are required. For example:

> *Unit psychiatrist:* The patient is nearly always suspicious of
> other people's motives, but now that we're talking about it, it's
> clear that he has been verbally abusive and blatantly irrational
> only when he's been taken by surprise. I think I'll advise the
> staff both to see if this does seem to be true, and to give him
> early gradual notice of upcoming changes. This way he may
> be able to stay on the open ward.

In other instances, with permission from both the other professional and the client, I may drop by to see the client in his or her own setting so that I can help to make concrete just what the focus might be. For example, I ate breakfast where Irene Kugel waitresses. There, I observed that the clientele are a rushed and impolite lot and that the short order cook bellows for her to pick up orders immediately no matter where she happens to be. These are indeed situational stresses, ones to which Ms. Kugel responds with increasing fluster and disorganization, which in turn eventuate in further demands from customers and bellows from the cook. As the breakfast crowd thins out, I see that Ms. Kugel now appears more efficient: she answers each call as it occurs until the work is done, whether the call is that of the cook, a customer's motion for his check, or a counter with dirty plates. Ms. Kugel and I wave, and I later telephone her counselor to suggest that they might explore some of the other "whens" and "when nots" of these ways of being. Perhaps they will indeed find a more suitable work setting; but they will also explore ways through which she might address calls before they become shouts.

In still other instances, the referring professional, the client, and I carry out the above explorations as a threesome. This requires more total hours, but in this way we all know firsthand the concrete referents of our assorted understandings and abstractions.

Engaging the client. In the case of a self-referred client or when the above contextualizing requires futher exploration and reflection, the client and I pursue the assessment ourselves. I briefly inform the client of the other professional's original and concretized/contextualized referrals, and then ask him to fill me in on his understanding of why we're getting together and what the referral is about as he sees it. At first the client responds in a socially perfunctory manner, awaiting my further questions from which he assumes I will draw my expert conclusions. This expectation is disrupted as I refuse to deal for long with generalities or actuarial facts, instead respecting the client's expertise about his own life. My role is to guide him, through my specialized training, to engage actively in delineating the ways and occasions in which he gets into difficulty as well as the pivot points already available for trying out alternatives.

However, even with the self-referred client, the initial "presenting problem" is usually as overgeneralized and abstract as that of the professional referral. For example: "My inferiority complex has caused me to fail all my job interviews"; "I just hate myself . . . I've never been any good to anyone"; "I want you to give me an IQ test to see if I should apply for a management position." So here too, we begin by concretizing/contextualizing. I might ask, "Tell me about the last time you 'failed an interview.' " Together, we try to discover what was similar among several of these occasions, how the client comported himself into and through these, what other situations were similar (perhaps being turned down by a potential date), and when he managed to comport himself through kindred situations successfully (as when he asked an apartment neighbor to return a favor). Sometimes this sort of discussion provides the client with all he needs to experiment with some alternatives on his own, with or without return visits for follow-up assessment/counselling.

Since our primary data are his actual life events as he reconstructs them for us and as he lives new ones in our sessions, the client understands that his active, responsible participation is critical. He now frequently interrupts to share new recollections that modify one of our earlier understandings. We both experience ourselves as working progressively toward useful comprehensions rather than as looking for causal explanations or precise truth. As we enter this stage I tell the client that all of our time will be spent in this same manner, even as we use test materials, make field visits, perform role-play options, or whatever. I also tell him that before I write a report (if one is required), I will share what I have in mind and it will be up to him to let me know of any problems that my formulations might involve with particular readers. Later, he will review the entire report.

Using test materials. Often, the client and I talk our way to a certain point of understanding, but aside from some truisms, we still don't know what could be done. At that point I decide to use test materials, not so much to obtain scores as to go beyond talk into joint activity. As I observe the client copying Bender gestalts (geometric designs) or solving intelligence test arithmetic problems, I am open to being surprised by the client's particular way of doing these things. Even while I view through my experience of what other clients have done and what my books and journals have told me, I find that this person both does and does not fit my expectations. If my observation seems relevant to our focal interest, my remarking upon it may raise to awareness something the client has taken for granted. For example, I interrupt Ms. Kugel, the waitress (referred for continued assessment), to ask how it is that both the parallel lines of the last drawing are turning out to slant. "Oh," she says, "well I didn't notice that the first one wasn't straight, and I just used it to copy for the second line." Sure enough, we discover that that's how the earlier columns of dots gradually changed direction of slant from the original drawings. Moreover,

Ms. Kugel laughingly suggests that she "Benders" her way through her apartment on the way to work; each completed task points to the next one. If she happens to catch sight of her uncombed hair on the way to the bathroom, she may forget to brush her teeth as she goes on to put on her make-up after arranging her hair. So too in the restaurant she follows the lead of dirtied tables and impatient glances rather than that of a prearranged plan.

Awareness of these habitual ways of getting about allows us to try out different ways of moving through the test materials, to discover viable alternatives. More about that in a moment. The tests are not used to uncover traits, but to provide situations similar to others in the client's daily life. The assessment events can serve both of us as a living metaphor for structurally similar past events, which become more readily available to us in these concrete ways. We are attuned to the unitary fullness of events rather than to their intellectualized aspects such as "cognition," "affect," "emotion," "motivation." An example is the sixth grader who couldn't explain how he managed to turn in "messy" spelling papers even when he knew all the words. After looking from his Bender copy to the card to me, and back to his copy, he grimmaced, and began erasing and resketching. "Spelling!" I said. "Yes! Just like with Mrs. Morrison! My stomach hurts, I don't feel very sure, the letters don't look neat enough, so I erase. . . ."

Locating assessment events in daily life. Several examples of this practice of collaborative assessment already have been provided, but it bears emphasizing and saying again that assessment events simply are specialized instances of the client's past and future comportment.

Besides locating, that is, identifying and contextualizing, events similar to those that occur during the assessment, the client and I also identify those occasions when he or she does not get into such difficulty (the "when nots"). For example, Irene Kugel mused that she *has* carried out a planned agenda, and in a relatively undistracted manner, on at least two recent occasions: when she took over care of her preschool niece during a family emergency, and when she planned a two-week vacation tour for herself. Eventually we concluded that in these circumstances she had experienced herself as the only person who could handle the task if it were to be done properly, and that, unlike most situations, there had been few opportunities for others to gradually pick up responsibility or for her to slip into just letting things happen.

As the client engages in this sort of exploration, he discovers in a powerful way that his life is indeed in his own hands, that things don't have to be the way they have been, and that change can be self-initiated. Compare this with Irene Kugel's statement early in our session that she had thought that I might find out what "makes" her become rattled and distressed at work. She assumed that the counselor would then "work it out" (that is, "fix it"). There is a liberating power to this informed participation by the client in contextualizing the whens and when-nots of his or her difficulties. It is dramatically illustrated in the following summarizing comment by a women whose circumstances we had just unfolded as being precisely those in which she had attempted suicide on three other occasions: "You know, I feel so relieved and hopeful. I don't *have* a 'self-destructive' tendency afterall; I've just been trying to kill myself." (We followed up with a set of concrete environmental changes, to be overseen by a therapist, through which this woman could move herself out of her suicidal situation.)

Trying out alternatives. Collaborative assessment necessarily assesses not just the client but options available to him or her given his or her particular goals, perspective, style, and situation. Since there is no absolute psychiatric portrait from which to prescribe diagnosis-specific treatment, the client and assessor themselves devise and try out alternatives that fit the client's particular circumstances. This process of developing understandings and then options is a spiraling one, in which the nonviability of what looked like a reasonable alternative leads to revised understandings which in turn serve to suggest new alternative routes, and so on.

The trying out can occur in a variety of forms: different approaches to taking the intelligence test, role playing variations of a problematic event, imagining and describing several versions of a scenario, and specification of concrete actions the client will try out on-site.

Let us return to Irene Kugel. We started with a "when not" of her "Bendering" her way among demands, with the hope of expanding that style into other situations. Specifically, she described in detail how she had planned that vacation trip so that it would be sure to meet her expectations. I suggested that she describe for us just how she would like the Bender to turn out if she were to do it again. She floundered for awhile, saying that she didn't know what she should want. We nodded in recognition of a habitual pattern, and then Irene agreed to plan the Bender as though she were still the adventurous worldly vacationer who had brought just the right dress for every stop on the itenerary. The Bender was to be executed in light but unretraced lines. She would try to copy the patterns with quick approximations, paying more attention to the original design than to her own pencilings. She would draw five down the left margin, and then four down the right margin. As she began, we discovered something else about the context in which she is able to keep an advance plan in mind: it was easier when no one else was watching her. Nevertheless, I stayed, and she finished, surprised at how well it turned out. I next presented her with pictures of designs she was to build from colored blocks. As she finished the first one, she looked at me, as though for approval or instructions. Again we smiled in recognition, and this time Irene announced that for the rest of the designs she was going to decide for herself how to attack each design, and to know when she was satisfied with her own solution.

We continued in similar manner through several tasks, until we both knew that Irene could now recognize the feeling of letting developments tell her what to do next. On her own she could find a bypass to a now increasingly familiar place from which she could pause to plan the rest of her journey. Note that we were dealing not merely with physically visible sequences, but with the client's lived ways of traveling and experiencing her own terrain. My personal observation of the sequences alone would not have been adequate for helping her to modify *her* style.

Joint formulation of reports. Rather than writing a report about Irene Kugel, I called her counselor while she was still in my office and described in detail our successes and their evolution. I advised him that Irene was in favor of looking for another job, still waitressing, but where she could get a fresh start at planning her waitressing. During the ensuing weeks they used the assessment explorations as a point of reference in discussing Irene's newer ventures. Later, they also reflected on the similarities to (and differences from) Irene's social relations and their own relationship.

Sometimes my report is in the form of a letter to the client, summarizing what turned out to be the thematic moments of our session(s) and reminding him of the concrete on-site tryings-out upon which we had agreed. If a copy of the report is to go to another professional, I remind the client (in the letter) of that person's concerns and of how our assessment work is relevant to them. Rarely is there anything in the letter or report that the client and I have not already discussed. If I do have an afterthought, I label it as such.

In short, before the client leaves me, he or she is already informed about what I think are the critical points to be recorded. Occasionally a client will request that I not divulge some particular fact, such as a homosexual encounter. If I agree that it does not seem essential to our goals, I ask the client to provide me with incidents that make the same point with different content.

So long as I formulate the report in terms of everyday life, there is no need to disguise my findings. Most clients regard our conclusions in this manner: "Nothing really new, although I never thought of it this way before; and now I can do something about it." Thus I have included diagnostic labels while discussing with patients their neurological impairment, paranoid delusions, suicidal state, and so on without undue disturbance, defensiveness, or surprise on their part. Although the labels may be politically deleterious, operationally they are simply gathering devices for difficulties with which the client is already quite familiar.

I write my reports in first-person form, and try to let the reader see who I was and how I contributed to the conclusions that emerged between the client and myself. Where possible, I include the client's actual words, so that we may all stay in touch with his sense of things rather than with my abstractions. There is no unexplained jargon. Test behavior is reported only as an introduction to similar everyday events, which in fact make up most of the report. Everything that is mentioned must meet the "so what?" criterion for practical implications. In other words, overall my reports strive to embody my beliefs that truth, even scientific truth, is necessarily perspectival and value laden, and that the professional knowledge that advises and guides me is not more fundamental than the life events as they are lived by the client. Moreover, it is only within life events that the client and his significant others can intervene constructively. There is a marked contrast between these reports in which life events are the data and already tried out alternatives are the results, and the traditional reports in which test scores are the data and traits and diagnoses are the results.

Client's commentary and instructions. Where there is a formal record or report, I ask the client to read it, and to add his comments and signature. If the assessment process itself has been collaborative there is nothing new in the report. Any corrections are usually along these lines: "The part about my family is true, but it seems a bit overemphasized"; "Actually, my mother died when I was nineteen. It's my stepmother we were talking about"; "I don't want it to appear that these problems dominate my life; they're important, but I'd like to emphasize the part about my also being a successful salesman and a contributing member of my lodge." Although these changes are usually minor, the fact of the client's involvement as a commentator is powerful: first, it encourages the assessor to stick as closely as he can, in his own formulations, to the client's experience; second, the client knows for sure that he continues to be seen as responsible for participating fully in directing his life. When I believe that the client understands the interpersonal and nonfinal nature of the report, I provide him with his own copy. Along with his written commentary and signature, the notation about the client's possessing his own copy of the report goes a long way toward impressing other readers with the client's readiness to participate actively in any further helping relations. Moreover, client and readers alike share common referents, namely actual events, as they discuss further implications of the report. Again, the professional's competence here lies not in his knowledge of scientific notions, but in how well he helps the person to cope with his own daily life.

The client's commentary also informs the assessor and readers of discrepancies, beyond those already noted in the report, between the client's and assessor's views. For example:

> *Mr. Ruckles's commentary:* Dr. Fischer has accurately portrayed my tendencies to create a hostile environment through my defensive aggression. However, she has failed to give adequate attention to the conspiracies that are spawned even in my absence. She made no mention of my therapist being in the employ of the Communist Party.

Whoever works with Mr. Ruckles will have to contend with Mr. Ruckles's perspective while keeping in mind the understanding that he nevertheless developed with the psychologist. In less dramatic instances, the client may point out a previously implicit difference in values: "I'm already working on our recommendations for initiating conversations, but it still seems to me that social relations are not as important as how well one does his work."

Sometimes the commentary indicates growth since the writing of a report. For example:

> *Joan's commentary:* I've already begun to take time out when I find myself plunging into things (like on the ink blots). But I've discovered that I can seek my own counsel best when no one else is around. So I'm going to practice with school work and housekeeping before trying out in social settings.

This last excerpt also illustrates that the commentary phase is an occasion for continued assessment, as are the client's tryings out in his daily life. The report is not an x-ray of immutable traits, but a progress report on changing comprehensions, growth, and suggestions, similar to therapy or counselling notes.

Additional excerpts

The following excerpts are all from one report, written for a state mental hospital on a fifty-four-year old retired coal miner. In answer to the diagnostic referral, I concluded that his delusions were not schizophrenic but were related to brain damage suffered in (documented) mining accidents.

As I found myself lapsing into swapping social pleasantries with Mr. Clark (for example, recipes for frying rabbits, soil conditions for cantaloupe, reputation of the hospital), I realized that for the moment I had forgotten his delusions about being a six-star general, and that he could no longer correctly add four plus four. I suspect that in a similar way his family and neighbors often either forget, or find it seemingly inappropriate, to check out with him his understanding of new plans or agreements. . . .

Mr. Clark worked attentively with the Kohs blocks for much longer (ten minutes on one design) than most testees will. He said that it felt like puttering in his workshop—he'd keep "fooling" with it until the "danged thing" worked out. Sometimes, when he's available, Mr. Clark's (adult) son has been called on for advice about a resistive project. But sometimes Mr. Clark has shouted and argued, thrown tools around, and insisted that his son is disobedient, that he (Mr. Clark) is the "commander-in-chief." He described such incidents when I asked him when else had been like "just now, with me (psychologist) pushing you to go faster, the nurse interrupting us to say that you have to miss garden assignment to take medication, and your leg hurting." I'm not clear about what his household variations of these conditions are; perhaps Mrs. Jayson (unit social worker) could develop some leads on this with the family. . . .

Mr. Clark and I eventually named this sequence "impatience," and practiced his "standing for [his] rights" by asking for clarification or assistance whenever "impatience sets in." We practiced this on the Bender, where he finally "stood" for his "rights" by asking directly if he were doing okay, and in a "pretend" interview in which he finally announced that he was "confused" and "impatient" and that I would have to get help from someone else for my answers. Ward staff and family could continue this terminology and practice with Mr. Clark to help him bypass those situations in which confusion, frustration, and what I suspect must be a sense of impotence, have led to delusional assertions of competence.

These excerpts illustrate several of the themes from above: the assessment context, including my own kind of presence and approach, is represented; test performance is presented as instances of the patient's daily comportment and as my vehicle for trying out alternatives; the language we used in the sessions is made available for continuity in relating with the patient; and finally, the report tries to evoke a sense of the patient's living of his world—its fluctuating physiognomy for him as he moves through it in variations of his way. While physically visible events are the touchpoints for the patient, myself, and his other helpers, we must try to reach him "where he lives" if we are to help him to recognize those changes in the face of his terrain that ought to announce: "Danger: Take Alternative Route."

Mr. Clark did not comprehend several of the sentences and the thrust of the report. So I focused on his understanding of our concluding set of recommendations and of how the staff would behave with him. In addition I tried to clarify for him his understanding of why he was in "the loony bin." I assured him that he did not have a "split personality" (his definition of "crazy"), but that it was his familiar periods of "confusion," "filling in" or "exaggerating," and "getting in trouble" (his characterization of fighting with a storekeeper, threats of violence to his family, and so on) that had led his son to hospitalize him. I explained that his difficulties in "recollecting" and planning started with damage to his nervous system sustained in the mining accidents, and that although medication and periodic examinations might help, it was up to him to learn to live with this "unfairness" as he had other "hard times"; others could help him, but "staying out of trouble" was still largely up to him. Of course this message had to be represented in multiple, repeated, and consistent ways by staff and family, but Mr. Clark again understood and experienced himself as "[his] own man, like in the old days."

Tallent (1975) has published a full psychological report that I wrote several years ago. It illustrates most of these collaborative assessment practices. Additional lines of discussion and examples can be found in Fischer, 1969, 1970, 1972a&b, 1974, and in Fischer and Rizzo, 1974. Before going on to respond to some questions typically raised about collaborative assessment, let me mention that all that I have said about psychological reports also holds true for other records. If the above practices are followed, client access to files should present no problem.

Elaboration

As Mr. Clark's case illustrates, the nature of the client's informed participation varies drastically from person to person. Admittedly, the earlier illustrations were from verbal, fairly reflective persons—always the easiest with whom to be a clinician! On other occasions, when the client cannot help me himself, I ask his significant others to help me locate the "whens," "when-nots," and pivot points. In short, the *practices* are malleable in order to meet each situation. But the *theoretical principles*, to be summarized in the next section, serve the goal of all cases: for the client to expand whatever experience he has of himself as sharing a world in which he can participate in shaping his own life.

Collaborative assessment does require more time than traditional assessment. In the long run, however, it is more efficient. The outcome includes not only a portrait of the client, but already tried-out entries into his daily life, and a first-stage set of concrete recommendations. The client already is feeling better able to cope with his situation. If he is referred or returned to a longer-term therapist or counselor, the transition is a smoother, more efficient one than in the past. Client satisfaction is higher, recidivism is lower, intensive individual therapy is assigned more judiciously, and staff's sense of achievement is greater.

The data and notions developed by objectivistic approaches, whether MMPI (Minnesota Multiphasic Personality Inventory) profile predictions or psychoanalytic interpretations, should not be overlooked. They too should guide the professional's understandings and queries. But they are realms of reflection, not of some truth underlying or causing behavior and experience.

This sort of common sense approach does result in a loss of mystique about psychology. I frequently hear from my graduate students' clinical supervisors that their reports were received enthusiastically by all involved as maximally useful, but that "they really weren't very psychological." Collaborative assessors learn to accept being ordinary, and earn their prestige on the basis of accomplishment with clients. This does require that the professional be much more than the technician he often has been in the past. It is his or her opinions that are presented, not "what the test says." Scores are starting points; they are not "results." The professional is answerable for his own values and assumptions, which must be reexamined as he confronts each new client. In a way, he is a consultant to clients, offering his impressions and suggestions, and perpetually refining and correcting procedures as his clients let him know the extent of his usefulness.

There are indeed touchpoints with other contemporary trends. For example: contingency management client contracts, self-control behavior modification, client participation in program evaluation, and humanistic psychology's therapies and workshops on self-discovery and self-help. Where this particular approach to informed participation differs, however, is in the theoretical foundation that allows it to go beyond the just-mentioned techniques to respect and work with the person's humanness, especially his lived world, in a fuller and more sustained manner.

GUIDING PRINCIPLES

Because most practitioners are more interested in successful techniques than in theory, this chapter has emphasized actual practices. At this point it seems important to review the human-science framework and to name explicitly the principles that guide the practices of collaborative assessment. This may attenuate readers' tendencies to yea-say the practices, or to reject them out of hand, without critically comparing them to their own assumptions and practices.

Human-science psychology in general

To summarize, psychology as a human (versus object) science takes explicit account of the individual's goals, values, and ways of forming and experiencing his milieu. Objectifiable physical conditions are also taken into account, but not as independent, more real, or as causal. Human science accepts the complexity involved in respecting the multiperspectival character of human reality. It foresakes the precision of object-science methods in the interest of staying in closer and more effective touch with the necessarily ambiguous and fluid structure of human affairs, including the inherent unity of experience and behavior. Ambiguity and flux are not chaos, however. There is order, but one for which the goals of anticipation and influence are more appropriate than those of prediction and control.

This human science approach allows professionals to be both scientific (rigorous, empirical, reflective, disciplined) and humanistic (promoting personal growth and capacity for experience). It encourages us to bring the idealistic preambles of our assorted codes of ethics (for example, "respect the dignity and worth of the individual") into consonance with our explanatory theories. A human science approach allows us to bypass the "yes, buts" and "never minds" to address the individual client in his own right while still being guided by general knowledge of human expression, options, and limitations. Finally, such an orientation necessitates the client's active involvement as an informed participant.

Among the relevant writings of the increasing numbers of existential, phenomenological, and humanistic authors, the ones addressed most directly to psychology as a human science are Giorgi's *Psychology as a Human Science* (1970) and volumes one (1971) and two (1975) of *Duquesne Studies in Phenomenological Psychology*.

Guiding Principles for Collaborative Assessment

I have named my own practice of human science psychological assessment in terms of the *collaborative*, jointly responsible, relationship between the client and assessor. But it also is characterized by several other interrelated guiding principles; collaborative assessment is *descriptive, contextual, structural, and interventional*.

Its data are on-going events from daily life and the assessment sessions, *described* as well as possible without recourse to reductionistic abstractions. Such descriptions try to present the *context* of the event—the observers' perspective and participation and at least an evocation of what seems to be the client's vantage points and involvement. Human-science assessment comprehends *structurally* rather than causally or reductively. That is, we understand an event in terms of its all equally essential, distinguishable but inseparable components rather than as a product of underlying forces. (For example, we understood Ms. Kugel's "Bendering" as occurring *when* she has no personally appropriated plan and standard for action, *when* there are others around to direct her, and *when* she perceives others as expecting her to be her old self; we did not attribute her conduct to "dependency," "social immaturity," or "impulsiveness.") The structure is understood in terms of the participants' situated experience rather than in terms of one privileged observer's objectifying perspective. This approach acknowledges that any assessor necessarily influences his client's participation in the assessment as well as his own perception of that participation. Finally, it encourages planned *intervention* within the client's accustomed ways of dealing with tasks. Thus we surpass identification of restrictions to explore personally viable expansions.

If the reader does not follow these or related principles in his or her professional work, then that person should specify just how his or her practices do take into account any human differences from objects. If he or she sees no significant differences, then shouldn't prospective clients be informed of that fact? For those readers who do find themselves in general agreement with a human-science approach to psychology, perhaps these guiding principles can help to bring practices into closer consonance with beliefs.

REFERENCES

Craddick, R. A. 1975. Sharing oneself in the assessment procedure. *Professional Psychol.* 6:279–82.

Dana, R. H. and Leech, S. 1974. Existential assessment. *J. Personality Assessment* 38:428–35.

Fischer, C. T. 1969. Rapport as mutual respect. *Personnel and Guidance J.* 48:201–4. Also in C. E. Beck, ed. 1971. *Philosophical guidelines for counseling.* 2d ed. Dubuque: Wm. C. Brown.

———. 1970. The testee as co-evaluator. *J. Counseling Psychol.* 17:70–76. Also in A. Giorgi, W. F. Fischer, and R. von Eckartsberg. 1971. *Duquesne studies in phenomenological psychology*, vol. 1. Pittsburgh: Duquesne University Press.

———. 1972a. Paradigm changes which allow sharing of results. *Professional Psychol.* 3:364–69.

———. 1972b. A theme for the child-advocate: shareable everyday-life events of the child-in-his-world. *J. Clinical Child Psychol.* 1:23–25.

———. 1973. Contextual approach to assessment. *Community Mental Health J.* 9:38–45.

———. 1974. Exit IQ: enter the child. In *Clinical child psychology: current practices and future perspectives*, ed. G. Williams and S. Gordon. New York: Behavioral Publications.

Fischer, C. T. and Rizzo, A. A. 1974. A paradigm for humanizing special education, *J. Special Education* 8:321–29.

Giorgi, A. 1970. Psychology as a human science: a phenomenologically based approach. New York: Harper and Row.

Giorgi, A., Fischer, W. F., and von Eckartsberg, R., eds., 1971. *Duquesne Studies in phenomenological psychology*, vol. 1. Pittsburgh: Duquesne University Press.

Giorgi, A., Fischer, C. T., and Murray, E. L., eds. 1975. *Duquesne studies in phenomenological psychology*, vol. 2. Pittsburgh: Duquesne University Press.

Riscalla, L. M. 1972. The captive psychologist and the captive patient. *Professional Psychol.* 3:375–79.

Szasz, T. S. 1961. The myth of mental illness. New York: Harper and Row.

Tallent, N. 1975. Psychological report writing. New York: Prentice-Hall.

Vane, J. R. 1972. Getting information from school and clinical psychologists. *Professional Psychol.* 3:205–08.

4.

Coercion and Reciprocity in Psychotherapy

DONALD N. BERSOFF

Psychotherapy, like any other social influence enterprise, is . . . a process in which the therapist arranges stimulus conditions that produce desired behavioral changes in the client.

—Albert Bandura (1969)

One point of origin in the modern history of inappropriate client manipulation may be found in the psychotherapeutic treatment of a fearful Viennese five-year-old named Hans. Hans's analysis in 1909 provided the first case material used by Freud to substantiate his theories of infantile sexuality and the existence of the Oedipus complex. Little realized is the fact that the therapy itself was highly impersonal—it was kept secret from the patient and was applied by a psychiatric surrogate. The fact is that Hans was seen by Freud only once. The therapy itself was accomplished by Hans's father who frequently consulted Freud either in his office or through the mail. Thus, all the insights so omnisciently exposited in "The Analysis of a Phobia in a Five-year-old Boy" were actually based on Freud's interpretation of Hans's father's perception of Hans's behavior. Hans never knew his behavior was being observed so that it could be reported and analyzed; he did not know that he had been labeled as a "little Oedipus" libidinously longing for his mother and paradoxically frightened and angry toward his father; neither did he realize that his behavior was being systematically managed and controlled so that he would be purged of those feelings.[1]

Freud may have been guilty of what today we would regard as rather flagrant violations of good practice in his relationship with the manipulated Hans, but in no way should he be singled out for special penance. Psychotherapy is merely an instance of social interaction and, in such interaction, the behavior of each participant significantly and directly affects the other. All therapists control and, to some extent, coerce, their clients. Psychotherapy is a special case of social interaction only because clients so frequently perceive their therapists to be benign, democratic, and nonmanipulative, a perception often shared by therapists themselves. It is primarily this failure to recognize the power and control inherent in any therapy relationship that has led to the perpetuation of abuses in it.

This paper, therefore, has a two-fold purpose: (1) to make explicit some of the behaviors therapists of various persuasions engage in which lead to the (for the most part) unintended coercion and subordination of their clients; and (2) to describe practices, some already existing, some emanating from the author's fantasy, that may hopefully correct some of the unacknowledged harm we do to our clients. The first task is relatively easy, the second admittedly more difficult.

COERCION IN PSYCHOTHERAPY

Behavior is not independent of the situation in which people are observed to be behaving. Yet many therapies are based on the notion that behavior occurs in relative isolation, predominantly the product of what are called response dispositions—"a bewildering phantasmagoria of putative underlying mediating structures and mechanisms" including "needs, traits, drives, cathexes, and a whole host of energy transformations apparently involving as many structures and mechanisms of change as there are therapists" (Wallace 1966, p. 132). Somehow, the environment is neglected despite the importance of the stimulus in theory. Treatment modalities based on such internal mechanisms proceed on the premise that behavioral disturbances reside primarily within the person, despite lip service to the client's own responsibility for change.[2]

Such practices are not congruent with what is known about behavior. All situations in which behavior occurs are also characterized by environmental events which evoke the behavior (antecedent events) and after its occurrence, either accelerate, decelerate, or maintain it (consequent events). Behavior is thus stimulated and consequated by the action of others.

The two views of behavior may be exemplified through the following illustration. A child must be in front of his house by 8:00 A.M. if he is to catch the school bus by that time. One morning, because the alarm does not ring, he fails to waken and his mother yells at him, "Hurry up, it's late." If after that admonition the child does not get out of bed he may be called lazy, irresponsible, or passive-aggressive. Such name-calling is an overt expression of a theory which places responsibility of behavior primarily within the target of change. However, the failure of the child to be aroused can be alternately ascribed to the failure of the mother to evoke effectively the behavior she wanted. Assume the mother altered her command from "Hurry up, it's late" to "Hurry up, it's five minutes to eight," and was successful in achieving the desired result. There would have been no change in the "personality" or psychodynamic construction of the child. The change would have occurred in the nature of the stimulus conditions arranged by the mother. In like manner, if the son did get up on time but received no recognition for this appropriate behavior, it is likely he would not continue to engage in that behavior consistently. But, if he were to be praised for evidencing the behavior desired by his mother, such behavior would most likely continue at a rather high rate.

The mother, then, arranges the conditions in which the behavior of her son is to occur and influences the rate that it will be emitted in the future. The psychotherapeutic environment can be analyzed in the same way. The therapist designs the stimulus conditions for the evocation of behavior and becomes a potent source of its consequation. In this way, psychotherapy can be seen as another instance of behavior control. This view has been overlooked because, as Perry London (1969) has pointed out, psychotherapy has relied on a relatively ineffective means of control. Psychotherapy is basically a verbal enterprise in contrast to such therapies as hypnosis, drugs, and faradic shock. Language, with its imprecision, misleads us into thinking that words are not really control devices. It is noteworthy that therapy has come under closer scrutiny as a coercive exercise with the increasing popularity and established effectiveness of the behaviorally-oriented therapies that rely more on action and less on words. As London (1969) asserts, "mental health practitioners have been in the business of individual behavior control for a long time, via psychotherapy, but it has been such a slow and sometimes useless means of influence that they have not been forced or felt the need to see it as an effort toward that end" (p. 7).

London's historical perspective nevertheless somewhat underestimates the many ways clients have been coerced and manipulated in what they thought was a deconstraining and nondirective verbal milieu. The ensuing discussion focuses on some of the ways therapists have been responsible, unwittingly or wittingly, for the subjugation of their clients.

The nonbehavioral therapies will continue to receive the brunt of criticism here, but only because those forms of therapy, even when expertly conducted, run special risks of being coercive. This danger is inherent in any system where the change agent assumes that he is more knowledgeable than the client about what is "really" going on. However, while behavioral therapists are less disposed by theoretical commitment to see themselves as the experts on personal reality, their *practices* too are the target of the following discussion.

Structuring the Stimulus Conditions

In general, therapists determine the structure of the therapeutic relationship. For many clients, the therapist's silence and ambiguity constitute the setting in which they are asked to interact. Such an environment did not develop full blown from theory, however. When Joseph Breuer saw Anna O., the young, attractive patient he had been treating with uneven success for some time, writhing on the bed playing out the fantasy that she was giving birth to her doctor's child, he was inescapably faced with the realization that ministering to a "hysterical girl" may have some unanticipated consequences.[3] The experience was so powerful that Breuer lost almost all interest in pursuing this new form of medical treatment and left its development in the hands of his younger colleague, Sigmund Freud.[4] To preclude the reoccurence of such discomforting events, Freud decided that the absence of both personal involvement and self-revelation would not only reduce the therapist's responsibility in any transference reactions, but would heighten the responsibility of the client to solve his own problems. Such reasoning, underlying almost all brands of insight therapy, is summarized by London:

> The patient himself must assume responsibility for virtually all the subject matter of the therapy sessions. . . . The onus rests on him to initiate discourse and to conduct it, with the

therapist there to guide the stream of patient's consciousness, not to interfere with it. Everything the therapist does ... is supposed to encourage and reinforce the patient's exploration of himself, not to put new contents in his life. Not only does the insight therapist avoid pressing his own opinions on the patient ... but ... he also avoids significant disclosures about himself. This anonymity further forces the patient to be responsible for himself; otherwise, by knowing too much about the therapist's personal life, he might pattern his own behavior after this potential model [London 1969, p. 47].

The clearest manifestation of avoidance of self-disclosure is silence. If such behavior increases client responsibility, it also has some unintended side effects. Two of these effects, frustration and anger, are expressed by Tom Prideaux in a short poem:

> With half a laugh of hearty zest
> I strip me off my coat and vest.
>
> Then heeding not the frigid air
> I fling away my underwear.
>
> So having nothing else to doff,
> I rip my epidermis off.
>
> More secrets to acquaint you with
> I pare my bones to strips of pith.
>
> And when the exposé is done
> I hand a cobweb skeleton.
>
> While you sit there aloof, remote,
> And will not shed your overcoat.[5]

Silence, however, is only one weapon in an arsenal that critics of psychoanalysis claim heightens not client responsibility, but therapist power. To critics, these techniques (Jay Haley 1969a, calls them Freud's ploys) are all designed to maintain therapist omnipotence. Equating psychoanalysis with one-upsmanship, Haley describes it as a

dynamic psychological process involving two people, a patient and a psychoanalyst, during which the patient insists that the analyst be one-up while desperately trying to put himself

one-down, and the analyst insists that the patient remain
one-down in order to help him learn to become one-up. . . .
Carefully designed, the psychoanalytic setting makes the superior position of the analyst almost invincible [Haley 1969a,
pp. 12–13].

In less humorous terms, John Marquis has castigated the analytic
relationship on the same grounds:

A classical psychoanalyst may go for six months without doing
anything but instructing the analysand in the techniques of
free association, and interpreting his resistances. Almost everything that the patient says is considered as being wrong. At
best it represents some sort of derivative of his unmentionable
impulses filtered through ego-mechanisms whose primary
function is to deceive the patient and the others about him. At
worst it is a deliberate attempt to evade and subvert efforts to
help him. The analyst is the expert on everything, including
how the patient feels [Marquis 1972, pp. 43–44].

If silence is characteristic of psychoanalytically oriented forms of
psychotherapy, its counterpart, ambiguity, is found in almost all
other nonbehavioral therapies. Such ambiguity is most prevalent in
the setting of goals and the delineation of therapy strategies.

Humanistic forms of psychotherapy, such as sensitivity training
and T-groups, which on the surface seem to possess many of the
features one would like to see in a genuinely noncoercive therapy
setting, are specifically designed to be ambiguous. Most usually,
such groups are initiated without a predetermined agenda, without
any clearly defined rules for participation, and without an explicit
statement of learning goals:

One is deprived of cognitive maps of the situation. Everything
is possible and yet nothing is sanctioned. No means to one's
personal ends are ruled out nor are any prescribed. The
criteria which usually exist in social situations for choosing
among courses of action become blurred and fuzzy. The experience is of being in a setting in which one does not know how
to do anything [Harrison 1965, pp. 4–5].

By working through the anxiety, confusion, and fear engendered by
the ambiguity, by sharing these feelings, by receiving feedback,
and through the intense group interaction evoked by the lack of
structure, it is generally hypothesized that the outcomes will be

increased openness, authenticity, and sensitivity to self and others. Just as silence produces unintended consequences, however, so does ambiguity.

Lack of structure, whether it be silence or ambiguity, produces a condition known as response uncertainty (Fulkerson 1965). Any situation can be classified as possessing either certainty, risk, or uncertainty. The more the situation is structured and the more the rules of behavior are explicitly expressed, the more the person responding will be able to evaluate his own behavior. But, situations that are deliberately designed to provide little structure or direction prevent the behaver from responding in ways that allow him to accurately monitor the effectiveness or appropriateness of his action. Lack of structure, especially when it includes the failure of the clinician and client to cooperatively develop therapy goals, deprives the client of power to the extent that he is unable to determine if the therapist is indeed moving him toward the intended outcomes. In a satirical essay Haley includes as a central tenet of his twelve points on how to fail as a therapist, "a continuing refusal to define the goals of therapy. If the therapist sets goals, someone is likely to raise a question whether they have been achieved" (Haley, 1969a, p. 694).

Situations with a high degree of response uncertainty enable the therapist to maintain power in other ways. In such a setting, where one person possesses the guidelines for behavior and the other does not, the uncertain behaver is more likely to accept the opinion of the one more knowledgeable. Thus, the therapy setting is one in which conditions facilitate the occurrence of modeling. Bandura (1969) and his colleagues have demonstrated in both laboratory and field research that learning can occur on a vicarious basis through observation of another person's behavior and the consequences that behavior has for the one observed. Such observational learning, or modeling, has been found to be enhanced when the modeler is, in the perception of the observer, a prestigious person. London has stated that "the extent to which the patient is likely to buy the therapist's interpretation . . . probably depends more on their personal relationship than on any other single factor, including the wisdom or accuracy of the interpretation" (London 1969, pp. 50–51). If this is true, by virtue of his status as a therapist and insofar as he does not reveal himself as a person, the therapist is in an almost unassailable position to influence his client. Furthermore, the effects of modeling are known to continue in the modeler's absence, allowing the therapist to influence his client's actions though he may no longer serve in that role.

Clients would have little difficulty in evaluating whether they

were being unduly or inappropriately influenced by their therapists if they had some objective basis for making that decision. But,
by keeping goals vague, and by making interpretations about traits,
complexes, or ego-states, all unobservable nonbehavioral
phenomena, the therapist prevents the client from making such an
evaluation. Additionally, it has been found that clinician's judgments concerning therapy outcomes are indirectly based on how
well the client has modeled and internalized the therapist's value
system. Rosenthal (1955) found that therapists rated those clients
who changed their values in the areas of sex, aggression, and authority toward greater congruence with the therapists' values as
showing the greatest improvement.

Thus, psychotherapy, to the extent that its practitioners structure
the therapeutic experience ambiguously, produces a situation in
which clients become victims of coercion and subtly induced conformity, while their ability to monitor whether they are moving
toward their own goals is highly attenuated. In such a setting, only
the therapist knows where he is moving the client, at what rate he is
moving him there, and when he has transported the client to the
final destination.

Symptoms as Diseases and Symptoms in Isolation

The probability for mutual disclosure and person-to-person re-
latedness is reduced when the therapist perceives a client problem
as either a disease or an expression of an underlying conflict. Much
of the criticism concerning the correlation of psychological
symptoms to physical disease has been stimulated by Thomas
Szasz. In a prolific outflow beginning about 1960 he has attacked
the concept of mental illness and the process of diagnosis. To Szasz,
"psychiatric classification is not a 'scientific' activity; it is a social
act, designed to demean the patient by casting him in the role of the
mental patient and to legitimize the psychiatrist's intervention by
defining it as a medical-therapeutic endeavor" (Szasz 1966a, p. 41).
Mental illness, in any of its diagnosed forms, is merely a name used
to denote a deviant social role. The inherent immorality of such
classification is that the deviant role is acquired involuntarily.
Many roles are assumed by individuals with their consent—persons who marry agree to accept the role of spouse. But, very few
people graciously and willingly accept the role of mental patient.

Because the consequences of being called mentally ill (for example, disenfranchisement, involuntary incarceration) are so negative,
Szasz (1966b) calls diagnostic labels "semantic prisons" and those

responsible for bestowing those labels "behavioral classification officers" who by their acts define an individual's personal identity and legitimize condemning a person's social role.

Labeling can lead not only to the loss of many freedoms, it can also lead to the rejection of the labeled person himself (Phillips 1963). Assuming that symptoms are derivatives of disease, the therapist is more likely to see himself as separate from the client. He will be more likely to act out the doctor role and treat the client as sick. Medical practitioners rarely disclose personal information about themselves; neither are they likely to inform an ill patient about his illness or the specific interventions they will use to cure him. Thus, a disease model of symptomatology is likely to isolate the client from human encounter with the therapist and increase the probability that decisions will be made *about* a patient rather than *with* a client.

As for the consequences of perceiving symptoms as symbolic expressions of hidden dynamic forces, Bandura has made one of the most cogent statements:

> [In] the psychodynamic model . . . any behavior, no matter how trivial or apparently irrelevant, tends to be viewed as a derivative of concealed psychodynamic forces and is therefore subject to analysis and reinterpretation in terms of the therapist's theoretical predilections. Thus virtually no aspect of the client's life—his social, marital, and sexual behavior, his political and religious beliefs, his vocational choice, his child-training practices—escapes the therapist's repeated scrutiny and influence over a period of several years. Since this approach tends to regard behavioral difficulties as superficial manifestations of more fundamental and often unconscious internal events, influence attempts are primarily directed toward subject matters of questionable relevance. It is not uncommon, therefore, to find clients whose beliefs systems have been thoroughly modified despite little amelioration of the behavioral difficulties for which they originally sought help [Bandura 1969, p. 84].

A suggested solution to such a situation has been a behavioral model in which the specific task of the therapist is symptom removal. The therapist views himself, in this context, as a kind of super-technician:

> The relationship is as direct and straight-forward as that of the

therapist consulting his attorney about a legal matter, or his accountant about his income tax. The expert is supplied with data, and a request for help with a specific problem, although the expert may also be called upon to formulate the problem more precisely. Perhaps a better example would be the more personal and complex relationship of the architect using his technical skills to design and build for the client a house which matches his needs and his lifestyle [Marquis 1972, p. 48].

Psychotherapy built on such a model may have much to commend it. Of genuine benefit is the fact that it differentiates the therapist and his client only insofar as their genetic endowment and life experiences have been dissimilar. The therapist does not view himself as any better or healthier than his yet unredeemed neurotically sick patient. Symptoms are merely seen as maladaptive learned behaviors modifiable through the application of a variety of effective techniques.

However, while the behavior therapist may view himself as neutral, such a perception can be challenged as illusory and naive. Seymour Halleck in *The Politics of Therapy* has been most vocal in this regard: "At first glance, a model . . . based on the contention that people should just be helped to learn to do the things they want to do seems uncomplicated and desirable. But it is an unattainable model" (Halleck 1971, p. 19).

Halleck views any therapy as a political act. Defining politics as the science of how power is sought, distributed, and exercised within social systems, he asserts that because treatment has an impact on the distribution of power within the various social systems of which the client is a part, all therapeutic intervention must be viewed as having political consequences. The specific consequence of a symptom-removal-only approach is preservation of the status quo. If one views certain symptoms as behaviors arising from the need to influence an oppressive environment (and Halleck perceives symptoms this way), the behavior therapist who does not go beyond modifying behavior protects the system. Any time therapists teach clients to live better within the environment they are helping to preserve the milieu in which the symptom occurs. As Halleck says, "A person who might have confronted the existing social order can, as a result of undergoing psychotherapy, become more tolerant of the status quo" (p. 47). Within this framework, Halleck views behavior therapy as more repressive than more traditional forms of therapy: "because symptomatic treatment makes it so easy for the patient, the therapist, and the community to deny that social factors create human misery, it can be used as powerful instrument of social control" (p. 68).

In many ways Halleck's arguments are overdrawn and not consonant with the reality of behavior therapy. For example, assertive training, a mainstay within broad spectrum behavior therapy, is a technique designed specifically to alter abusive environments or the oppressive actions of others. Furthermore, in many cases behavior therapists have helped clients reduce anxiety concerning (or did not interfere with their continuing) behavior which society might condemn as illegal or immoral (cf. Kraft 1972). But the cautionary message that Halleck offers is important for all therapists. Insofar as any practitioner becomes insensitive to the political implications of his work, that practitioner will be helping to sustain the present order through the behavior control of his client. Almost all therapies, not merely behavior therapy, neglect the client as he interacts within the environment and overlook the complexity of behavior as a function of situational influences, both in its evocation and consequation. In their assessment techniques and intervention strategies, mental health professionals have concentrated on fixing the person rather than on seeking ways to restructure the environment in which the disturbing behavior occurs.

Providing Consequences for Client Behavior

Thus far it has been shown how clinicians structure the therapy situation in ways that evoke, influence, control, or coerce clients' behavior. However, these outcomes also occur as a result of therapist response to client behavior. Verbal conditioning studies (Greenspoon 1962, Krasner 1958, Salzinger 1959, Salzinger and Pisoni 1958, Verplanck 1955) have indicated that interviewers (that is, therapists) can accelerate parts of speech, self-statements, discussion of particular subject area, and presumably any other language variable by the mode and frequency of interviewer response. For example, Salzinger and Pisoni (1958) experimentally altered the rate of emission of affect statements simply by following these statements by some kind of positively toned remark to accelerate them and subsequently ignoring those statements to extinguish them.

In most therapeutic interaction the conditioning that Salzinger demonstrates goes on without intention or awareness, producing covert compliance over which neither the client nor the therapist has any control. As Salzinger, Portnoy, and Feldman indicate:

> Even though the interviewer reinforces the interviewee's be-
> havior unknowingly, he may still do so in a lawful way. For
> the interviewer who considers sex problems to be the core of
> abnormality, the interviewee's statements about these will
> constitute reinforcing events for the interviewer who believes
> social causes to be crucial for abnormality, statements con-
> cerning these factors will act similarly. Each kind of inter-
> viewee statement would in turn be reinforced by the respec-
> tive interviewer. In this way, the theory or bias of a given
> interviewer will determine what reinforces him, what he rein-
> forces, and therefore, what theory he will confirm [Salzinger,
> Portnoy, and Feldman 1964, pp. 846–47].

Client-centered therapy has been pointed to most often as a form
of therapist-client interaction which avoids the danger of selective
reinforcement.[6] Central to a client-centered relationship is noncontingent, nonselective responsiveness by the therapist. The therapist has no constraining theoretical orientation or agenda other than
to develop an atmosphere in which empathy and warmth abound. A
setting such as this, characterized by genuineness and uncondi-
tional positive regard, is seen as the most supportive environment
in which to evoke self-determined constructive change in the
client.

The notion of noncontingent responsiveness in client-centered
therapy is more a myth than a reality, however. Truax (1966)
analyzed the tape recordings of a long-term therapy relationship
between Carl Rogers and a client. He found that Rogers responded
selectively with differential levels of warmth, directiveness, and
empathy to such client behavior as: (1) learning discriminations
about self and feelings; (2) lack of client ambiguity (client clarity
was reinforced); (3) expressions of insight; (4) verbal expressions
that were similar in style to the therapist's way of expressing himself; and (5) problem orientation. Furthermore, of these five classes
of client behavior to which Rogers selectively responded, four
showed significant changes over the course of therapy:

> When the patient expressed himself in a style similar to that of
> the therapist, the therapist was more empathic, more warm
> and accepting, and less directive. When the patient expressed
> himself in a style quite different from that of the therapist, the
> therapist tended to show significantly less empathy, less ac-
> ceptance, and more directiveness [Truax 1966, p. 5].

In addition, such contingent responsiveness served to accelerate the behavior of the client in the direction desired by the therapist. If this phenomenon exists in a setting specifically structured to prevent its occurrence, one can only conjecture at the unmonitored consequences of similar reinforcement of therapist values in other therapy situations.

A Final Constraint

It may seem in the context of this paper an outrageous exaggeration to say that therapists have been bought by the "establishment." However, this is not as radical a statement as it first appears if one thinks carefully about how most therapists are trained. Because most mental health professionals have been financially supported by those who construct and administer current government policies, they will, in some ways, be wedded to the status quo. Halleck makes this point clear in his description of a psychiatrist's education:

> Most of his training has been supported by the state. It is virtually impossible today for a man to go through four years of medical school, a year of internship, and three years of residency training without having had a major portion of that training paid for by a government agency. One cannot even practice psychiatry unless his credentials and ethical standards have been approved by professional and state agencies. Only in exceptional circumstances would the healer be inclined to radically reform the system that nurtured and affirmed him [Halleck 1971, p. 238].

The majority of practitioners have been supported in a similar manner. NIMH training grants may be the most prevalent example. But, not only is the training of clinicians underwritten by the government, the sites in which most therapists work are also supported by government monies. Mental health clinics and other community agencies are traditionally financed by local funds generated by United Way campaigns and by state funds raised through taxes. Therapists hired by public schools, state hospitals, vocational rehabilitation agencies, the military, the Veterans' Administration are all supported by one or a combination of local, state, and federal dollars.

The strain of working within institutional bureaucracies for those committed to helping individuals has been expressed by Ernest Keen:

As psychotherapists, we find ourselves trapped in a conflict between two traditions, two sets of values, two definitions of what is important in life; bureaucratic and therapeutic values. . . . Bureaucratic values tend to define my work as making people who are different more like everyone else—"productive members of society." Therapeutic values tend to define my work as making people who are like everyone else different. . . .

The modern role of psychotherapists has always been an uneasy compromise; we have told *ourselves* that we work for the truth of men, of our patients, and we have always told *society* that we work in the service of efficiency and productivity [Keen 1972, p. 13].

Since they are financed by the system and in danger of losing money if they violate community standards, it is difficult to conceive of many clinicians teaching clients new behaviors—or removing barriers to old ones—that might lead to the challenging of society's tenets. While such therapist inhibitions may be defensible, it should be made clear that such inhibitions may be a direct violation of the client's request as well as a manifest preservation of the environment in which the client lives—another instance of how psychotherapy may legitimately be construed as a political act and a means of social control.

RECIPROCITY IN PSYCHOTHERAPY

The problems so far presented do not lend themselves to easy solutions. Covert manipulation, subtle reinforcement, and political influence are incredibly complex issues hardly considered, much less systematically mitigated, by many therapists. It is doubtful if therapist coercion and influence can be eliminated entirely but their effects may be reduced by adopting suggestions similar to the following.

Psychotherapy as an Experiment

The least repressive form of psychotherapy is one conceived of as a scientific experiment. Such a flat statement may appear to be a contradiction of terms and the idea is not entirely new,[7] but it may be wise to look at the contention afresh and see in what ways it may be helpful in the context of reciprocity and coercion.

Research, like therapy, tried to solve problems. The difference between them, however, is that in research all known important facets of the problem-solving strategy are disclosed so that the work of the researcher can be easily verified. The aim is replication. Others must be given sufficient information to do the experiment themselves. Hypotheses must be stated, methods for testing the hypotheses specified, the description of the working rules for conducting the experiment and interpreting its results clearly delineated, data yielded from the procedure presented, and conclusions drawn from the data fully discussed so that objective observers can judge the validity of the interpretations made. In like manner, it is suggested that the client be conceived of as a consumer of his therapist's experimental methodology.

Yet, some important distinctions must be made between an experimental and a therapeutic procedure. In an experiment both the delineation of hypotheses and the delineation of methods to test those hypotheses are the responsibility of the researcher. These components have as their counterparts in therapy the setting of goals and the specification of the strategies to achieve those goals. Unlike the research situation, these tasks do not belong exclusively to the therapist. Bandura (1969) suggests distinct roles for client and therapist in the setting of goals and the designing of interventions. Goal setting requires a value judgment while strategy construction is primarily an empirical decision. Thus, the client would have responsibility for suggesting goals and for making judgments concerning outcomes, while the role of the therapist would be limited to fabricating techniques which he felt would be most effective in achieving those outcomes.

In such a relationship the therapist would have the right to reject aiding his client in securing goals he felt were antagonistic to his own or the community's value system. The client would have the right to reject strategies or implementations he perceived as inimical to his values or behavioral style. Once goals and strategies were agreed on, the therapist would develop the therapy situation in such a way as to increase the probability that the client attained the outcomes he had chosen. The therapist's role, as specified by Kelly, would be as follows:

> The psychotherapist helps the client design and implement experiments. He pays attention to controls. He helps the client define the hypotheses. He helps the client avoid abortive undertakings. He uses the psychotherapy room as a laboratory. He does not extort results from his client to confirm his own systematic prejudices nor does he urge his client, in turn,

to seek appeasement, rather than knowledge. Finally, he recognizes that in the inevitable scheme of things he is himself a
part of the validating evidence which the client must take into
account in reckoning the outcome of his psychotherapeutic
experiments [Kelly 1955, p. 589].

From a different perspective, the experimenter role has been
conceived as that of task and social leader. The therapist becomes
both an engineer and facilitator "responsible for the attainment of
treatment objectives and . . . the continuance of the relationship
through providing patients with at least a minimally acceptable
level of immediate outcomes" (Rosen 1972, p. 330).

Specification of Outcomes

Mutual defining of client goals is one part of an initial therapeutic
relationship that strives for reciprocity and openness. At the very
least, three aspects of a goal need to be specified: (1) the behavior
itself; (2) the situations in which this behavior is expected to be
performed; and (3) the criterion for evaluating whether the behavior has been performed successfully (Mager 1962). To concretize, a
behavioral goal as delineated by a "socially inhibited" adolescent
might be:

On Wednesday evening between 7:00 and 8:00 P.M. I will dial
Alice's telephone number and speak to her. Criterion for goal
achievement will be a conversation of at least one minute's
duration in which both she and I speak a minimum of 50
words.

Such a definition may appear sterile. But defining concerns so
that they can be understood by the client makes it difficult for the
therapist to reinterpret problem behaviors within a theoretical
model he has not shared with the client. It also clearly informs the
client of what the therapist is going to do and allows him to monitor
the performance of the therapist and himself as he is helped to
engage in the designated behaviors. This mutual specification of
goals also enhances the concept of client individualization. Goals
are seen as important in their own right. Neither problems nor
anticipated outcomes are seen as symbolic expressions of universal
themes.
One of the advantages of the behavior therapy technique of systematic desensitization is the joint establishment of the anxiety
hierarchies by the client and therapist as a prelude to the desensiti-

zation procedure itself. These hierarchies are personalized and specific to the unique determinants of an individual's phobia. Standard hierarchies have been developed for many fears (for example, test anxiety, speech anxiety) and have found to be effective; but unreflective use of standard hierarchies may prevent the therapist from more closely investigating the individual nature of the fear and its potential consequences if extinguished.

Thus, specification of outcomes can not be limited to a mere definition of terminal behaviors. The client and therapist ought to explore the consequences to both the individual and to the community that deceleration of a behavioral excess or acceleration of a behavioral deficit may have. Only after such exploration can the client decide whether he is genuinely interested in altering his behavior.

It would be naive to assume that many clients come with well-defined target behaviors they wish changed and well-defined terminal behaviors they wish established. Much of the initial phase of therapy (behavior-oriented therapies at least) is concerned with the particularization of outcomes because clients often come to a therapist with vague, abstract, unspecified problems. There is always the danger, then, that the client may be influenced to move toward the outcomes preferred by the therapist, simply as a consequence of delineation and redefinition. While the therapist may patiently and objectively aid the client in goal setting, it will be almost impossible for him to outline the entire range of behavioral possibilities. More importantly, the therapist may lay different stress on the potential consequences of the outcomes the client chooses. As Bandura admits:

> Some encroachment on the client's decision-making primacy in the value domain is inevitable. If the change agent's value preferences are explicitly identified as his personal biases and not represented to the client as scientific truths, this problem is much less serious [Bandura 1969, p. 102].

In sum, it is felt that the chances for systematic coercion are greatly reduced within a therapeutic relationship in which outcomes are defined and tied to specific situations, and their consequences identified.

Treatment Contract

Behavioral definitions of client goals enable the client and therapist to jointly monitor progress toward those goals. Piaget (1972),

3 1303 00060 6203

215016

Friedman (1972), and others make it a practice to draw up a written contract in which the outcomes are designated. Intermediate goals may also be itemized so that there are short term as well as long term indicators of progress. It has also been suggested that such goals be time-limited; that is, that certain goals be projected for specific dates. It has been Piaget's (1972) practice to have such a contract signed by both the client and therapist. The contract thus represents a coconstituted plan in which the client knows what behaviors are to be changed and how effective the therapist is in modifying those behaviors.

A treatment contract prevents unilateral and unshared redefinitions of the client's reason for being in therapy. Such a redefinition is more likely to occur in those relationships in which the therapist does not feel that the client knows what is "really wrong with him" and when the therapist considers symptom alleviation as a superficial machination. Such a point of view very likely leads the therapist to pursue objectives that may be significantly different from the client's original intent.

Some therapists may be successful in convincing their clients that disturbing behaviors are simply derivatives of more important underlying problems and encourage the use of "insight" methods to uncover the hidden dynamics that have led to the eruption of symptoms, but as Bandura states:

> A therapeutic contract involves an obligation on the part of the therapist to modify the problems presented by his clients. A therapist may market a particular brand of insight without raising ethical objections provided he adds two important qualifiers: First, he informs his clients that the insights they are likely to gain reflect his own belief system and second, that attaining them is apt to have little impact on the behavioral difficulties that brought the client to treatment [Bandura 1969, p. 103].

The formal development of a treatment contract is not meant to calcify therapy or lock the therapist (and the client) into goals and plans that may turn out to be inappropriate. Part of any intervention strategy is the careful monitoring of the effectiveness of the approaches used by the therapist to help the client attain the intended behavioral outcomes. Along with such monitoring is a continual questioning and restructuring of goals. Initial achievement of goals may lead to changes in the contract. Some of the goals may seem ill-contrived considering the consequences experienced as a result of initial behavior changes. Other goals may become trivial or useless. New goals may arise as new behaviors are integrated into the person's repertoire. Thus, any therapeutic contract is accorded provisional status and may be changed at the mutual agreement of both the client and the clinician.

Mutual Feedback

Specification of outcomes and their formalization through a written contract does not guarantee their achievement. In large part, as has been described, the therapist is responsible for structuring the setting in the most effective way possible. It has been a favorite task of those concerned with psychotherapy to propose guidelines for establishing the most productive therapy environment. A rather new attempt in this regard appears to be relevant for the theme of this paper.

Aaron Rosen (1972) has suggested that two crucial variables related to outcome in a treatment relationship are stimulus-response congruence and content relevance. Stimulus-response congruence he defines as the extent to which a response provides feedback to the other participant that the message he sent was received. Simply, this concept deals with being heard and understood. Content relevance refers to the extent to which the content of a response is perceived by the other participant as relevant to and in agreement with his definition of the interaction situation. Again, more simply, this concept deals with "on task" behavior; is the therapist dealing with the problems raised by the client?[8]

How successful the therapist and the client are in achieving stimulus-response congruence and content relevance are hypothesized by Rosen to be positively associated with the level of favorable outcomes. But, these variables are rarely designed as part of a therapeutic relationship except in broadest terms. In fact, most therapy situations are constructed to be antagonistic to such interaction. If congruence and relevance are important, the question then becomes, how can the setting be organized to enhance, rather than inhibit, these desirable behaviors in therapy? The initial step is sharing and disclosure. Seldom in any kind of relationships do "participants share their expectations and definitions of interactional goals and content" (Rosen 1972, p. 333). Yet, successful outcome in therapy may be directly linked to the commonality between therapist and client definition of treatment. Rosen has detailed in what ways such sharing may be accomplished:

> Careful and early orientation of patients to treatment, its setting, functions, processes, and subject matter emphasis should

contribute to commonality of clinician-patient definition of the situation and to the content relevance of the clinician's responses. Patient's perception of the instrumentality of the treatment relationship could be enhanced by careful explication of treatment content and its sequences in relation to patients' objectives.

Clinician's orientation to patients' objectives . . . is as important for maximizing content relevance as is the orientation of patients. Information regarding patients' definition of the treatment situations and their goals and objectives . . . should serve to guide the content relevance of clinicians' responses and should be used for timing, manner, and content of patients' orientation to treatment (p. 335).

Sharing and disclosure may set the tone and create the atmosphere for congruence and relevance but it will not insure that such interaction occurs. Central to its maintenance is monitoring and feedback. In most therapy situations feedback is one-sided, from therapist to client. But, it may be possible to establish situations in which the client can provide immediate information to the clinician with regard to his perception of how well he is being heard and how well therapist input is related to the client's goals.

One specific suggestion is an adaptation of an idea originally offered by Craddick (1972). Many psychiatric wards have instituted token systems in which patients receive some symbol (poker chips, beads, check marks) indicating that they have engaged in appropriate behavior. These tokens can be traded in for privileges (cigarettes, private room) at a later time. Craddick advocates that patients be given the opportunity to dispense tokens to those caretakers of whose behavior they approve. His position is that present token systems are unfair; patients receive tokens for behaving in an acceptable manner, but those responsible for their treatment (aides, nurses, psychiatrists) are never so evaluated.

The reciprocity that Craddick suggests on the psychiatric ward may be just as possible in a therapy setting, though in less tangible forms perhaps. Certainly the paradigm, implemented in some way mutually agreeable to client and therapist, would furnish the client a means of providing continuous feedback to the therapist concerning stimulus-response congruence and content relevance. Behavioral definitions of these terms could be drafted. They would then be evaluated during each therapy session through some signal from the client that the therapist was listening and helping him move toward coconstituted goals. One concrete method of implementing this idea is the use of lights. Lights can be placed beside the therapist and his client. They remain lit as long as one feels the other is being congruent and relevant. When one or the other condition is not being met by either party the offender's light is turned off. Such a signal would be an overt indication of dissatisfaction, providing the occasion for some reorientation of the interaction.

Completion by the client of postsession rating forms (see examples in Lazarus 1971) is a technique that, despite its actual rarity on the therapy scene, probably seems familiar and hence more comfortable for both therapist and client. In this case, therapist accountability is pursued in a more reflective manner, that is, after the session is over and each participant seeks his own counsel, the client while writing and the therapist while reading. These session evaluations can be used alone, or as a forerunner to the in-session feedback described above, or in conjunction with other efforts toward therapist congruence and relevance.

A more radical suggestion, but one offered seriously, would be to make payment of therapist's fees contingent on movement of the client toward attainment of the treatment contract. Obviously, a procedure like this would involve trust, especially on the therapist's part. But, assuming there would be a way to collaboratively monitor client behavior to insure that the intervention strategies designed by the clinician were actually being carried out, the therapist's fee would be based on overt evidence of successive approximations of terminal behaviors. Such a contingency would be handled on what in operant vocabulary is called a "response cost" basis. In response cost, presently available pleasurable stimuli (reinforcers) are withdrawn when behavior that is judged inappropriate occurs. For example, a child will be allowed to watch a favorite television program as long as he does not hit his brother. When he does he is removed from the television room. Such a model could be adapted in therapy. Assume that the practitioner's fee is $30.00 per session. Based on predetermined criteria the client would pay the therapist the full amount or deduct specified amounts. In part, the criteria might be within the congruency-relevancy framework. If the signal light idea were implemented, "light off" time might serve as the objective measure of those variables. There might be some agreed-upon baseline time the light would be off without penalty. Any time above that baseline would result in fee reduction. The therapist, in turn, would feel free to complain about inordinate penalties and renegotiate the contingencies.

Of course, the whole matter need not be handled so compulsively, and the author admits to never having put into practice his own suggestion, but it is the idea which commends itself rather than the particular design. There is very little accountability in psychotherapy. The only indications that clients are dissatisfied come through passive, self-defeating measures such as refusal to pay bills or discontinuance. In most cases, these maneuvers are usually interpreted by the therapist as client resistance, lack of motivation, or untreatableness (Rosen 1972). But since any kind of dyadic interaction is characterized by interdependence, each participant's behavior is directly evoked and consequated by the other. If the theory offered earlier concerning the nature of a therapeutic relationship is valid, the responsibility for behavior change lies primarily with the therapist, not the client. Feedback, through mechanical or verbal signals, contingent payment of fees, or other means, may help to reorder the traditional parent-child relationship found in therapy and make it more reciprocal.

Coming to Terms With Political Influence

If Halleck's (1971) assertion that all therapeutic intervention is also a political act is correct, then some means must be found to deal directly with this aspect of intervention. It is in this regard that the principles of openness and mutual disclosure are most applicable. If goals and strategies are rooted in both scientific principles and personal values, it is imperative that therapists inform the client of those aspects of the decision-making procedure that have been dictated by personal judgment.[9]

Halleck feels that the only protection the client has against political coercion is the knowledge the therapist discloses concerning political matters and the preferences he has for therapy outcomes. Halleck is especially concerned that the client know how changes may affect his ability to deal with and influence the social systems in which he is immersed, as well as how such changes would affect his outlook on social problems. In addition, Halleck has begun informing his clients about his views on such matters as premarital sex, drugs, divorce, and other social, political, and moral issues.

Such self-revelation, he says, "does not fully protect the patient from the political outcomes of therapy that he may not anticipate or desire, but it gives him a fighting chance to resist the potentially indoctrinating effects of psychotherapy" (Halleck 1971, p. 56). Responding to the potential dangers of disclosure Halleck replies:

It is true that when the psychiatrist reveals himself he loses the opportunity to deal with the kinds of interesting transference reactions that sometimes develop when he presents himself as a "blank screen." But this loss is, in my opinion more than compensated for by the self-revelation that allows the psychiatrist to present himself as a real person. If the therapist is open about himself, he is in a stronger position to interpret whatever irrational fantasies the patient brings to the therapeutic encounter (pp. 56–57).

The last comment is not the strength of the argument as much as is Halleck's willingness to present himself as a "real person." Most people coming for therapy are motivated by interpersonal dissatisfaction. When therapists hide themselves through enclosure in a professional cloak, they deny their clients their own humanness. The situation they create in the office becomes unlike the functioning situation clients will meet in the everyday world. Thus, changes that occur in the office may be ungeneralizable to most situations in the environment. As Kelly (1955) suggests, therapists are most effective when they act as samples of the client's social world. A close to ideal relationship between client and clinician may have been most succinctly described by Halleck:

> The [therapist] would have no secret knowledge, no diagnostic intuitiveness to use as "trump cards" against his patient. Each of his moral judgments would be open to question. Patients could enter into dialogues with their therapists and would have the opportunity to convince their therapist what life styles might be preferable for them [the patients] . . . Each behavior would be analyzed in terms of how it affected the patient's humaneness [Halleck 1971, p. 198].

TWO FINAL POINTS

The End of Ideology

In the beginning of the twentieth century psychodynamically oriented clinicians were accused of being ideologues. A singular theoretical focus made them almost immune to perceiving and investigating the possibly divergent meanings of their clients' symptoms. Symptoms were redefined within the particular psychodynamic theory adhered to by the therapist, whose orientation determined both diagnosis and treatment. In the second half of the century, the last decade especially, the supremacy of those elegant theories has been challenged by behaviorally oriented practitioners. But it has not been enough to simply challenge. A theory as formidable as psychoanalysis, which seeks to explain all forms of human endeavor, could not be supplanted by anything less than another all-encompassing formulation. So many behavior therapists claim that all they do can be interpreted within a learning model. And, because of such claims the behavior therapists have become the new ideologues.

Thus argues Perry London (1972) in a provocative indictment of what he considers the current ideology. Behavior therapy, by asserting that its practices are imbedded in laboratory-derived principles of learning, is not only engaging in irrelevant colloquy but is sadly mistaken, he feels. And it is true that many of those who call themselves behavior therapists admit that what they do cannot be completely subsumed within an operant or classical conditioning framework (cf. Kraft 1972, Lazarus 1971).

It is London's wish that all therapists turn from proving that what they do fits into theory to finding out if what they do "fits the facts of human experience" (London 1972, p. 919). Further he says "the only treatment question of relevance is that of the functional relationship between the problem and the solution. The process is what matters and nothing else" (p. 915). I share his concern and wish. Clients are better served by those therapists who design interventions that are helpful in accomplishing the goals of the client than they are by those who impose an orientation that may be theoretically esthetic but empirically ineffective.

The End of Psychotherapy

Despite all that has been said about the potentialities for creating genuinely reciprocal relationships in psychotherapy, one cannot help but wonder whether most clients would be better served if they never saw office-bound therapists. The very nature of the traditional therapy setting precludes it from being the most efficient milieu for intervention. Even in an extreme depth analysis, client-clinician interaction may only consume 5 of the 168 hours a person spends living a week. Ninety-seven percent of the time while involved in this most intense form of therapy,[10] the client lives in the natural environment. Actual manifestation of problem behaviors occur infrequently in the therapist's office. Most often the therapist deals with equivalents, rather than actual "symptoms," or sometimes only with verbal descriptions of them. In contrast, behavior is modified more effectively by treating real events and when treatment programs are conducted in natural settings (Bandura, Blanchard, and Ritter 1968; Fairweather, Sanders, Maynard, and Cressler 1969). It might be more helpful, therefore, if therapists shifted from office-bound verbal interaction to coordination of "out-in-life" intervention programs, using in-office visits to develop strategies and monitor treatment programs.

Such an approach, to some extent, has been adopted by those advocating behavioral approaches to assessment and intervention. But behavior modification is most successful when the change agent is that person with whom the client has the most contact. For example, parents and teachers have been taught to act as "therapists" with children in their charge, and have produced significant results in comparison to children taken out of classrooms or homes and engaged in some form of in-office psychotherapy. (Lindsley 1966, Thomas, Becker, and Armstrong 1968; Zeilberger, Sampen, and Sloane 1968). In these cases, behavior therapists have acted as treatment coordinators while the concerned adults have been the ones who helped the child produce actual changes.

It should be pointed out, parenthetically, that there are dangers to even this approach. The child is likely to be ill-managed and covertly coerced, like little Hans, unless he is assessed as he interacts with his family or teacher, and all the variables affecting the behavior of the child are observed and evaluated. Like the adult client, the child's behavior is evoked and consequated by those around him, and the target of change may turn out not to be the child but the significant others in the environment. If the child (or any potential client) does become the object of change, he should be informed of the reasons for the proposed intervention in his behavior and of the particulars of the change process itself. Indeed, the child's development is facilitated by his very participation in evaluating his own behavior and in revising interventional programs. Especially where such reciprocity is practiced, the use of nonprofessional psychotherapeutic agents (Guerney 1969) is advocated.

Many of the value, control, and coercion problems in therapy may be overcome if the therapeutic function is carried out by indigenous peers. While teachers, parents, and institutional nonprofessionals (for example, ward attendants) have been used as adjunct personnel in therapy roles, they are still "doers-to" and separate from the client's everyday life. The ultimate reciprocity may come when the major responsibility for helping others with problems in living falls to those cultural kinsmen with whom a client comes in daily contact. Such an approach has three advantages: (1) the inappropriate modeling that occurs when a client interacts with a statused professional will be ameliorated; (2) the client will be relating to someone whose cultural values are similar to his; (3) it is unlikely that a peer will have been nurtured and bought by the "system." Admittedly, there are problems in the concept—it is difficult to fully conceive of ways in which indigenous personnel may be trained and yet not coopted into the dominant cultural value orientation. But the idea yet may be the most appropriate solution to the quest for genuine reciprocity and openness between client and helper.

CONCLUSION

This chapter's criticisms of current practices were not intended to denunciate any particular psychotherapy, but to alert therapeutic personnel to the coercive potential in all psychotherapy. The suggested alternatives were not offered as solutions, but as an impetus for continual effort to embrace in the client-clinician relationship those democratic and ethical traditions that we value in all our relationships: noncoercion, mutuality of disclosure, self-direction, and fully informed involvement in one's own life.

NOTES

1. There is a trenchant critical examination by Wolpe and Rachman (1960) of the case of little Hans in which Freud's data is reinterpreted to show that Hans's horse phobia was not a symbolic expression of castration anxiety but a true fear of horses.

2. For a fuller discussion of this point see Tillman, Bersoff, and Dolly (1976).

3. An interesting description of the nature of the relationship between Breuer and Anna O. is presented in Lucy Freeman's 1972 book, *The Story of Anna O.*

4. *Studies in Hysteria* (1895), based largely on Breuer's interaction with Anna O., was coauthored by Breuer and Freud. Yet, Freud may have met the patient only once, and that meeting is undocumented. Furthermore, the data on which Freud developed the psychodynamic underpinnings for paranoia (the Schreber case) came entirely from the patient's diary. Thus, three basic psychoanalytic analyses come from evidence secured by, at the most, two personal patient contacts.

5. Author unknown; as quoted in Karl Menninger (1959).

6. Rogerian therapy has been faulted on other counts, however. Marquis (1972) asserts that a nondirective setting constitutes a hostile environment in that the therapist refuses to answer a direct and reasonable request for information. Haley feels that the client-centered approach "is an inevitably

winning system for the therapist. No one can top a person who merely repeats his ideas after him" (Haley 1969b, p. 20).

7. The concept was first described at length by George Kelly (1955).

8. The question may legitimately be asked in reverse. At times, it will be entirely appropriate for the therapist to monitor the behavior of the client with regard to content relevance.

9. It may be remedial simple to try separating the theoretical, empirical, and subjective aspects of therapist functioning. Indeed, even science and empiricalism can be seen as embodying a certain philosophy and value system.

10. It is recognized that group experiences may last an entire week or longer. But that is often short term, rather than a continuous experience, as in psychoanalysis.

REFERENCES

Bandura, A. 1969. *Principles of behavior modification*. New York: Holt, Rinehart and Winston.

Bandura, A., Blanchard, E. B., and Ritter, B. 1968. The relative efficacy of desensitization and modeling approaches for inducing behavior, affective, and attitudinal changes. Unpublished manuscript, Stanford University.

Breuer, J. and Freud, S. 1895. *Studies in hysteria*. Lippzig: Deuticke.

Craddick, R. A. 1972. A different use of the token in mental hospitals. *Professional Psychol*. 3:155–56.

Fairweather, G. W., Sanders, D. H., Maynard, H., and Cressler, D. L. 1969. *Community life for the mentally ill: an alternative to institutional care*. Chicago: Aldine.

Freeman, L. 1972. *The story of Anna O*. New York: Walker.

Friedman, P. H. 1972. Personalistic family and marital therapy. In *Clinical behavior therapy*, ed. A. A. Lazarus. New York: Brunner/Mazel.

Fulkerson, S. C. 1965. Some implications of the new cognitive theory for projective tests. *J. Consulting Psychology* 29:191–97.

Greenspoon, J. 1962. Verbal conditioning and clinical psychology. In *Experimental foundations of clinical psychology*, ed. A. J. Bachrach. New York: Basic Books.

Guerney, B. G. 1969. *Psychotherapeutic agents: new roles for non-professionals, parents, and teachers*. New York: Holt, Rinehart and Winston.

Haley, J. 1969a. The art of being a failure as a therapist. *Am. J. Orthopsychia*. 39:691–95.

———. 1969b. The art of psychoanalysis. In *The power tactics of Jesus Christ and other essays*. New York: Avon.

Halleck, S. L. 1971. *The politics of therapy*. New York: Science House.

Harrison, R. 1965. *Cognitive models for interpersonal and group behavior: a theoretical framework for research*. Washington, D. C.: NTL, NEA.

Keen, E. 1972. Bureaucratic and therapeutic values. *Voices* 8:12–16.

Kelly, G. 1955. *The psychology of personal constructs*. vol. 2, New York: W. W. Norton.

Kraft, T. 1972. The use of behavior therapy in a psychotherapeutic context. In *Clinical behavior therapy*, ed. A. A. Lazarus. New York: Brunner/Mazel.

Krasner, L. 1958. Studies of the conditioning of verbal behavior. *Psychol. Bullet.* 55:148–70.

Lazarus, A. A. 1971. *Behavior therapy and beyond.* New York: McGraw-Hill.

Lindsley, O. R. 1966. An experiment with parents handling behavior at home. *Johnstone Bullet.* 9:27–36.

London, P. 1969. *Behavior control.* New York: Harper and Row.

———. 1972. The end of ideology in behavior modification. *Am. Psychol.* 27:913–20.

Mager, R. F. 1962. *Preparing instructional objectives.* Palo Alto: Fearon.

Marquis, J. N. 1972. An expedient model for behavior therapy. In *Clinical behavior therapy*, ed. A. A. Lazarus. New York: Brunner/Mazel.

Menninger, K. 1959. *Theory of psychoanalytic technique.* New York: Harper Torch Books.

Phillips, D. L. 1963. Rejection: a possible consequence of seeking help for mental disorders. *Am. Sociol. Rev.* 28:963–72.

Piaget, G. W. 1972. Training patients to communicate. In *Clinical behavior therapy*, ed. A. A. Lazarus. New York: Brunner/Mazel.

Rosen, A. 1972. The treatment relationship: a conceptualization. *J. Consulting and Clinical Psychol.* 38:329–37.

Rosenthal, D. 1955. Changes in some moral values following psychotherapy. *J. Consulting Psychol.* 19:431–36.

Salzinger, K. 1959. Experimental manipulation of verbal behavior: a review. *J. Genet. Psychol.* 61:65–94.

Salzinger, K., and Pizoni, S. 1958. Reinforcement of affect responses of schizophrenics during the clinical interview. *J. Abnormal and Soc. Psychol.* 57:84–90.

Salzinger, K., Portnoy, S., and Feldman, R. S. 1964. Verbal behavior of schizophrenic and normal subjects. *Ann. N. Y. Academy of Sciences* 105:845–60.

Szasz, T. S. 1966a. Discussion of Dr. Robbins paper. *The classification of behavior disorders*, ed. L. D. Aron: Chicago: Aldine.

———. 1966b. The psychiatric classification of behavior: a strategy of personal constraint. In *The classification of behavior disorders*, ed. L. D. Aron. Chicago: Aldine.

Thomas, D. R., Becker, W. C., and Armstrong, M. 1968. Production and elimination of disruptive classroom behavior by systematically varying teacher's behavior. *J. App. Behavior Analysis* 1:35–45.

Tillman, M., Bersoff, D. N., and Dolly, J. 1976. *Learning to teach: a decision-making system.* Lexington, Mass.: D. C. Heath.

Truax, C. B. 1966. Reinforcement and nonreinforcement in Rogerian psychotherapy. *J. Abnormal Psychol.* 71:1–9.

Verplanck, W. S. 1955. The control of the content of conversation: Reinforcement of statements of opinion. *J. Abnormal and Soc. Psychol.* 51:668–76.

Wallace, J. 1966. An abilities conception of personality: Some implications for personality measurement. *Am. Psychol.* 21:132–38.

Wolpe, J., and Rachman, S. 1960. Psychoanalytic 'evidence': a critique based on Freud's case of little Hans. *J. Nervous and Mental Disease* 130:135–48.

Zeilberger, J., Sampen, S. E., and Sloane, Jr., H. N. 1968. Modification of a child's problem behaviors in the home with the mother as therapist. *J. App. Behavior Analysis* 1:47–53.

5.

From Violence to Mutual Obligation in Psychiatric Treatment

ERNEST KEEN

The violence that permeates current psychiatric treatment must be understood within its cultural context. In this and every culture, people understand themselves and others in a particular way. Psychiatric treatment is a particular extension of these assumptions into institutional practice. If it is violent, it is an extension of our cultural violence. In this chapter we will first look at some standard practices of psychiatric treatment in and of themselves. We will then consider that treatment, and its violence, in its cultural context. We shall try to see clearly its connection with our popular assumptions and cultural forms. Third, we will conclude with a description of some alternative, nonviolent assumptions and cultural forms. These have been and might be translated into a psychiatry that encourages mutual obligation—a reciprocal respect for individuality.

CURRENT PSYCHIATRIC TREATMENT

Diagnosis

The official act of psychiatric diagnosis is the seminal violence. Other examples of psychiatric violence are derivative from this perceptual and political act. The act of diagnosis is violent in that it is an extreme form of the most common violence to which we are all subject: the definition of one's self from the outside. What makes psychiatric diagnosis particularly offensive in a society where we are already constantly defined by others is its official and power-laden character. Being defined by my students as a slave-driver and by my wife as a fool may hurt me, but I can always move from one to the other in escape from the one. With psychiatric diagnosis there is no such luxury. The judgment pervades every aspect of my hospitalized, and most aspects of my posthospitalized, life.

In a purely logical sense, it does violence to the integrity of any object to focus on one attribute and make it definite of the whole object. When that object is a molecule and its weight is taken as definitive of it, thus letting other aspects of its particularity fade from sight, no one is likely to become upset. But when that object is a person and his symptoms are taken as a definition of who he is, thus letting his particularity fade from sight, then the violence has come to have an important human cost.

Through diagnosis a number of social changes are accomplished. From the point of view of professionals, diagnosis is a way to classify the work, relieving the cognitive strain that would emerge from considering patients one by one in their particularity. From the point of view of the public at large, diagnosis is the definition of evil. Such definitions are needed in stressful social situations, and they play directly into the hands of our popular readiness to pronounce judgments on ourselves and others, in terms of good and evil, thus to solidify our own identities.

Therefore, the individual who is diagnosed as "neurotic," "immature," "character disordered," "hostile," "a poor prognosis," or "out of touch with reality," suffers a double judgment—from his family, friends and neighbors on the one hand, and from medical authorities on the other hand. Although he is likely to be hurt by such a judgment, he may be less as well as more indignant than we are. He will be more indignant than we are because he does not have our distance. We can understand that people will be people and professionals will be professionals in about the best way they know how, and that few people or professionals maliciously set out to hurt others intentionally. He is locked into an interaction with them in which the stakes are high.

On the other hand, he may well be less indignant than we are about diagnosis because the processes of judging and being judged do not strike him as atrocities. Psychiatric diagnosis is a particularly bad judgment against him, perhaps the worst imaginable, but the act of judgment itself does not offend him. It is the stuff of life as he has been trained to understand it in modern society. Moreover, the troubling or troubled citizen may temporarily welcome the giving up of personal accountability that attends his transformation, by socially revered authorities, into a "patient."

Medical Records

Goffman, one of our most astute observers of the psychiatric process, has said of the case record:

> This dossier is apparently not regularly used, however, to record occasions when the patient showed capacity to cope honorably and effectively with difficult life situations. Nor is the case record typically used to provide a rough average or sampling of his past conduct. One of its purposes is to show the ways in which the patient is "sick" and the reasons why it was right to commit him and is right currently to keep him committed; and this is done by extracting from his whole life course a list of those incidents that have or might have had "symptomatic" significance [Goffman 1962, pp. 155–56].

Hence, the critical significance of the medical record is that it is an extension of the diagnostic process into written form, thus solidifying the judgment and documenting it beyond refutation.

It is a fact of in-patient life that patients know that the record exists and that they may not see it. One could hardly better design an arrangement to undercut someone's definition of himself, and to produce that insecurity born of knowing that there are great powers over oneself that nevertheless remain ambiguous and unknowable. The experience can be compared to primitive men's belief in all-knowing, all-powerful, but essentially capricious and temperamental gods.

The psychiatric patient is made to understand that he may indirectly affect the contents of the medical record, for the staff of the hospital may write in it at any time. However, the patient has power over the content of the record only to the extent that he has power over the opinions of the staff. The staff therefore become the priests who mediate the way to the gods in the murky heavens above.

There have been some important innovations in medical records in the last decade. One of these is computerization, which makes the record into a research tool[1] as well as a clinical document. In order for information to be processed by a computer, categorization of observations must precede the observations themselves. Such categorizations as "less interaction with others," "less aggression against staff," or even more abstractly, "improved," "unchanged," are commonly used. The scientific meaning of such data is questionable, and computerization even further mystifies the record and its meaning for the patient. But the political meaning of computerization is fairly clear: judgment can now be made by merely checking a box, and the retention and recall of such judgments can be electronically perfect. In short, the patient himself is removed still further from the decision of what is to be written about him.

Another innovation is the "problem-oriented chart." This sort of patient record specifies the problems precisely in concrete, behavioral terms and then organizes all subsequent progress notes, laboratory and testing results, and summary data according to the identified and numbered problems. This kind of chart has two noteworthy virtues. First, diagnostic labels are avoided and problems are concretely described ("hears voices condemning him" rather than "schizophrenic symptoms with depressive features"). Second, by defining a problem, the staff has made itself accountable for the outcome of treatment in terms of the problem, not in terms of some vague judgments about the degree of "contact with reality," and so on.

In practice, however, problem-oriented charts have more the effect of increasing precision than of lessening the violence of medical records. It is still the staff, or the complainant in the family who defines "the problem" and not necessarily the patient himself. It is still other people's right, but not his, to see what is written about him. Nevertheless, combined with assessment techniques as described by Fischer (1970), the problem-oriented chart has the potential of becoming a cooperative working document rather than a symbol of judgmental power.

The Case Conference

Case conferences have two official functions and several unofficial ones. Both official functions are violent; unofficial ones are even more so. Officially, case conferences are first of all for teaching trainees. Patients' lives therefore become captive teaching material. Second, the case conference is a way to put together information and expertise in order to devise a treatment plan. Naturally, this routine reinforces the general social structure in which staff have the power of decision and patients have only the power of accepting or rebelling against such decision.

Unofficially, the case conference functions as a "degradation ceremony" (Garfinkel 1956) in which the patient's definitions of himself are undermined by the paternalistic listening to what he has to say (so its real meaning can be discussed after he leaves the room). In addition, the congregation of a number of high-powered experts suggests the technical difficulty of the patient's problem. The case conference is also frequently an unofficial, and perhaps, unconscious, intimidation technique. Typically, a case conference is called if (1) the patient is presenting the staff with a "management problem" or some other occasion of puzzlement, such as refusing to take unpleasant medicine, being "AWOL" from ceremonies, therapies, or mopping the dayroom floor. Whatever the specifics, the usual expectations of the staff for the patient's behavior are not being fulfilled; or (2) a patient is about to be discharged, transferred, or some other decision of great moment is about to be made. In both of these situations, the case conference is, in effect, a formal notification of threat and a display of power that enforces the general notion that the staff and not the patient is in charge of the future.

It is not uncommon for the case conference to take on the social trappings of a trial, even in the distribution of the furniture. Certainly it is often seen that way by the patient, who also notes that his defense attorney (his own therapist) has a prior contract with and loyalty to the judge (visiting expert, consultant). If it is a court, it is a kangaroo court. If it is science, it is violent science in which the integrity of the individual is lost from view. Stemming as it does from traditional hospital routines such as "rounds," its violence is obscured from view. Even the patient, who has or is about to yield up his right to define himself to the wisdom of experts, usually acquiesces. Indeed, perhaps the most excruciating feature of case conferences is how unquestioningly and routinely most patients accept them.

The Ward System

Most mental hospitals have a hierarchy of wards in which some are relatively more open and privileged and others are relatively closed or literally locked. Other wards may have a hierarchy of statuses within their own population, and patients may have to wear badges or a certain color or style of clothing to indicate to the staff and the public their rank within the system. The status difference, and the symbols that make it vivid, amount to a class system within the hospital that copies one of the least attractive aspects of our social world outside the hospital.

The status system serves three functions. First, it helps the hospital staff to organize its work. Like color-coding library cards, staff can tell at a glance whether a patient is privileged to leave the ward, to smoke, and so on. For patients who are classified as suicide risks and must be watched at all times, color-coding their clothing is an unmistakable convenience for staff. Second, the status system is used by the staff as an inducement to change. It is a consistent and predictable reward system where concrete, understandable privileges are directly contingent upon certain kinds of behavior. In token economy wards (Ulrich et al. 1966), patients' behavior-reward sequences are tightened up by the issuing of tokens that can be used as money to "buy" beds, meals, and so on. This system is refined into an elaborate set of routines and norms that often look military ("You should be standing by your bed for the rating. If you are making your bed at the time the rater arrives, you will not receive a chip" [*Veterans Administration Hospital*, 1972].) Third, the status system has an obvious threat-of-punishment function, where a lowering of one's status involves loss of such privileges as cigarettes, off-the-ward or out-of-room mobility, access to activities, and so on.

Patients can readily understand the rules of this system. At the same time, however, we may say that it is very destructive to a patient's sense of himself, or his sense that he has a valid perspective or point of view of his own. Truth, goodness, and beauty are definitively established without his participation. There is, of course, the straight and narrow path to discharge, but there is no latitude. Everything expresses and reinforces the essential power situation: the staff has all the power, and he has none. Most important of all, patients learn that the only way to control one's life is to manipulate the perception of the staff (Braginski, Braginski, and Ring 1969). The patient must learn to see the world and himself through the eyes of staff if he is to avoid a collision. The reciprocal process, of seeing the world and the staff through the eyes of the patient is not one of the traditions of the hospital, and the new patient who expects it as an ordinary part of social life will soon learn not to.

Policy Decisions

It is exactly this lack of reciprocity that makes the unequal distribution of power so anomalous for a psychiatric institution. Power may perhaps be an inevitable part of social structures of any kind, but for psychiatric patients in particular, it should be handled with an acute awareness of its psychological meaning.

Centralization of power, is, psychologically speaking, a lack of reciprocity in who is obliged to understand whom and who can count on being understood. To place power in the exclusive hands of the staff is to put the patient in the position of having to understand staff without the staff being obliged to understand him. In other words, the violence of centralization results not only from the fact that the staff has (nearly unlimited) power over patients. Even more important are the inevitable assumptions people come to make about one another. Being a patient eventually yields the conclusion that the interpersonal field, the arena of one's relationships with others, is nonreciprocal and asymmetrical.

In response to some sense of this violence, many wards and even hospitals hold "community meetings" that run according to a town meeting model. Patients and staff alike are "the community." There is great variety in the styles of these meetings, which range all the way from pure farce to a serious attempt at some degree of democracy. However, given the role structure of the hospital into "staff" and "patients," there is no way that these meetings can overcome paternalism, tokenism, and pretense. As long as patients are defined as "patients," the meetings have the inevitable taste of sham. And as long as staff tolerate this sham, the meetings have little possibility of dislodging the role definitions, which in turn supply the continuing backdrop that guarantees the tokenistic meaning of the meetings.

For example, a committee may be formed to decide the cigarette policy of the ward: which patients get them, when, who pays for them, and so on. There may be some real latitude between various possible arrangements, as long as the results do not contradict hospital or ward policy. But the unchallengable existence of this policy requires patients to understand and accept it without any obligation of the policy to be understanding or accepting of patients. One might argue that the hospital thus mirrors the outside world, where it is not the citizen's prerogative to question certain laws. To the extent that this is true, society is violent, for denying an individual reciprocity of understanding is violent. As in the class system, the hospital again copies the least attractive and most violent aspects of society at large. To justify hospital policy on these grounds is to say, "If they can live here, they can live anywhere." That hardly constitutes imaginative psychiatric treatment.

However, the justification for the exclusiveness of staff power is more usually the role definitions themselves: they are sick and we are well. Thus we see again that diagnosis is the seminal violence from which all other violence in psychiatric treatment is a specification, solidification, and implementation.

THEORY

We wish to examine theory in a complex way. In the first place, theories of psychiatry and psychology articulate a number of assumptions of our culture as a whole. These assumptions must be made explicit and criticized. Second, such criticism is therefore not only a professional and intellectual matter, but it necessarily also becomes something of a cultural critique. But third, it is clear that the assumptions about the nature of man that are implemented in psychiatric treatment are not the only bases of relationships among us in our culture. Alternative, nonviolent assumptions are also a part of our cultural heritage, although not the part currently embraced by violent psychological institutions.

Therefore, a theoretical critique among professionals in this case amounts to more than just a theoretical critique. Our theoretical assumptions are articulated into practice and shape our institutions which shape popular consciousness to a large extent; the latter, in turn, feeds back as support for our profession. We must understand this situation in all its complexity if we are to see the importance of the innovations described in the last part of this paper.

Cultural Forms

The term "assumption" above may be misleading if it is taken in the cognitive sense of a logical premise. In fact, we must examine those assumptions that are *not* explicitly thought, but rather are *lived* by us in our everyday lives. Hence I will not focus on intellectual systems, such as manipulative science and existential humanism, but rather on the way we live—the implicit sense of ourselves and others that we enact every day. Specifically, I will describe two cultural forms that are part of how we understand ourselves and others, and I will, perhaps a bit artificially, polarize them for our own convenience: *obligation* and *competition*.

By obligation (from the Latin *ligare*, to bind), I intend to describe that network of mutual expectations, which we share with our friends and relatives: to respect them and to treat them decently. Although this network has usually escaped theoretical notice, except to be criticized as irrational superego morality, our lives are built upon it. These expectations come to us from a heritage of moral and religious thought which, while mostly abandoned as doctrine, remain a living cultural form within which we make ourselves and others intelligible to ourselves. As human beings we find ourselves *bound by* this cultural form that *binds us to* others.

To be human is to be embedded in a reciprocal social matrix. Regardless of our individualistic ideologies, we could no sooner be who we are without this network than we could survive without a physical body. Everyone exists within a *circle of obligation*, and we derive an essential sense of personal security from it.

By competition, I intend to describe how we grow up in a society in which we learn there are winners and losers. Much of our training revolves around the symbols of winning and losing; we are trained to tell the differences and pass this training on to our children. We also learn that everyone else learns these symbols and will judge us according to them as well. Hence we are thrust into a network of people judging and being judged. We judge in self-defense in such a network. We learn to be cruel as protection against having cruelty perpetrated against ourselves.

Both of these themes are present in our culture and supply part of the rich matrix of expectations we have of one another every day. They are more than themes; they are forms—frameworks of already existing meanings within which we understand ourselves. There are other such forms, typically studied by social scientists under the rubric of roles, norms, and world-view. I have pulled these two forms into focus because they are historically and contemporaneously important, because they permeate our experience of ourselves as modern Americans, and because they enlighten us about the origins and stakes of violence and nonviolence in psychiatric practice.

Psychiatric Treatment and the Cultural Forms

I shall use the term "disobligate" to refer to that social process by which individuals are excluded from the "circle of obligation." It is a double process. If I disobligate you, I am, first, refusing to be obligated to you, and I am, second, refusing to make you obligated to me. Both of these refusals are denigrating and undercut your status as a human being. Since the "circle of obligation" is a reciprocal and dialectical social arrangement, binding me to you and you to me and both of us to the arrangement, disobligation cuts both sides of the reciprocity. Both of us are freed from and deprived of the obligation both to give and receive the respect and dignity usually accorded human beings. Disobligation ruptures the cultural form obligation, and thus changes the very meaning of you to me and me to you. It violates (and hence is violent to) that culturally given, already present, sense of what it means to be a person instead of a thing.

Once one is recognized as mentally ill, then it is popularly assumed that professional experts will take over, and the rest of us may feel free of responsibility; the individual is cut loose from our everyday circle of obligations. Thus, professional diagnosis perpetrates disobligation, and disobligation perpetuates the need for professionals. And thus do the rest of us rely on diagnosis to disqualify ourselves from the ranks of the helpful. And thus is diagnosis a procedure that holds together the implicit agreement between professionals and the rest of us—an agreement from which everyone benefits—everyone except psychiatric patients.

Against this backdrop of collusion between professional experts and the rest of us, psychiatric treatment takes place. Psychiatric treatment has become a codeword for (1) get them out of our hair, (2) change them to fit us so that the rest of us don't have to change, and (3) make sure we can prosecute those who offend us even though they may break no laws and hurt no one. Psychiatric treatment—a medical specialty dedicated to saving lives and enhancing health—has somehow evolved into a set of rituals and routines, collusions and scapegoating, that violate even the most elementary obligations of decency and respect for fellow men. How could this have happened?

Before we can answer this question, we must see more clearly *what* has happened. The obligation form teaches us that we can count on decency from our fellows and are obliged to be decent to them. The competition form teaches us to defend ourselves against our fellows who are struggling to be winners and to make us losers. On a personal level, we have all experienced this contradiction. On the level of ideology, we can see the contradiction between the capitalist and Judeo-Christian ideals. Personally we all find some way to juggle such contradictions. With respect to psychiatric treatment, that juggling has been facilitated by a certain combining of the forms: the best way to defend oneself is to enhance one's inclusion in the circle of obligation by explicitly excluding others from it.

Not everyone can win, but most people do not have to lose either. Most of us can win at least a place in the circle of obligation, as long as we agree to exclude others. Insofar as that agreement has become obligatory, the obligation form has been subverted by the competition form. At the very least, the agreement requires a minimum attunement to the judging-being-judged format of relationships, and we dare not forget it. Should we forget it, we may lose our bearings as to who we are, and having lost that, we may be in for the big loss: being a loser.

There are all degrees of being a loser; the symbol system is quite complicated and the distinction is nearly always relative. My losing is usually not as bad as that of someone else. And so I may catch myself before I hit rock bottom and work my way back up. This is humane; everyone is given a second chance, provided he is willing to get back into the running. God help him if he is not, however, for he has forfeited himself. He becomes the absolute loser against which the relative-loser-system and its complicated symbols work.

The absolute loser is necessary to ground the entire operation. Without him, the system has no base, the symbols become meaningless, and the judgments float in mid air. The absolute loser is the most important symbol of all; he is the zero point that makes the numbers count, the ultimate evil against which degrees of goodness can be reckoned, the stopping that makes the running make sense. We have come to need the disobligated in order to assure ourselves a place in the circle of obligation.

Human consciousness has the peculiarity that the system of symbols given from outside comes to populate us inside. We cannot live without symbols, and the symbols from popular culture, once learned, are not just known, they are lived. We therefore live our judgments and our being judged; to give up these symbols is not only to have it said by others that we have forfeited ourselves. It is to forfeit ourselves.

Some psychiatric patients are diagnosed. Some diagnose themselves. In either case, the same violence is perpetrated upon them—the competition form has precluded for them the obligated form. They are disenfranchized, dehumanized, objectified, and most seriously of all, they are disobligated.

Psychiatric treatment, which is officially dedicated to welfare and happiness (obligation), has unofficially become an instrument of another official system—of judging and being judged (competition). Traditional psychiatric treatment is the capitalism of human relationships.

In its definition of itself, psychiatric treatment has failed to understand that it is not a unilateral operation. It is not a matter of the doctor combatting an illness. It is rather a matter of two persons, both caught in the obligation-competition contradiction, finding different solutions to the problem of survival. They are both defectors from the obligation form and have found a place in the competition form. The doctor's solution has been to become the master judge; the compliant patient's solution has been to become the master-judged.

The fact that psychiatric treatment has become a code-word for various kinds of violence is the inevitable outcome of psychiatry having been annexed by the judging-being-judged system without knowing it. Both doctor and patient have defined themselves, but the symbols available to them for self-definition have not been well chosen. Once accepted, the symbols sign and seal our identities. The vision necessary to undo one's identity in a psychiatrically violent society is available only by reclaiming obligation. This requires no great intellectual feat; it requires only that we see the importance of the circle of obligation in our own lives and in the culture.

But it is also not easy. We need a vision, in order to escape. In order to gain a vision, our only leverage is to flail and rant and rave at our own absurdities until something becomes clear.

Changing Psychiatric Theory

In the last part of this paper, I will describe some recent innovations in psychiatric practice. Here I want to describe some concomitant changes in psychiatric and psychological theory. Both are explicit expressions of an implicit sense of obligation, a redressing of the balance between communal and individualistic, respectful and manipulative, nonviolent and violent cultural forms. Theoretical shifts affect practice, practice affects popular consciousness, and popular consciousness supports institutions that shape practice and theory. No one factor in this matrix is autonomous or can change lastingly, without the others changing.

Diagnosis, in psychiatric theory, has been subject to recent criticisms (Szasz 1961, Leifer 1969, Taylor and Heiser 1971, Honigfeld 1971). The logical error is clear: a part comes to define the whole. A person in our population who scores under seventy on an IQ test is "mentally retarded." That defines him, regardless of how sensitive he may be to music, how skillful with his hands, or how kind to others. His particularity as a person is lost in the swamping effect of his label, and he is treated identically with everyone else who shares this IQ peculiarity. The theoretical questioning of diagnosis is in part a rebellion against the loss of our common humanity, community, and decency—in a word, obligation.

Second, theoretical definitions of "the problem" are changing from a malfunctioning psyche within the individual to the pattern of relationships within which the individual is embedded. By calling *him* psychotic, professionals had implicitly located the problem within him and set themselves the task of changing *him*. That definition of the problem amounts to a judgment of him as a loser among winners. It disobligates him, makes him into an object of scientific intervention, thus explicitly excluding him from the circle of obligation. The current redefinition of "the problem" as interpersonal instead of intrapsychic shifts the focus of professional attention away from what is wrong with him to what is going on in the circle of his relationships. This shift amounts to a new perceptual and theoretical focus on how he has been disobligated instead of how he has become a loser. The growing professional interest in family therapy (Eisenstein 1956; Boszormenyi-Nagy and Framo 1965; Lidz, Fleck, and Cornelison 1965; Laing and Esterson 1970; Esterson 1972; Howells 1971; Zuk 1971; Ferber, Mendelsohn, and Napier 1972; and the volume by the Group for the Advancement of Psychiatry 1970) expresses this important theoretical shift. Similar expressions are found in the trend toward community psychiatry, and even in the Skinnerian emphasis on the situational nature of behavior (for example, Tharp and Wetzel 1969).

Regardless of theoretical innovations, the nature of psychiatric treatment does not change until practice changes. The importance of changes in practice has more than the obvious effect of changing how patients are treated. It also mightily affects public attitudes and the quality of our self-understanding. It does not matter that professionals liberate themselves from the shackles of diagnostic thinking unless it changes their behavior. But their change of behavior fundamentally alters how we experience ourselves and others. Once professionals refuse to see all under-seventy-IQ persons as alike, and instead treat them in their particularity, they encourage, even force, family and community to do the same. Closing the doors of institutions for our dispossessed and disobligated is just such a decisive action that forces a more honest confrontation, in family and community, with the forms of obligation. It reacquaints us with that network of shared expectations and mutual respect upon which we all desperately depend. It establishes a consciousness of our own cultural forms and frees the obligation form from its servitude to the win/lose routines of the competitive form. It pulls into focus the already existing but too often denied sense of the circle of obligation that makes us as civilized as we are. It restores a balance between our communal and individual identities. It breaks the collusion through which the professionals aid and abet the population in our security operation of solidifying our own place in the circle of obligation by excluding others. The experience of having to deal with a former loser necessitates a review of the grounds by which he was defined a loser. These results are inevitable for the general population if and only if the *practice* of psychological and psychiatric service changes.

INNOVATIONS TOWARD NONVIOLENT PSYCHIATRY

It is impossible to describe all the innovations in a nonviolent direction in the last few, very creative, years. What follows is, perhaps, a representative sample of how both professionals and nonprofessionals have attempted to articulate their growing vision into institutional forms.

Modifications of existing institutions

Because professionals themselves have some growing recognition of the violence of traditional psychiatric treatment, some rather extensive tinkering with existing routines is taking place. We can see that most of these modifications eliminate one or a few of the occasions of violence, often retaining others because (1) modifications are within, rather than apart from, existing institutions, and (2) institutions are where the money and the legitimacy are. Later, I will discuss more radical, new beginnings, which do not have these limitations.

In general, concepts of "community psychiatry" are sweeping through the profession. In many cases, this trend is little more than an extension of psychiatric violence: diagnosis, elaborate record keeping (with the additional violation of privacy through computerized, interagency information retrieval systems), nonreciprocality, and other forms of disobligation. However, any change of routine that tries to prevent hospitalization is a step in the positive direction of avoiding the totalism of institutions, thus confronting the population with its disobligated members. Specifically, day treatment centers allow the individual to live at home during the night and on weekends, while attending the therapeutic program during the regular working hours. There is considerable financial saving in eliminating residential facilities even while forty hours of treatment a week is provided. Group therapies, seminars on problems like money, sex, and employment, and other creative and recreational activities in a group setting characterize these programs. However, drugs are often used heavily to take up the slack in control lost by letting patients go at night. Most of these programs are "voluntary," although the continuing power of the state to lock patients up seriously compromises this concept.

Other institutions are increasingly involved in family work. For example, stattelite programs for "aftercare" involve entire families of previously hospitalized, or future-hospitalizable, persons one or more nights a week. Again, family work is sometimes merely an extension of the violence, especially violation of privacy, but the current term, "identified patient," indicates an awareness among family therapists that the family that "identifies" the patient as such is as much a part of the problem as is the "identified" person. Insofar as family work by-passes diagnosis and keeps people out of the hospital, it is a nonviolent innovation. Insofar as it deals with families, it is an explicit attempt to reclaim a circle of obligation.

Institutions have also created halfway houses (Raush and Raush 1968). Generally, the closer the tie to the traditional parent institution, the more the violent rituals and routines are maintained. But it is also true that merely leaving the hospital grounds and entering the community, even on the basis of a second-class-citizenship, is a concrete gain.

Finally, "community mental health centers," following the mandate of the President's Commission on Mental Health and Mental Illness (*Action for Mental Health* 1961) have sprung up, nourished by federal money, across the land. This kind of institution is definitely the wave of the future (Glasscote et al. 1964), but its continuation of most of the medical routines characteristic of mental hospitals makes it more of a fertile ground needing, rather than an example of, the Prometheus principle. Let us, therefore, look at some of the complexities of innovating in such institutions.

Innovation in a Community Mental Health Center: The Concept of Underground Treatment

Often, the staff of community mental health centers can barely find time to be helpful, for they are saddled with many time-consuming routines that serve to maintain the bureaucracy. In a state-supported institution in New York a worker cannot talk to a prospective client, even on the phone, without filling out a form for admission that requires such data as social security number and family income. One cannot continue a relationship without recording every contact with a client, his family, his employer, or his minister. Progress notes, three- and six-month summaries, codified diagnoses, and other trappings of medical routine not only absorb great quantities of time, they give the entire relationship a certain "official" character that is destructive of a client's trust and a therapist's spontaneity.

It is said often enough that institutions must perform these rituals primarily for the purpose of justifying public support, that is, documenting to the legislature that work is being done. And it is recognized commonly enough that, while wasteful, such routines are a necessary accommodation to the politics of mental health. A certain cynicism is inevitable; cynicism seems to be the only reasonable response to having one's integrity compromised by the political realities of professional work. However, there is another possibility: underground treatment.

Underground treatment occurs when someone who has the official role of publicly supported professional helper helps someone in distress without any of the official bookkeeping: no admission forms, no recording of every contact, no summaries, none of that accountability to the institution and its political backdrop. Accountability is between the helped and the helper; records follow the needs of these two parties rather than standard formats; no one is given an official status as patient; the helper gets no "credit" for the work done. Underground treatment is like stealing from the company store. My skills, which are essentially sold to the state during the workday, are stolen back by me and allocated by my judgment to those I want to help.

Underground treatment, like any underground movement, is less effective if it is kept totally secret. If the secrecy is successful, all the time one spends on underground treatment will be unaccounted for, according to bureaucratic data routines, and one will eventually lose his job. Should an entire institution develop a sizable underground treatment program that remains a secret, it will be unable to justify itself to the legislature and it will lose its funding. Hence it is necessary that underground treatment not be a secret. What really matters is just how the secret is leaked.

There are essentially two kinds of leaks, the double message and the single message. Double message leaks occur when professionals tell their administrative superiors what the administrators want to hear and simultaneously let them know, "I am only saying what you want to hear; actually I'm using my time in a much more useful, interesting, and valuable way." Double message leaks have the elegance of responding in kind to the double message received from administrative superiors who say that the client's interests are all that is important in such a way as to let you know that justifying the institution to the legislature is all that is important. Double message leaks are preferred by the most cynical of underground treatment professionals.

Single message leaks occur when professionals openly resist bureaucratic routines and simply proclaim their priorities always to put helping people above institutional accountability. Single message leaks are less ambiguous and support a style of communication within the institution that is healthier and cleaner. Single message leaks are preferred by the less cynical of underground treatment professionals.

Double message leaks allow everyone to save face and avoid an open confrontation that will inevitably be won by those who have the most power—most likely, the institutional authorities. However, their ambiguity clearly perpetuates cynicism and surrenders the possibility that administrators and professionals could talk honestly. Single message leaks have the advantage of keeping open the possibility of honest communication within the institution, but they clearly run the risk of open confrontation which the institution in its overwhelming concern with preserving itself may well win at the expense of the professional and his clients.

Underground treatment, again like any underground movement, is more effective if it is practiced by more than one person at a time. The development of a group who practices underground treatment is more or less inevitable in a sizable institution, and such a group will develop its own social structure—roles, rules, and routines. These parallel social structures exist in any organization, and they always present problems. Unofficial leaders are a threat to official leaders, and intramural conflicts between competing social structures can be destructive to everyone concerned. Therefore, it is important for underground treatment professionals to decide how much conflict and threat should surface. The issue is the character of visibility, which is clearly related to the kind of leaks that are used.

Single message leaks, especially in staff meetings, polarize the official and unofficial social structures. They are a more threatening visibility. In fact, to opt for a threatening visibility is to assume an already existing polarization. It is a precipitous option, forcing administration and staff to choose sides in an intramural fight. Such fights are justifiable only when there is promise of lasting positive change in the institution.

Intramural fights also tend to corrupt underground therapy from within by complicating the therapist's goals. In the heat of the fight, it is difficult to remember that the issue is helping people and not dethroning authority. The goal is to go around, not against, authority. How can underground therapists maintain their goal of helpfulness to clients when they are tempted to become angry at official authorities? The more polarization, the more difficult this is.

Ideally, underground treatment influences the organization without destroying either the organization or itself. No one pretends this is easy. When confronted with the threat of defunding, underground treatment professionals have the complex task of persuading their superiors to pass the leak and the visibility along to *their* superiors. This is bound to be difficult for, say, an administrative head or chief to do, because he feels the contingencies of his life are laid down by the bureaucracy above him and that he must, and his organization must, conform.

Mental health administrators are more likely to pass the leak upward and to insist on alternative models of accountability if they feel their professional staff is behind them. Underground treatment professionals can offer this support by helping the administrator invent ways of justifying the funds without strict numerical accountability. For example, a clear, concise description of the services, in narrative rather than numerical form, with examples that reflect the variety and subtlety of the work, should always be tried. Even though it is the administrators' job to write these, underground professionals can help by writing them or giving the administrator clear material from which to write.

At some point in the negotiations, the issue will surely come up whether it is easier to lie with numbers or with anecdotes. It is possible that there is less trust in numbers higher in the bureaucracy. It may be that the fetish with numbers is perpetuated by people on each level because they *expect* those above them to be impressed. The situation may be one in which the king has no clothes and someone must be courageous enough to say so. This generous assumption must at least be made once to test the rigidity of the bureaucracy at every level. Bureaucrats who cooperate can often work around a "numbers freak."

New "Noninstitutions"

Since tinkering with existing institutions only partially eliminates violence, entirely new institutions have also developed. These institutions usually define themselves as noninstitutions, and in the sense of old-style "mental institutions," they are right. However, they are "institutions," in the sociological sense and will be discussed as such.

In their attempt to avoid completely those routines that have produced so much violence, these institutions generally have adopted a strong, even militant, nonprofessional stance. This stance emerges from a sense that much of the violence of psychiatric treatment stems from its "professionalism." By professionalism is meant (1) the definition of a certain group of people ("professionals") who have the exclusive right and competence to work with certain kinds of problems, which (2) mystifies the problems to the general population, leading them to believe they cannot and should not try to understand certain people (for example, "psychotics"), which in turn (3) gives the general population an excuse for not trying to understand, for becoming judgmental (for example, "He's insane"), and for disobligating their outcasts, which in turn (4) keeps professionals in business. One way to attack this vicious circle of collusion that perpetuates psychiatric violence, and to reclaim the circle of obligation, is to operate successfully with people's problems nonprofessionally.

The most ambitious of these new institutions are the "free clinics" (Smith et al. 1971, Schwartz 1971) set up in urban areas to deal with problems that regular clinics will deal with expensively, insensitively, or not at all, such as drug crises, unwanted pregnancies, and even venereal disease. The style of these clinics covers a wide range, but they have the common feature that they are cost-free to clients. This breaks the "professionalism" at one point, that of keeping the professionals in business, for the economic motive for professionalism is simply not there. Most of the staff are volunteers putting in time beyond their regular jobs. Being cost-free not only makes them available to people who otherwise would not get help, it also redefines the concept of "professionalism" from the trade union exclusivity it has become to the technical conscientiousness that it should be. Even so, it sustains the "expertise" feature of professionalism and tends to lead the population to its wanted conclusion that they, just ordinary people, have nothing to contribute to the solution of certain problems which are "for experts only." This does not mean that professionals cannot combat this mystique; they can. And it is in the free clinics where this is most likely to happen.

Less ambiguous on the professionalism issue are "rap centers" and telephone "hot lines" that are largely conceived, staffed, and sustained by nonprofessionals. These institutions range in their offerings from only telephone counseling to home visit crisis intervention, referral, and follow-up. Sociologically, these centers are a new presence in a community. They are an attempt to put into touch with one another two large groups of people, those who want to help and those who want to be helped. This is an explicit attempt to reclaim and expand the circle of obligation.

Our traditional arrangement for putting these two groups together has been extraordinarily awkward and stilted. In order to be helpful, one had to undergo extensive education, most of it irrelevant, to become "qualified," thus accepting the role of "professional" and submitting to the expectations of one's colleagues for proper "professional" behavior. And in order to get help, one had to undergo the degradation ceremonies of diagnosis and total loss of privacy and to accept the role of "patient," thus submitting to the expectations of one's fellow patients and especially of professionals for proper "patient" behavior. Like medical routines, these customs ignored the circle of obligation and obscured it. Informal, nonprofessional institutions by-pass all this ritualizing, routinizing, and role-defining, and instead propagate simpler, clearer, and more successful help.

We cannot say that such institutions do not have their problems. Since their staff is largely volunteer, the institutions must trade on the rather uncertain tradition of volunteer services. In our culture, the volunteer tradition is very close to the tradition of charity, which is perhaps the weakest expression of the obligation form. Their predecessors in our culture, the Salvation Army and the settlement houses, could draw on religious commitment to firm up their staff's obligation and reliability. The contemporary lack of such religious ties enables these institutions to draw from a larger pool of potential helpers, including middle-class housewives and retired businessmen. But on the other hand, the youth and often counter-culture style of the central people in these modern institutions tend again to limit the range of participants. Some of these problems will be taken up in the next section.

Yet another new institution is the "growth center," which is largely a spin-off from the sensitivity-training movement so popular only a few years ago. These institutions typically advertise themselves as "enriching" rather than therapeutic, aimed at "growth *from* normal" more than "growth from abnormal *to* normal." This is a wholly salutary move; it is assumed that persons are already normal and that they might nevertheless want to grow. The general thrust of these centers is inherently pluralistic and nonjudgmental. Their aim is to encourage differences among people rather than to make people all alike (that is, "normal"). In their zealous enthusiasm, these centers may not entirely avoid pushing people into the same mold, but they lack the coercive power, the diagnostic paraphenalia, and the popular "people-fixing" legitimacy of conventional psychiatric treatment. Therefore they avoid the collusive vicious circle into which professional psychiatry has fallen.

The most elaborate and famous of these centers is the Esalon Institute at Big Sur, California, a center that has suffered a good deal of notoriety and acquired the inevitably destructive mystique that goes along with it. Many large cities and some rural areas have less elaborate and less well-advertised programs that typically offer weekend encounter groups of all kinds: for married couples, for single parents, for those interested in Yoga and other Eastern religious pursuits, and even astrology and palmistry.[2] Their staffs vary widely from well-known professionals to not well known nonprofessionals who have proved that they have something substantive to offer to the institution.

A rather special case of new institutions is the currently popular "Transcendental Meditation," which is neither transcendental nor meditational, but which offers effective techniques in relaxation and concentration that are helpful to many people. Unfortunately, this institution, like the growth centers, charges clients substantial fees in order to sustain themselves, which limits their constituency to middle and upper classes.

Perhaps the most direct and relevant new institution is the Kingsley Hall kind of center envisioned and implemented by R. D. Laing in London (Gordon 1971). This institution is based on the following premises, all of which are nonviolent and which directly counter the more violent assumptions built into psychiatric practice: (1) people do have intense personal crises that stem largely from the judgmental consciousness and social structure of modern times; (2) these crises are not to be "cured," but rather are opportunities for self-discovery and integration beyond what is "normally" possible in our society; and therefore (3) persons undergoing such a crisis ought to be encouraged to go through, instead of to back away from, the intense anxiety that accompanies profound personal change (Laing 1967).

Kingsley Hall was a place where such a process could take place. There were a small number of permanent residents, including Laing himself, and a small number of "guests," whose stay at the residence was for the explicit purpose of going "out of their minds"—that is, to escape the judgmental competition imposed by modern social structure and to explore other possible ways to be human. The permanent residents supplied a supportive, encouraging, largely noninterfering but occasionally prodding social context in which one could experience his own inner world more fully without having either to conform to the outer social one or be diagnosed and psychiatrically treated back to where he started.

Laing's experiment, and certainly Laing himself, are quite controversial among professionals (Beldoch 1970). From the point of view of professionals, Laing's thought and his institution are most unprofessional. But of course that is the point, given the tenets of professionalism and how it has established itself in our society.

Kingsley Hall is now closed, but its concept and spirit are not (cf. Jourard 1968). We should see it, I think, as a bold experiment in nonviolent psychiatry.

On Creating a New Institution: The Concept of Co-option

Unlike innovating within an institution, where the crucial political interface is between the innovators and established powers, creating a new institution engages one directly in an interface with the public. Both contexts are important, not to mention the interface between oneself and one's client. Here I would like to discuss some problems and some solutions involved in creating a new institution.

Suppose one wanted to begin a crisis switchboard, or rap center, or drug treatment center, on a nonprofessional, no-cost basis that would attempt to reclaim the circle of obligation and implement a nonviolent vision of how people might help people. Such a desire would presumably stem from a perception of social reality that is sensitive to the obligation form. The first problem is that this perception will almost certainly be different from both popular and professional perception in the community. Indeed, if the population and professionals shared this perception, there would already be such an institution.

There are understandable reasons why the population and the professionals may not see what, to obligation-sensitive eyes, is an obvious need. For example, if there is a drug problem involving growing numbers of adolescents and no facility where they can be "talked down" from their crises, the general population and professionals are busy (1) denying that there is a problem at all, and (2) desperately looking for people to blame for the problem, thus (3) scrambling to appear blameless. These reactions are understandable, given the competitive form and its popular judgmentalism in our culture. The experts are judging the parents badly and the parents are judging the experts badly and both know it.

Understandable as it may be, however, this judgmentalism does not put the professionals and the population into a position to cope effectively with the problem. Initially, the most likely scapegoats will be the disobligated "deviants" themselves, who, when so judged, have even less a stake in fulfilling the expectations of their parents, or rejoining a circle of obligation.

The initial reaction to the creation of a nonprofessional rap center aimed at the drug problem will be salutary to the clients but devastating to the center. Personnel at the center will partially replace the "deviants" themselves as the perceived source of the evil: "We didn't have a drug problem till those people moved in." This is not a wholly incorrect statement; the center brings into focus a skeleton that was under heavy lock and key in the community closet. This focus unmasks a number of pretenses and exposes parents, police, and professionals alike to "blame." The search for a scapegoat intensifies.

Innovative and realistic people who thus wanted to solve a problem they saw clearly but others did not are now accused of causing the problem they sought to solve. This is an insult as well as a serious misunderstanding, and many innovative projects fail at this point. Antagonisms escalate and the innovators are driven out. Such a fight obviously serves the disobligated clients, the "deviants," very badly indeed. They are caught between the new institution and the community and the new institution is caught in the crossfire between their clients and the community. Political hassles may engage such issues as funding, building codes, zoning laws, taxation, and licensure. The thicket can become quite dense.

Although most of these problems are inevitable, given the predominantly judgmental structure of popular consciousness, they can be mitigated by a careful process of co-option. Co-option is usually described as pulling a rebel into an establishment cause by allowing him to rebel in a controlled way. As long as his rebellion is under establishment control, any widespread, latent rebellion is defused. Thus, the status quo is protected by letting it be attacked in an ineffective way. There is no reason, however, why the concept cannot be turned around. Parents, professionals, and police may be co-opted by an innovative institution.

Considerable groundwork must be laid before the new institution becomes publicly visible. At first, all one might expect and all one needs is agreement to be left alone to operate for a short period of time. This operating will have to be on a small scale with low visibility. After some solid achievements have occurred, such as the arrest of a pusher, the salvation of a youth, and the development of workable concrete relationships, the crucial process of co-option is possible. Achievements in hand, the institution can now become publicly visible, giving all the credit to those whose opposition could harrass or destroy the institution: professionals, the police, educators, parents.

Such a procedure requires nearly superhuman humility. After juggling the various political footballs with excruciating care, and working hard with clients, one feels one deserves a bit of credit. Indeed one does, but to take it, even when offered by well-meaning advocates in the community, is to put everyone else in the position of losing face in the judgmental eyes of one another. This strategy is no lie. In truth, every solid achievement of such an institution does rely on an initial passive participation by established powers in the community. Later, the mayor, the department of mental hygiene, even the FBI, cannot resist an opportunity to increase their public stock. If they publicly commit themselves to seeing individuals in their particularity, and join the effort to reclaim obligation, the new institution will have been a success.

However, let us not be sanguine about the process of creating a new institution. Even though both real and apparent benefits can accrue to everyone involved in the community, suspicions die hard. When the issues are as emotionally loaded as drugs and mental illness, there is a constant danger of explosion. Genuine security of Promethian institutions is possible only when the population itself begins to forgo its judgmentalism, to perceive individuals in their particularity, and to live the obligation form that is inherent in our culture. This growth may already be identified here and there, but Prometheus is a long way from being nationally and officially adopted, and he may never be.

Political Innovation

Our third focus of interest in nonviolent innovations explicitly takes up popular consciousness and official policy. Unlike the modifications of existing institutions and the creation of new ones, political innovation is not directed toward the delivery of services. It is aimed at the political-social backdrop against which all services are delivered and acquire their meaning.

The American Association for the Abolition of Involuntary Mental Hospitalization (AAAIMH) was founded in 1970 by Thomas S. Szasz, George J. Alexander and Erving Goffman. Although it is officially dedicated to ending legal involuntary mental hospitalization, the organization is concerned with a range of civil liberties and how the psychiatric profession, in conjunction with the government, infringes upon them.

Involuntary mental hospitalization is violent not only in its occurance, but also in its threat. How voluntary, for example, is an admission to a closed ward in a mental hospital when the individual is told, as he often is, that he may as well go along "voluntarily" or else he will be legally committed without his consent? Indeed it is this final club of official authority that underlies the clout of less drastic psychiatric control. No matter what small thing I may be ordered to do by a psychiatrist, I am obliged to do it as long as I know I cannot defend myself against his weighty power of accuser, judge, and jury.

That such a situation exists for each and every one of us in modern society is an impressive fact. It is itself a cultural form. In a subtle but powerful way, it is decisive for how my experience is structured. I do not often reflect explicitly upon how this or that behavior would lead to my hospitalization, but some real possibilities for how to live my life appear closed to me precisely because they would be considered grounds for involuntary mental hospitalization. I am not, because of this threat, permitted to cry uncontrollably, to shout obscenities at my psychiatrist when I see him on the street, or to be too disagreeable to people in my own behalf, no matter how oppressed I might actually be. These activities might be guaranteed and protected for me by the Bill of Rights. Nevertheless, somewhere in the back of my mind, next to the guilt-inspiring question, "Is it right?" stands the equally powerful shame-inspiring question, "Will it be perceived as sane?"

Another, less visible, movement from the side of patients accompanies the AAAIMH: The "Insane Liberation Front," or "patient power." It is significant that this movement is seen by all of us as less respectable than the AAAIMH. They are, after all, finally "just patients" (we should add, to say it fully: "not real people"). We know who the losers are. Even though their political sensibilities have as much right to a hearing as the group of professionals that make up AAIMH, patients are inherently disobligated. They do not have the organization that Szasz has been able to build, nor even the possibility of attracting the high-level professional support that Szasz's group might acquire.

The AAAIMH is "non-sense" in the same way that Pinel was "non-sense." What they want does not fit our current understanding of ourselves and of one another. But the image of a group of inmates stalking the administrative offices of a mental hospital in search of their civil liberties is not only "non-sense," it is downright frightening. Here we have an indication of the extent to which we have disobligated mental patients. They want to be accorded the rights of human beings, which include the right to be heard, to be obligated to others, and to demand obligation from others. They too want an end to involuntary mental hospitalization.

We must take up the question seriously because of both groups. As one who has been responsible for making the decision to "arrest" someone who has committed no crime but has convinced me that he may well do so, it is with genuine ambivalence that I support these movements. When Mr. X, who was brain damaged and alcoholic, threatened his wife and six children with knives, I was not convinced that more harm than good was done by the legal commitment procedure. I could only imagine a stabbed child, and I was grateful that I could legally intervene through involuntary mental hospitalization.

However, involuntary hospitalization was my last resort. My resources were exhausted; he would not even speak to me. My profession lacked any provision by which I could see that someone stuck with him twenty-four hours a day, or whatever it may have taken to overcome his already advanced disobligation. It is not often the case that such extreme services are demanded of professionals or of a community, but when they are demanded, they ought to be there. As long as it is possible instead to call the police and have it over, they will not be developed. And they should be.

This leads us, finally, to the last political action group that I would like to report. I know of only one such institution, the Eleanor Roosevelt Developmental Services (ERDS) in New York State. This is not a national movement, but it deserves discussion here because of its direct attempt to influence our cultural self-understanding through changing the structure of society. This state-supported institution is singularly dedicated to the task of developing direct community action.

It is interesting how poorly understood ERDS is among professionals. It is popularly accused of "getting everyone else to do its work," that is, of getting people, nonprofessionals, in the community, to take care of their own "emotionally disturbed" and "mentally retarded" children. The accusation is made from the assumption that these are problems "for professionals only"; the practice is exactly what the accusation literally says—it aims at making professionals superfluous by developing community resources, churches, clubs, families, and rap centers, to the point that "deviants" need not be sent to "experts" but can find a supportive and healthy social context right where they are. It is a direct and blatant attempt to reclaim the cultural form, obligation, as a framework for self-understanding.

ERDS, and all other community organization efforts, is in constant political trouble, for it threatens to establish a network of loyalties and obligations that runs counter to the existing system of ward healers and bosses that constitute the professional establishment. The outcome of such work, if it is successful, will be to heighten people's awareness of one another in their particularity, within that reciprocal framework of meaning that we have called obligation. The question is, as ever, whether it can survive the political storms it creates long enough to succeed. If it does not, another attempt at community organization will later take its place. It is a complex task to organize a community so as to put professionals out of their traditional business, to ensure that persons defined as "deviant" come to be tolerated, supported, and perceived in their uniqueness. Everyone, once he thinks the whole situation over, will have to support it—everyone, that is, except those whose self-definition is grounded in the competitive form of winners and losers. Unfortunately, that includes all of us to the extent that we have not seen clearly the role of culture, particularly of this highly competitive culture, in our self-understanding.

EPILOGUE

We have flailed and ranted and raved at some of our own absurdities and some things have become clear. Perhaps the clearest thing is the enormous vitality and creativity of individuals and groups who are trying to separate out and eliminate the violence of traditional psychiatric treatment.

Equally impressive, however, is the depth of the problem as soon as one takes seriously its presence in popular consciousness as well as in institutional forms. One of the most recurrent observations about current psychiatric treatment is the extent to which patients accept its routines without objection. Once disobligated, it is possible to remain so indefinitely. Although this acquiescence may be a deceptive appearance, the psychiatric patient in our society has no power to define his behavior as a reasonable rebellion when it is so powerfully interpreted as a sign of mental illness. Except for initial "adjustment" and later occasional "crisis" or "decompensation" phases, it appears that patients understand how they are being treated and why, and they accept it. From our perspective, the rebellious phases are encouraging. They indicate that the spirit has not been broken, that a demand for dignity and reciprocity still finds expression, albeit in a currently ineffective, "crazy" way.

Paradoxically, the normal, general population gives us somewhat less encouraging data. We are all caught up in a collusion with professionals in which we have come to feel that our only protection against disobligation is to disobligate others. However, Promethean initiative in rupturing popular consciousness has begun to have some effect. As our institutions continue to evolve, we can hope the Prometheus principle will become more central to our personal, professional, political, and cultural lives.

NOTES

1. It must be realized, of course, that research using medical records of psychiatric patients is rarely performed for the purpose of discovering truth. Its most common purpose is to justify the institution and to support its claim that it should grow.

2. A partial list of those centers that advertise nationally is: *Quest*, Bethesda, Md.; *The New England Center*, Amherst, Mass.; *Tori*, La Jolla, Cal.; *Aegis Institute*, Haverford, Pa.; *Aurean Institute*, New York, N. Y.; *Human Development Institute*, Chicago, and a publishing/co-ordinating organization *University Associates*, Iowa City, Iowa.

REFERENCES

Action for mental health. 1961. Final Report of the Joint Commission on Mental Illness and Health. New York: Science Editions.

Beldoch, M. 1970. R. D. Laing and the search for ecstasy. *Psychia. and the Soc. Sci. Rev.* 4:13–16.

Boszormenyi-Nagy, I., and Framo, J. L., eds. 1965. *Intensive family therapy.* New York: Harper and Row.

Braginski, B. M., Braginski, D. D., and Ring, K. 1969. *Methods of madness: the hospital as the last resort.* New York: Holt.

Eisenstein, V. W. 1956. *Neurotic interaction in marriage.* New York: Basic Books.

Esterson, A. 1972. *The leaves of spring.* Harmondsworth, Middlesex, England: Pelican.

Fairweather, G. W., Sanders, D. H., Cressler, D. L., and Maynard, H. 1969. *Community life for the mentally ill.* Chicago: Aldine.

Ferber, A., Mendelsohn, M., and Napier, A. 1972. eds. *The book of family therapy.* New York: Science House.

Fischer, C. T. 1970. The testee as co-evaluator. *J. Counseling Psychol.* 17:70–76.

Garfinkel, H. 1956. Conditions of successful degradation ceremonies. *Am. J. Sociol.* 56:420–24.

Glasscote, R., Sanders, D. Forstenzer, H. M. and Foley, A. R., 1964. *The community mental health center.* Washington, D. C.: Joint Information Service of the American Psychiatric Association and the National Association for Mental Health.

Goffman, E. 1961. *Asylums.* Garden City, New York: Anchor, 1961.

Gordon, J. S. 1971. Who is mad? Who is sane? *Atlantic* January: 50–65.

Group for the Advancement of Psychiatry, Committee on the Family. 1970. *Treatment of families in conflict.* New York: Science House.

Honigfeld, G. 1971. In defense of diagnosis. *Professional Psychol.* 2:289–91.

Howells, J. G. 1970. *Theory and practice of family therapy.* New York: Bruner/Mazel.

Insane liberation front. 1971. *Radical Therapist* 2:15.

Jourard, S. 1968. Society's need for respectable "check-out places." In *Disclosing man to himself*, S. Jourard. New York: Van Nostrand Reinhold.

Laing, R. D. 1967. *The politics of experience.* New York: Pantheon.

Laing, R. D., and Esterson, A. 1970. *Sanity, madness, and the family.* Harmondsworth, Middlesex, England: Pelican.

Leifer, R. 1969. *In the name of mental health.* New York: Science House.

Lidz, T., Fleck, S., and Cornelison, A. 1965. *Schizophrenia and the family.* New York: International Universities Press.

Raush, H. L., and Raush, C. L. 1968. *The halfway house movement.* New York: Appleton-Century-Crofts.

Schwartz, J. 1971. Free Clinics: new approach to neighborhood health care. *Radical Therapist* 2:4–5.

Smith, D., Bentel, D., and Schwartz, J. 1971. *The free clinic: community approaches to medical care and drug abuse.* Beloit, Wis.: STASH Press.

Szasz, T. S. 1961. *The myth of mental illness.* New York: Hoeber-Harper.

Taylor, M. A., and Heiser, J. F. 1971. Phenomenology: an alternative approach to diagnosis of mental disease. *Comprehensive Psychia.* 12:480–86.

Tharp, R. G., and Wetzel, R. 1969. *Behavior modification in the natural environment.* New York: Academic Press.

Ulrich, R., Stachnik, T., and Mabry, J., eds. 1966. *Control of human behavior.* Glencoe, Ill.: Scott, Foresman.

Veterans Administration Hospital. 1972. *Token economy handbook.* Unpublished manuscript. Albany, N.Y.

Zuk, G. H. 1971. *Family therapy: a tradition-based approach.* New York: Behavioral Publications.

6.

Rights of Medical Patients

ROSEMARIE R. PARSE

It matters not how strait the gate,
How charged with punishments the scroll,
I am the master of my fate;
I am the captain of my soul.
W. E. Henley

To think that we are or ever can be masters of our own fate in any significant way may be a self-delusion, one of the "vanities of human wishes," to paraphrase the thesis of Pico della Mirandola's Renaissance philosophical tract. Given on the one hand the premise that we have to be in control, and on the other hand the morass of Orwellian thought engineering, half-truths, and biased reportage that bombard us every day from every medium, it would seem that self-determination is almost beyond our reach. The critical word here, however, is "almost".

In the last decade, a countermovement has emerged in this country, a "right-to-know" movement to put people in control of their fate at least partially—if not significantly. Truth in lending, truth in packaging, consumerism, the demise of the Corvair, the publication of the Pentagon Papers, and the precedent-setting Escobedo and Miranda Supreme Court decisions are all touchstones in this new wave. And Ralph Nader, Jack Anderson, Daniel Ellsberg, and the

121

members of the Warren Court are the high priests in this attitudinal reformation. Unfortunately, in many sections of American life, attitudes change slowly. And without a Ralph Nader to prod, a Jack Anderson to publish, and an Earl Warren to adjudicate, some attitudes change not at all. The area of health care is one sector of American life that has remained insulated, at least somewhat, from the "right-to-know" movement.

An examination of the situation, as it exists today, shows clearly that health care consumers are underinformed about their conditions and have little to say about their care. They do not significantly participate in decisions regarding their own health and neither do they participate in policy making for health care practices in institutions or in the community at large (Sparer 1971).

Persons seeking health guidance are frequently treated impersonally, stripped of their autonomy, and given very little information about their health status (cf. Sparer 1971). These people are approached autocratically by health professionals with prescribed expectations and are too rarely looked upon as individuals uniquely experiencing a health problem. In accordance with hospital policy, questions to the nurse such as "What is my temperature today?" or "Do you think I have a tumor" are often answered by "You'll have to ask your doctor." And, if the physician should be asked these questions, he frequently sidesteps with: "The temperature is OK" and "I'm not sure whether you have a tumor or not" (even if he is sure), or even "Don't worry yourself about that; I'm taking care of everything." Picture the young father with chronic colitis being scheduled for surgery (which might result in total reconstruction of the bowel) without access to information regarding his general health or knowledge of the ramifications involving such surgery. How about the mother of three who has been told only that she may be developing arthritis when all the laboratory studies show and the physician's notes state conclusively that her illness is chronic progressive rheumatoid arthritis. And the 58-year-old store owner with metastatic lung cancer who is discharged from the hospital completely unaware that a note on his chart states "terminal stages of cancer—two weeks to six months." Numerous examples of this could be listed; they are not atypical. One study was conducted on fifty or more doctor-patient relationships in a large medical clinic. It showed that more than one-third of the patients were given no explanation whatsoever about tests being done on them; one-half were told only that a particular organ was investigated, and the remaining 14 percent were given some explanation of the results

(Sparer 1971, p. 28). It seems as though patients are perpetually uninformed.

To make matters worse, health professionals have even gone so far as to set expectations for patients' behavior. The "good patient" is described as one "who accepts medical decisions without debate, follows orders without serious questions, returns faithfully for follow-up and expresses gratitude and continuing dependence appropriately" (Tisdale 1970, p. 387). Professionals have implied that compliance with the medical authorities will in itself contribute to healing. Ways are continually being sought to increase compliance behavior in patients (cf. Vincent 1971).

Where health professionals have continued to abdicate their responsibility to inform their patients, a health worker known as the patient's advocate has appeared on the scene. This health worker is not at present a professional, but is becoming more and more prevalent. In fact, the American Hospital Association sponsors a Society of Patient Representatives for those persons who work for the following purpose:

> To humanize the patient's hospital experience.
>
> To act as the patient's friend from his time of admission until his time of discharge.
>
> To interpret the purpose and philosophy of the hospital to the patient.
>
> To interpret the patient's problems and opinions to Administration.
>
> To explain patient's needs to Administration and hospital staff (New York Hospital 1970).

Introduction of this worker, sometimes referred to as a hospital ombudsperson, into the overall scheme of health care delivery has only perpetuated the situation in which health professionals are not accountable to consumers and has magnified the intrinsic problem of lack of communication between patient and health professional. The hospital ombudsperson intervenes, intercedes, and interprets for the patient when problems arise. He generally answers questions and seeks information on behalf of the patient. When the information sought is medical or nursing oriented, the ombudsperson is, in fact, interrupting the line of communication between patient and health professional and in so doing supports the reluctance of health professionals to share information.

MEDICAL RELUCTANCE

This is the way it is. It sounds like a very black and white situation: the patients or consumers are the good guys, the health professionals, the bad guys. Not so, at least not completely so. Some of the factors that have influenced the evolvement of this situation can illuminate the gray areas of blame in both camps. This section will discuss some understandable sources of the medical profession's reluctance to encourage informed participation by patients. The following section will indicate some of the ways in which medical consumers have failed to pursue their own rights and personal responsibility.

First, and most significant, is the Code of Medical Ethics (American Medical Association Judicial Council, 1971). Section 9 of this document contains the following two relevant statements: (1) "The physician should neither exaggerate nor minimize the gravity of a patient's condition. He should assure himself that the patient, his relatives or his responsible friends have such knowledge of the patient's condition as will serve the best interests of the patient and family" and (2) "Whether the contents of the report (health) are to be given to the patient rests with the decision of the doctor who knows all the circumstances involved in the situation" (p. 53). Both of these statements show that the admirable intention to "serve the best interests of the patient" is oversimplified into a strictly medical issue; and in strictly medical areas the doctor of course must bear most of the responsibility for medical decisions. The patient advocacy movement seeks to broaden the concept of "patient's best interests" by including patient participation in health related decisions.

Further, Section 1 of the Code of Medical Ethics states "the medical profession is to render service to humanity with full respect for the dignity of man" (p. 5). "Dignity of man" could be interpreted to include patient participation in decision-making regarding his own health. Historically, however, this has not been the case. So through the code of ethics of his profession, the physician has been encouraged, or at least given the opportunity, to maintain power over health care information and decisions. Other health professionals have followed the lead of the physicians. Nurses have been particularly negligent in seeking patient participation in decisions regarding care. Until recently most nurses have been considered and have considered themselves handmaidens to the physician. In many instances they have used physicians as role models. This scene is changing, however, and nursing is emerging as an independent profession. Hopefully, helping patients to make decisions will be an important part of that profession.

In addition to the general guidelines offered by the code of ethics, most health professionals have been explicitly schooled in and grown up with the traditional attitude that prescription, treatment, and caring were to be done *for* or *to* rather than *with* the patient. Coincidentally, these professionals have only been judged accountable to their peers (Sparer 1971); and this accountability has been very loosely interpreted.

It is important to remember, however, that these health professionals are frequently sensitive persons who have prepared themselves in a disciplined fashion to assist others with health problems. For many of them their raison d'etre is to heal. But they are constantly confronted with situations in which their knowledge and prescribed treatment do not result in cure. Perhaps the reluctance of health professionals to include the patient in decision making, consequently, is related to personal fears. It may be difficult to explain the health problem to the patient in terms he will understand. Or the professional may fear revealing his own fallibility. The patient may ask questions which the health professional cannot answer. For example, even if the physician can predict death, he cannot explain to the patient "Why me?" or "What now?." Indeed, most health professionals are particularly reluctant to tell the patient about imminent death. To inform a patient that death is imminent or that he will be permanently disabled is understandably paradoxical for one who has devoted himself to healing, caring, and above all, living. Nevertheless, some forward thinkers, like Dr. Kübler-Ross (1970), who have worked with dying patients for many years suggest that the question is not "should I tell," but "how can I share" this information with a patient.

CONSUMER RELUCTANCE

The health care consumer, as indicated above, is equally to blame for the lack of communication between the professional and the patient. His role evolved along with and, in a way, perpetuated the "prescription without consumer participation" attitude (Fanning, Deloughery, and Gebbie 1972). Consumers accept without question the health professional's right to handle information and make decisions about health care practice. Many times patients do not want to share in the responsibility regarding the treatment of their health problems. The truth is, though, that through consenting to the expert's initiative the consumer has always been at least indirectly responsible. No health care institution can insist upon that which the patient refuses. Patients can leave health care settings if they wish, and even prior to that, most care requires his participation, albeit often minimal (cf. Sparer 1971). Moreover, patients have always been responsible for signing legal documents to permit surgery or diagnostic procedures. This signing usually occurs without any request for information or any complaining about not being informed.

THE LEGAL PICTURE

When patients have questioned or complained, it has generally been after some injury has been sustained. Complaints are often in the form of law suits of one sort or another. Take for example the question of whether or not a patient should be told about his condition. In this case, legal requirements, arising from "malpractice" cases seem to make that question a matter of professional determination by physicians (*Natanson* v. *Kline*, Kan. Sup. Ct., 1960).

The jury instruction given in *Salgo* v. *Leland Stanford Jr. University Board of Trustees* (Cal. Dist. Ct. App. 1957) illustrates this point:

> A physician violates his duties to his patient and subjects himself to liability if he withholds any facts which are necessary to form the basis of an intelligent consent by the patient to the proposed treatment. Likewise the physician may not minimize the known dangers of a procedure or operation in order to induce his patient's consent. At the same time, the physician must place the welfare of his patient above all else and this very fact places him in a position in which he sometimes must choose between two alternative courses of action. One is to explain to the patient every risk attendant upon any surgical procedure or operation, no matter how remote; this may well result in alarming a patient who is already unduly apprehensive and who may as a result refuse to undertake surgery in which there is in fact minimal risk; it may also result in actually increasing the risks by reason of the physiological results of the apprehension itself. The other is to recognize that each patient presents a separate problem, that the patient's mental and emotional condition is important and in certain cases may be crucial, and that in discussing the element of risk a certain amount of discretion must be employed consistent with the full disclosure of facts necessary to an informed consent (p. 170).

More recently, however, "negligence" rather than "malpractice" has been the usual course of action where the physician failed to get a patient's consent based on full disclosure. *Wilson* v. *Scott* (Tex. Sup. Ct, 1967), where the physician failed to warn the patient that total deafness could result from a stapedectomy, is a good case in point. The decision against Dr. Wilson seems to indicate that the physician is responsible for informing his patient. But the jury instruction in Salgo seems to give the physician more discretion. In sum, the picture is far from clear.

CALL FOR CHANGE

It seems as though the Code of Medical Ethics, traditional practice by health professionals, the law, and consumer response all somehow contributed in the evolving of the health care delivery system as we know it today. Is there any reason then to consider a change that would alter the whole situation? Why encourage a change that would break with tradition, call for reinterpretation of the Code of Medical Ethics by physicians and lawyers, shift the power from professional to consumer in health policymaking, and make the consumer a member of the health care delivery co-op in matters of diagnostic processes, treatment and care? There are many reasons for encouraging such a change.

First, altering the situation would enhance the consumer's dignity by affirming his responsibility for his own life. It could promote personal growth of the consumer *and* of the health professional through the sharing of responsibility for health care decisions. Every health care consumer should come to realize that personal health is a personal responsibility, one that requires action (cf. Kramer 1972a). Consumer participation in medical decisions could personalize health care services as the health professional takes time to fully explain the medical data to the patient, and to discuss the patient's knowledge and feelings about the situation. With a more personal approach, how the consumer is experiencing his illness can be more easily explored so that consumer and health professional can grapple honestly with their differing understandings and priorities. However this personal approach is accomplished, we must take active cognizance of the now well-established knowledge that in order to enhance the effectiveness of treatment, the patient must be engaged in all aspects of the treatment process including evaluation of its usefulness (cf. Levine 1970).

As society generally is moving toward a more informed citizenry in all areas, persons seek more knowledge about and participation in matters of health. There are several indications of a move in this direction. In December 1970, the Medical Committee for Human Rights, a subcommittee of the Joint Commission on Accreditation of Hospitals (JCAH), prepared a document called "A Patient's Bill of Rights." Much of the document deals with the patient's right to privacy. However, one section read: "The patient has the right to communicate with those responsible for his case, and to receive from them adequate information concerning the nature and extent of his medical problem, the planned course of treatment and the prognosis" (p. 2). The degree to which this is accomplished is evaluated by the JCAH before hospitals can receive accreditation. But even though this document does not include any indication that patients should participate in policymaking, it seems to be moving in the general direction of consumer participation. In addition to this push from JCAH, several studies have examined how patients and professionals feel about consumer participation in nursing care planning.

In one such study (Dodge 1972) 139 patients and 62 nurses were asked to respond to questions regarding what patients wanted to know about their illness. The results showed that patients were most concerned about the chances of recovery and recurrence, the results of diagnostic studies, the causes of symptoms, the effects of their medications, and insurance details. Nurses on the other hand believed that patients wanted to know more about what to expect regarding their care. Both nurses and patients agreed though that patients should be informed about diagnosis, length of illness, and how they can participate in their own care. Another study (Fanning et al. 1972) found that both staff and patients agreed that care and treatment should be a joint effort and that patient participation in the care planning process should begin on admission.

Legislation has been necessary in some situations to provide consumer input in the health care delivery system. Neighborhood health centers, model cities programs, and comprehensive health care planning legislate the presence of consumers on their policymaking and planning boards (Parker 1970). Consumer education for the role of policymaking is complex, of course, as is education for the health professional for collaborative participation. Nevertheless, the Berkeley Consumer Health Training Project was a one-year demonstration program for consumer education (Kramer 1972a). The program was quite successful in preparing approximately forty-five lay board members for their role in health policymaking. It was evident from the results of this project that initiation of many such programs would be beneficial.

At a national conference on health education in 1969, Dr. Scott K. Simonds indicated that a value system in health education had evolved, centered on the patient. He listed the following points as the essence of this value system:

1. He shall be respected and cared for as a human being.

2. He shall be recognized as having a unique sociopsychological, cultural, and familial background relevant to his condition and to communication with him concerning his condition.

3. He shall have access to and the opportunity to obtain the information and guidance that he sees as needed to care for his condition and shall have the support for helping him use the information obtained.

4. He shall be provided an active and participatory role in his own care to the extent that he chooses and is able.

5. He shall be stimulated and guided through effective educational means to acquire new knowledge, attitudes, and actions that will promote his ability to care for himself more adequately and to maintain his health at an optimum level.

6. He shall be cared for through services designed and organized to promote and support learnings and behavior that are appropriate to his care and to the maintenance of his health (Lesparre 1970, p. 77).

There is some indication then, that the consumer is coming of age in participation in health care decisions. And more can be done to speed up this evolutionary process and to enhance the advances made by legislatures, the American Hospital Association, and some progressive health professionals and consumers.

Concretely, the following suggestions could enhance the move toward self-determination in regard to health issues.

Power Shift

The power should shift a bit from health professional to the consumer in order to equalize the responsibility for decision-making in matters of health. In order to bring this about effectively, a new relationship must be developed between consumer and health professional (Kramer 1972a). Attitudes of mutual trust and respect are essential as well as a real commitment to consumerism (Sparer

1971). Group conference sessions for health professionals and consumers could provide a forum for interaction between these two groups. The responsibility to initiate change and create a power shift should be assumed by health professionals. Consumers should be invited to participate at policymaking levels in all health care agencies before legislation requires it. This would give the consumer a strong voice in the development of community health services (Corey, Saltman, and Epstein 1972). Only actual participation at this level represents a shift in power.

Education

Perhaps the most significant move forward would be through education. Many groups must be educated before change can occur. The consumer needs education in two major areas to enhance his effectiveness in health policymaking and to prepare him for informed participation with his own health care decisions. Education for attitude change and health responsibility should begin in early childhood in the home and continue formally throughout public school. In addition to learning proper health habits in such conventional areas as nutrition and hygiene, children should learn about their personal responsibility for health management and maintenance. The child should be helped to gain an understanding of what it is to be human and the interrelationship of freedom and responsibility in relation to health. He should understand that he has the freedom to make choices in matters regarding his health and that he bears responsibility in regard to these choices. Information, including basic anatomy, physiology, and common disease processes, should be disseminated so the individual will grow up with some understanding of his resistance and vulnerability to illness. Knowledge of the uses and danger of common drugs could be most valuable as well as general information about ecological contaminants. The child should be familiarized with criteria upon which to evaluate and utilize health information. All of this data will provide some input for participation in policymaking for health agencies. In addition, educational programs for consumers like the Berkeley Consumer Health Training Project (Kramer 1972a) could be established. These activities could prepare the consumer to participate in general health care responsibility and planning. When the consumer becomes a patient, he should participate explicitly in decision-making about his own diagnosis, treatment, and care. The patient should be taught the law and agency policies regarding his rights of access to his own health information. Of course, as a citizen he should have participated in some way in determining the law and policies of the health agency.

Education for the health professional or provider of care is just as essential as that for the consumer. A full commitment to patient welfare will evolve only after an orientation toward consumer rights and consumer accountability begins to develop within the health professions (Sparer 1971). Such basic issues as the right to information about treatment and prognosis are difficult for the health professional to understand from the consumer's point of view; much discussion is required. Health professionals then must learn *how* to share information with consumers and how to invite them to make decisions about treatment and care.

Medical Care Records

Family health histories could be owned and maintained by the family and used by all health professionals involved with the care of the family. Some persons have suggested central maintenance of a "whole life record" for persons living in a particular region (Sparer 1971, p. 30). The family history or whole life record, which should remain the property of the individual, could be utilized as basic resource information when a person was hospitalized or treated in any health agency. Medical information written in these records would be in terms the patient can understand and, of course, would be discussed with the patient. The medical record would actually be kept at the patient's bedside along with the nursing plan of care. The nursing plan would be "written with the patient and his family, in the patient's room." (Kramer 1972b, p. 33). A comprehensive, accurate problem list could be maintained on each patient. This problem list is the responsibility of the whole health team including the patient, and would include those problems the patient was experiencing during his current hospitalization (Schell and Campbell 1972).

The patient would be encouraged to write on the problem list and the nursing care plan, and the total health record could be available to him. The problem-oriented charting system currently in widespread use in major health agencies could be the vehicle through which to begin sharing information with the consumer. Some health professionals may cringe at this, arguing that "the patient will not be able to understand the information on the chart," or "the patient will become more anxious when he reads all this medical jargon." But this is not necessarily so. First of all, the information on the chart could be written in simple language; and secondly, the health professional could spend time with the patient discussing the items recorded to lessen apprehension. Time consuming? Yes. But definitely a more humane and personal way of dealing with the health consumer.

Differential Roles of Health Professionals

The nurse and the doctor could work closely with the consumer to make this medically related experience more personal and dignified. The physician's major contribution to health care delivery would be through his expertise in diagnosing and treating pathological medical conditions. The nurse's major contribution would be through her expertise in dealing with man-environment interrelations. And the nurse would be the one health professional concerned for the total well being of the patient.

The nurse's role would be broader than the physician's in that she would plan health maintenance as well as treatment of illness. The doctor and the patient would collaborate only on medical diagnosis and treatment, while the nurse and the patient would collaborate on the nursing care, follow-up, and health maintenance.

The doctor, responsible for explaining the diagnosis and treatment to the patient in language he understands, would prepare the patient for informed participation in decision making regarding diagnostic studies and treatment. The nurse would reinforce the information given to the patient by the doctor, and elicit the patient's assistance in determining a nursing plan of care. In relating to the patient, the nurse would assist him in describing his experience, evaluating his resources, and making informed decisions. All professionally educated nurses would work with patients in this fashion.

Nursing and medical students in some educational programs are already learning to share information with patients and assisting patients to assume responsibility for health care decisions. In some in-service programs for nurses, ways to include the patient in nursing care planning are being stressed. In these situations, both patients and professionals are more satisfied with health care delivery. Small beginnings, though, for a gigantic problem. All of the above suggestions, if carried out in a systematic fashion, would enhance self-determination in regard to health care and move toward solving the "right to know" problem.

CONCLUSION

Dr. Jonas B. Robitscher, physician and lawyer, has written on the subject of informed consent: "This is an aspect of law where the principles of special attention to the necessity of assent and the protection of rights of individuals are, for good or bad reasons, neglected" (Robitscher 1966, p. 68). The thesis amplified herein thus far shows how this situation can be rectified in the future.

The only remaining question is: *"Why?"* Why patients' rights should not have been and should not be neglected. There's a one-word answer: Humanness!

As indicated earlier, the patient-consumer is the raison d'etre for the health profession. And the patient is a human being first and foremost. Sparer has written, "It is the patient's human right [and soon-to-be, I hope, his fully recognized legal right] to know his condition, receive information and decide—if he wishes—among alternative treatments or non-treatment" (Sparer 1971, p. 29). The only way the patient can make this decision, of course, is by proper input from the health professional. But first, "the provider needs consumer 'input' to be better aware of the place where . . . the shoe pinches" (p. 34). And you can't have this kind of input from anything but a rational being, a human being.

Ralph Nader has not gotten around to the rights of health care consumers, at least not yet. When and if he does, he might do well to consider the words of Isaiah Berlin as the preamble to the patient's constitution:

> I wish to be a subject, not an object; to be moved by reasons, by conscious purposes which are my own, not by causes which affect me, as it were, from outside. I wish to be somebody, not nobody; a doer—deciding, not being decided for, self-directed and not acted upon by external nature or by other men as if I were a thing, or an animal, or a slave incapable of playing a human role, that is, of conceiving goals and policies of my own and realizing them. This is at least part of what I mean when I say that I am rational, and it is my reason that distinguishes me as a human being from the rest of the world. I wish, above all, to be conscious of myself as a thinking, willing, active being, bearing responsibility for his choices and able to explain them by reference to his own ideas and purposes [Berlin 1966, p. 16].

REFERENCES

American Medical Association, Judicial Council, 1971. *Opinions and reports of the Judicial Council*, including the principles of medical ethics and rules of the Judicial Council. Chicago AMA.

Berlin, I. 1958. *Two concepts of liberty*. Oxford University Press, 1958.

Corey, L., Saltman, S., and Epstein, M. F. 1972. *Medicine in a changing society.* St. Louis: C. V. Mosby.

Davis, R. C. and Woodcock, E. 1971. The nursing contract: an alternate in care. *JPN and Mental Health Services* 9:26–27.

Dodge, J. S. 1972. What patients should be told: patients' and nurses' beliefs. *Am. J. Nursing* 71:1852–54.

Fanning, V. L., Deloughery, G. L. W., and Gebbie, K. M. 1972. Patient involvement in planning own care: staff and patient attitudes. *JPN and Mental Health Services* 10:5–8.

Hochbaum, G. M. 1969. Consumer participation in health planning: toward conceptual clarification. *Am. J. Pub. Health* 59:1698–1705.

Joint Commission on Accreditation of Hospitals, Medical Committee for Human Rights. 1970. A patient's bill of rights. Addendum to *Patient's rights and advocacy workbook.* Chicago: Joint Commission on Accreditation of Hospitals.

Kramer, M. 1972a. The consumer's influence on health care. *Nursing Outlook* 20:574–78.

————. 1972b. Nursing care plans . . . Power to the patient. *J. Nursing Administration* 11:29–34.

Kübler-Ross, E. 1970. *On death and dying.* London: Macmillan Company.

Lesparre, M. 1970. The patient as health student. *Hospitals* 44:75–80.

Levine, R. A. 1970. Consumer participation in planning and evaluation of mental health services. *Social Work* 15:41–46.

Natanson v. Kline. 350, P2d 1093, 1960.

New York Hospital. 1970. Job description: Patient Services Coordinator. New York: New York Hospital.

Parker, A. Consumer as policy-maker—issues of training. *Am. J. Pub. Health* 60:2139–53.

Robitscher, J. B. 1966. *Pursuit of agreement: psychiatry and the law.* Philadelphia: J.B. Lippincott.

Salgo v. Leland Stanford Jr. University Board of Trustees. 317, P2d 170, 1957.

Schell, P. L. and Campbell, A. T. 1972. Problem-oriented medical records—not just another way to chart. *Nursing Outlook* 20:510–14.

Sparer, E. V. 1971. On the matter of "community relations": the consumer movement in health care and the Albert Einstein Medical Center. Paper presented at the Albert Einstein Medical Center, Long Range Planning Seminar, New York, June 1971.

Tisdale, W. A. 1970. The care of the patient: ideal and illusion. *Yale J. Biol. Medicine* 42:387.

Vincent, P. 1971. Factors influencing patient noncompliance: a theoretical approach. *Nursing Research* 20:509–15.

Wilson v. Scott. 412, S.W. 2nd 299, 1967.

7.

Prometheus in the Prison

STANLEY L. BRODSKY

Fully informed participation in human services may be openly pursued when the client is in a public school, a hospital or other place purporting to work explicitly for the client's good. It is an altogether different thing to be Promethean—that is, to promote genuine and informed client decisions—when the client is coerced to enter the setting and when the client is legally deprived of rights and privileges. The Prometheus principle is generally alien to prisons, and rarely present in either pretrial, postconviction, or post-release contacts of clients with criminal justice agencies. Because prisoners have been convicted and sentenced for having been antisocial, it is assumed that they now should become obedient wards. Behavioral requirements and living conditions are given to them without choice. Often there is an explicit punishment and deprivation philosophy, without any belief that it benefits the prisoners. Thus if the Prometheus principle applies here, it applies anywhere, for even treatment of the retarded and the mentally ill begins with philosophical assumptions of good being delivered to them, versus the implicit assumption of retribution being imposed on prisoners.

Prisoners participate in very few decisions. By definition, there is no choice of place of residence, or freedom to change habitat. Living quarters and food are not chosen by the prisoners. Indeed in some settings, not eating the proferred meals is a disciplinary offense. There is little or no freedom from supervision. Restrictions are placed on the range of possible sexual outlets, choice of roommates and company, employment, avocations, and leisure time pursuits. Health care alternatives are minimal; nonprescription medication is scarce and there is little availability of qualified physicians and dentists. There is an absence of active participation in routine as well as key decisions, which accumulates to an additional negative impact on the prisoner. Chaiklen has pointed out:

> The debilitating effects of prison stem not from physical or verbal brutality but from losing decision making ability by living in a totally bureaucratic environment.

> This creates a highly dependent institutional personality. Any resistance to following the routine is identified as deviant. Communication between offender and correctional personnel is liturgical; many words are exchanged, but there is little understanding. To get any response from institutional functionaries a man must display the right attitude: show respect, state that he has "turned himself around," and demonstrate an interest in institutional programs [Chaiklen 1972, p. 785].

This promotion of dependency is one of many similarities between prison settings and other human services institutions. They are all total institutions. Burns (1969) has pointed out for prisons, what also may be seen in some schools for the retarded in psychiatric hospitals, and in many public schools. They are miniature totalitarian states. There is a single ideology present: complete control of formal communication systems, control of the economy, use of secret police, and restricted entry and egress.

Let us examine the extent to which informed participation is approximated in existing correctional practices. When prison administrators discuss choices with a prisoner, they quickly explain that what happens to him depends on the prisoner himself. If he is hostile or belligerent, he will get few privileges. If he is cooperative, follows the rules, and behaves well, he can earn nicer living quarters, better hours, good times, and eventually parole. The practices are described as being just like those in the free world—one gets what one deserves. The prison staff, of course, is said to be there to aid the confined person in this process.

Inmate participation in the rehabilitation ideology is more apparent than real. The staff makes the governing rules, dispenses privileges unilaterally, and frequently arbitrarily, and seeks passive compliance rather than participation in active decision making. Abuses in the guise of free-choice rehabilitation and self-betterment are legion. For example, Mitford (1973) has described repeated drug studies in which prisoners have been disfigured as well as suffered medical injury. In these studies volunteerism is a function of being imprisoned; the subjects would not have volunteered in a free world setting. The American Friends Service Committee (1971) has identified abuses in treatment services for prisoners.

These issues bring us to the question: how can one develop genuine informed participation and sharing of power and decisions in prison settings? The remainder of this chapter presents several possible answers.

PAID EMPLOYMENT AND SHARED POWER

What is the expertise of the would-be helper, whether clinician or correctional counselor, that sets him apart from the inmate? It is not his proven effectiveness either in being of direct service to his client or in transforming him into a constructive citizen. Rather, expertise is defined, rather arbitrarily, in terms of academic credentials, access to information, power to make decisions, and paycheck sums. In this situation, the "helper" develops an implicit vested interest in maintaining his expert status and salary by keeping the client as a passive recipient of his services.

Instituting genuinely informed participation for prisoners could short-circuit this process by allowing helpers and helpees to work together. The client too could be paid for his own ideas and competence in any rehabilitation project. Let us take a look at how that might work in the criminal justice system.

At present, an appropriate model of services is imposed on the convicted person and the presumed delinquent. The rationale has been that whatever trouble he is in, the client arrived there because of something wrong with him. Our service models have not caught up with the current state of knowledge about how training schools, juvenile courts, and prisons place people into life-long tracks of failure via defined incompetence or deviance. Institutions continue to define and certify deviant status in disregard both of known law-violation among the general population ("normal delinquency") and of societal participation in individuals' failures and successes.

Once a deviant behavior problem is defined, then we develop programs to meet the problem. In one form or another, guidance and counseling programs are instituted. They serve the purpose of setting the client straight—and we operate on a priori, non-Promethean assumptions that we know what "straight" is. To run such a program, we need personnel to plan it, to do the "front-line work," to administer it, to evaluate it, and of course to solicit funds for it on a continually expanding basis (no program once established in justice agencies for delinquency intervention ever dies or levels off on its own accord). And what happens with the kids or convicted persons? The answer is Polk's law: "The more you do, the worse it gets." The program will do one thing very well and without question: it will entrench itself, including positions for professional staff, secretaries, and other workers.

The Prometheus principle could be inserted into this situation by paying for the services of high-risk target populations. Instead of the money going to a group of professionals who "know-what-to-do" to solve the problem, one pays the clients and gives them power to allocate other funds (which may include seeking of private counseling services). The target individuals would be paid for achieving the same overall objectives that the professionals would be paid to achieve: to reduce the annoyance and social discomfort arising from deviant individuals who disrupt nondeviant persons.

Paying them, changes them (Slack 1960, Schwitzgebel 1965). Now they have a piece of the action. There is no need to steal, disrupt, or diddle overly with the system to get the goodies of society. They have money, and they have to protect their new-found turf, just as the experts do. The way experts and target persons alike defend territory is to get allies—or more of their own into the good life. For experts or professionals, it means building staff and expanding operations. For the target groups, it means converting more people like them to the new-found success experiences and competence. In other words, they assume, in part by agreeing to take the money, the task of changing others to be like them.

What are the consequences of such a program? First, we initiate a procedure in which funds designated for the help of a disadvantaged group go directly to it, instead of to already-salaried others who are of uncertain help anyway. Second, we acknowledge in one uniform and unequivocal medium of worth, namely cash, that these individuals have the right to self-determine their futures in constructive ways. Third, we eliminate the concept of dependency of target individuals in justice programs, by sharing power and responsibility in a Promethean way.

We should note that there are a number of theoretical contexts in which such fiscal sharing can be viewed. In particular, Hirchi

(1970) views the reason one does not commit deviant acts as a result of the strength of his bonds to society and of his commitment to conventional activities. Cressy's (1955) notion of "retroflexive reformation" is that the person trying to persuade another to reform, himself becomes reformed.

The practical implications are broad. Let the target subjects have power, and they will set their goals consonant with society. In a related sense, Craddick (1972) suggested that we are operating our token economies incorrectly. What we need to do is let the residents of communities with behavior modification practices give the tokens for appropriate staff behavior. The voucher system in public schools, for all the problems encountered to date, reflects a similar major belief in the worth of the client's judgment. In justice work, where one admission ticket to the target population group is a functional disbelief in one's worth and desirability, this introduction of explicit money awards is an important step toward clients' competency and success. In short, give me thirty kids or convicts getting fifty dollars a week each to run a youth advocacy program or crime reform project, rather than thirty experts getting $100 a day to prevent delinquency, and both the clients-as-helpers and the clients-as-helpees will be better served.

DISCLOSURE TO THE CLIENT

The goal of informed participation calls for being informed as well as actively participating. The access to information about oneself in justice settings is usually very limited. It is not unusual to see prisons, court clinics, and parole offices gather large numbers of prior agency reports on the client, of unsubstantial life descriptions from the client's friends and relatives, diagnostic or classification judgments, and descriptions containing the client's own statements about his life. Such information is often in error, sometimes is misused, is inappropriately open to examination without the client's permission and frequently is used against him. Let us examine these misuses of information and reports.

When a convicted person is newly admitted to a prison, a dossier accompanies him, describing his offense and containing reports about him. Guards, or higher level staff, who read the reports of persons convicted of sexual crimes or assaultive acts, often laugh, snicker, or vicariously enjoy the person's illicit acts. While a case could be made for forwarding such data to a prison, it is unlikely that its common use in fantasy stimulation can ever be defended.

A more insidious use of this information comes about in institutional and parole decision making. The client is repeatedly retried after his trial, in institutional decisions. His living quarters, his opportunity for release, and his everyday treatment by guards and other prisoners are influenced by this information. He may become known as "that rapist" or "the child murderer" or "that con-man" and be treated harshly or differently (in the cases of a few offenders, this leads to differentially better treatment). His current behavior tends to be overlooked in the shadow of his offense and his identified deviance seems to call forth primarily negative information affirming his wrongness.

Several kinds of misinformation make their way into prison reports. For example, prison classification officers write to the families of confined persons, asking for background information. The fact that information comes from outside sources leads it to be called "verified." Such reports themselves are often biased, based on second hand sources, or reveal social problems reported in a misguided effort to help the convicted person. In the same sense, professional reports often contain descriptions of personal problems or unreported crimes by the client, which were otherwise not known to authorities. The client presents this information to a mental health or other helping professional with the belief that it will be used on his behalf. Instead it is almost always used to his detriment. The use of such information has led to the right in a few states to have an attorney present during mental health examinations, so that the clients do not reveal self-incriminating information without full consent.

The formal psychiatric or psychological diagnosis is another species of loaded datum against the convicted client. It has been pointed out that many mental health professionals unreflectively assume a causal model in evaluating offenders (Brodsky 1973). They believe that if an individual is in prison, then there must be something wrong with him psychologically. This individual-blame process leads to a search for a psychopathological label to place on the client. Indeed, some prison diagnostic taxonomies have no provision for labeling people as being healthy or normal. While it is probably fortuitous that most prison decision making processes have systematically discarded or ignored the psychiatric diagnostic recommendations, these labels are taken seriously by some persons and may follow a client into his future.

The sharing of reports and information with the client would serve a self-correcting function. Examination of his accumulated records by the client encourages correction of false materials that may be influencing key decision makers around him, allows the client to alter his strategy in terms of the data by which he is being judged, and encourages a sense of accountability on the part of those who have inputs into the files and records. I have suggested elsewhere (Brodsky 1972) that prisoners should have full opportunity to write their own statements or rebuttals in these reports, in order to correct inaccurate statements.

The same issues arise about the investigation report to the court prior to sentencing. However, in the court setting many judges choose to disclose the contents of the report to the defendant. Clark (1972) surveyed ninety-nine federal judges, forty-seven of whom disclosed either all or part of the presentence reports to the defendant or his attorney. While it has been argued that disclosure would make informants reluctant or fearful of providing information, Zastrow (1971) suggested that it helps the defendant understand the court's disposition of his case, that the client has an opportunity to refute damaging information and that "nondisclosure excludes the defendant from the sentencing process (p. 21)." Zastrow has found in five years experience that full disclosure to clients has not led to anticipated problems, but rather has resulted in more cooperative and helpful attitudes on the parts of the defendant and his attorney.

It would appear that the fear of opening information sources to clients is greater than any negative consequences of the act itself. If he is to be a partner and participant in justice goal-setting and in planning related to his life, the client cannot be denied access to information relating to him. The painless and productive experience of Zastrow in Wisconsin is likely to be repeated in every justice agency that takes this risk.

PARTICIPATORY MANAGEMENT

"What? Turn the prison over to the prisoners? You must be mad!"

It's easy to picture this sort of incredulous reaction to suggestions that prisoners assume active participant roles in running prisons. Yet this has been done and is continuing to be done on a small scale. The critical first step is finding a descriptive term which allows the process without mobilizing instant, impenetrable resistance.

In 1918 Thomas Osbourne relegated partial administrative control of the Portsmouth Naval Prison to the prisoners' Mutual Welfare League. This radical program's existence under conventional colors was successful, but short-lived.

The National Commission on Criminal Justice Standards and Goals in its volume on corrections (1973) described this process with the term "participatory management." Standard 14.7 recommended:

> Correctional agencies should adopt immediately a program of participatory management in which everyone involved—managers, staff, and offenders—share in identifying problems, finding mutually agreeable solutions, setting goals and objectives, defining new roles for participants, evaluating effectiveness of these processes.

The commission sought to change prisons so that "individuals may pursue their own and the organization's needs and objectives simultaneously." The immediate results of this process are seen as prisoner self-government, prisoner-operated community facilities, and resultant new roles for line staff.

The term chosen, "participatory management," is a good example of success in the semantic aspect of this struggle. Beyond the words, this recommendation by this most prestigious prison study group lends itself to a good likelihood of adoption.

A CASE STUDY

A discussion of principles and strategies tends to obscure what informed participation for both the convicted persons and the practitioners is like at a personal level. Once having met Prometheus—in one form or another—the client becomes joyous and elated, and unwilling to settle for less. The widespread patterns of professional and agency secrecy and autocracy become clearer while the possibilities of personal responsibility grow stronger. The sense of appreciation for informed participation is sharp, rewarding, sometimes humbling.

The staff member himself goes through changes in attitudes and feelings. Risks are taken of criticism by colleagues and possible violation of agency procedures. However, the rewards and pay-offs more than balance such risks.

After I had published a journal article (Brodsky 1972) describing shared results and informed participation with clients, I began corresponding with the director of a psychological clinic in a large probation department. This psychologist had been treating a young man on probation. The following excerpts from the psychologist's letters are presented verbatim with permission of both client and psychologist:

> His "problems" when first brought to my attention—were

numerous and complex. Diagnostically, he appeared to strad-
dle a combination of technical labels, as is so often found, it
seems to me, among "Probation Cases." He was markedly
schizoid, a sixteen year old child molester of lengthy record,
with marked phobias and debilitating hysterical symptoms.
He was very narcissistic and quite paranoid in his thinking.
Although nearly a school drop-out, his IQ was measured at
115. Even some organic-like "signs" were apparent on his
WAIS and Bender. Where to even begin was the essential
"problem." Only because he was determined to get some help
was I even willing to accept some sort of symptom relief therapy with him. Although highly manipulative, his plea for help
was bolstered by the fact that he returned to the Clinic after
having been sent, unexpectedly, to live with his father for a
year in a different county. Upon returning to his mother's
home, he immediately reiterated his need for help, and therapy was reinstituted that week. He was under no outside pressure to seek any help whatsoever.

Early in our endeavors, it became clear to me that communication between us might be enhanced if he were dealt with
openly regarding each step of his therapy. His paranoia was in
the way, for one thing. His schizoid movement in his capacity
to relate—as described by Guntrip so very well—might be
stabilized by this sharing of material, and the feedback of my
observations of him, during our session, seemed entirely too
disruptive if shared at the times they occurred. In addition, it
just felt right in some nebulous way.

In spite of my early training and twenty years of nonopen
experience, my intuition won out, and I opened his files to
him—including my folder of therapy notes. I risked whatever
needed to be risked, praying that I was not committing some
unforgivable professional sin. I recognized that it would be
my task to pick up the pieces if this were the wrong move on
my part.

Much to my relief—and amazement—he was not only in-
trigued with my findings—but in substantial agreement with
his entire file. Of particular interest to him were my therapy
notes—which had heretofore been sacrosanct. Some of my
comments angered him, some embarrassed him, and some of
them mystified him completely. These required further exploration—together. Where there was disagreement, we discussed our opposing frames of reference. It was in the discus-

sion of these notes that the greatest progress was made in his therapy. His narcissism had previously prevented any objectivity regarding how he appeared to someone else. He was truly at a loss for words regarding his own behavior, attitudes and comments made during his sessions. Yet, in a very short time, he began to truly pull himself together as he had not been able to do before. His paranoia was dealt a deathblow regarding our relationship, and it opened up areas which had never been discussed before. He could graphically see how he manipulated people and attempted to influence their behavior toward him. He began to relate some of his suicidal thoughts to the real target of his anger. I could go on and on. . . . Now, at the beginning of each session, we briefly review my observations regarding our previous session. Sometimes this opens up an entirely new channel of inquiry. Sometimes the previous notes are read, discussed very briefly, and new material comes forth which does not appear to have been triggered by the notes. I'm never too sure however, whether this is entirely true or not.

None of my professional acquaintances can believe that I actually share my therapy notes with the client about whom they are written. I generally meet with disbelief—if not a certain amount of head-shaking. Why I would do such a thing is invariably the question. In spite of the fact that it works quite well, it just isn't done! Thus, I have avoided confessing this technique upon most occasions, as it is obviously considered a most "nonprofessional" technique! Even though it works. Simply amazing, isn't it?

Would it always be appropriate? I can only ask, "Why not?" Have others tried it with their longterm therapy cases? I don't know. Clients may not be as fragile as we have assumed that they are. Clinicians may be more fragile than we care to admit that we are! Clients and therapist can both be manipulative. Is manipulation only a client's tool? Open files and shared therapy notes seem to deal directly with fragility and manipulation. I am delighted with the results I see in this young client. His record has been "clean for five years, his self-concept is undergoing profound changes, and the open quality of our relationship is far less of a "strain" on both of us. I can only assume that the open file and the continuing practice of sharing his therapy notes with him played and continues to play a positive role in his growth toward psychosexual maturity.

I will share your latest communication with my client this Friday, during our session.

His response to your request that portions of my letter be used in some fashion (I can visualize a footnote) was quite positive. Then he responded, "Guess what! I'm going to be in a book!!" This was of particular interest to him, as he has vague plans of becoming a writer some time in the future. Then upon further discussion of this possibility of being mentioned, it was suddenly brought into awareness the fact that even if you choose to "honor" him with a comment, he could hardly point out that the case described was him without rather embarrassing exposure to whomever he proposed to share this information! Although known to the Probation Department since eleven years of age as a firesetter—and "out of control,"—it was at fifteen that he came into the more serious difficulties involving child molesting. These latter offenses are certainly not of the same caliber as his earlier maladaptive behavior, and, while he could discuss with relative ease his early involvement with the law, he could hardly be expected to admit to the later difficulties he encountered! Only his immediate family is aware of his sexual acting out—besides those young males who participated in his aberrant behavior. Thus, his delight over even being mentioned in your forthcoming book, has understandably, been somewhat tempered by reality! However, his enthusiasm remains relatively high, although flavored with some regret.

Again, thanks for the material—which I will share with him as usual.

CONCLUSIONS

The research on psychological treatment success with inmates consistently has shown that treatment subjects recidivate as much, and maintain the same adjustment levels, as control subjects (for example, Kassebaum, Ward, and Wilner 1972). One possible interpretation is that prisoners are poor candidates for counseling and psychotherapy. An alternative explanation that grows out of the present frame of reference is that treatment cannot be imposed constrictively; success is dependent upon prisoners' assuming roles as active, informed, and informative participants rather than as passive recipients of programs.

New prisoner roles will accompany free access to files and voluntary, participatory treatment. Prisoners will engage in consumer evaluations of justice programs and collaborative redefinition of the purposes of justice agencies.

Expressions of staff discomfort and administrative uneasiness may be heard as Prometheus makes his way into prison settings and other justice agencies. Those welcome sounds will be telling us that changes are being made. Our reaction should be to broaden and expand the scope of Promethean changes. As Francis Bacon wrote: "It is a secret both in nature and state, that it is safer to change many things than one."

REFERENCES

American Friends Service Committee. 1971. *Struggle for Justice.* New York: Hill and Wang.

Brodsky, S. L. 1972. Shared results and open files with the client. *Professional Psychol.* 4:362–64.

———. 1973. *Psychologists in the Criminal Justice System.* Urbana: University of Illinois Press.

Burns, H. 1969. A miniature totalitarian state maximum security prison. *Canadian J. Corrections* 11:153–64.

Chaiklin, H. 1972. Integrating correctional and family systems. *Am. J. Orthopsychia.* 42:784–91.

Clark, D. R. 1972. Judicial attitudes at the federal level regarding disclosure of the presentence investigation report. Master's thesis, Southern Illinois University, Carbondale, Illinois.

Craddick, R. A. 1972. A different use of the token in mental hospitals. *Professional Psychol.* 3:155–56.

Cressy, D. R. 1955. Changing criminals: the application of the theory of differential association. *Am. J. Sociol.* 61:116–20.

Hirschi, T. 1970. *Causes of Delinquency.* Berkeley: University of California Press.

Kassebaum, G., Ward, D. and Wilner, D. 1972. *Prison Treatment and Parole Survival.* New York: Wiley.

Mitford, J. 1973. *Kind and Usual Punishment.* New York: Knopf.

National Advisory Commission on Criminal Justice Standards and Goals. 1973. *Corrections.* Washington, D. C.: U. S. Government Printing Office.

Schwitzgebel, R. K. 1965. *Street-corner research.* Cambridge: Harvard University Press.

Slack, C. W. 1960. Experimenter-subject psychotherapy: a new method for introducing intensive office treatment for unreachable cases. *Mental Hygiene* 44:238–56.

Zastrow, W. G. 1971. Disclosure of the presentence investigation report. *Federal Probation* 35:20–22.

8.

The Prometheus Principle in the Classroom

MARY R. CHISHOLM
and ROLF VON ECKARTSBERG

This chapter is written in two parts by separate authors, the first addressing the practice of informed participation in the classroom at a conceptual level (von Eckartsberg), and the second presenting a case history of actual practice (Chisholm). The reader may want to read only one or both sections in either order. The authors have taught together often, and have shared in the development of both concepts and practices.

CONCEPTUAL OVERVIEW

Our present educational system relies mainly upon the classroom as the accepted symbol of the formal teaching and learning situation, for it is here that teacher and students meet. They come together for a course of study on a selected topic. What is the nature of this process that we call teaching and learning? (We shall be focusing on the university, but our remarks are intended as relevant to all levels of education).

The process begins with the teacher. He is older in experience in regard to the subject-matter. Then there is the student, younger or less experienced in regard to the subject. Both are together as "distemporaries" (Rosenstock-Huessy 1971), each representing his own time with its own specific interests, desires, goals, and attitudes. The process of teaching is the dialogue which succeeds in joining these two times, these two divergent lifetimes, so that succession in time becomes possible. The student through time comes to take the teacher's place. The young and the old, the primitive and the educated, are linked together. Thus teaching lies at the heart of all social processes because it establishes generational succession and hence continuity of the social body over time. That is what society and education is all about: the creation of a "body of time."

This "body of time" is accomplished through dialogue which alternates between play and struggle, between play and seriousness. "Good teaching begins with a joke and ends with a challenge" (Rosenstock-Huessy 1971). The students represent play; they have not yet faced the seriousness of the questions with which the teacher has struggled in earnest. The teacher is concerned with the problem of how the thought and the truth discovered by him in his own time can survive beyond his own time. How can he call students into responsible succession?

> The teacher may infect the will of the student by combining his love for the truth and his love for the student. If the teacher testifies to his membership in the fellowship of truth and at the same time keeps his membership in the play community which he has formed with the student, his testimony may take the boy up into the serious fellowship [Rosenstock-Huessy 1971, p. 17].

So much for the social meaning of the teaching situation, which is of vital significance for the survival of society. What goes on when viewed from the psychological perspective?

Any student who wants to learn begins with faith in the teacher. He has to accept the teacher's word for the truth that he himself has not yet discovered. But he does not stop there. He must also bring into play his own biographical stock of experience. He has to examine his own experiences and to develop observational powers in order to test and perhaps then modify the truth presented by his teacher. How is this accomplished?

In teaching, when we talk about our disciplines, we employ a specialist language that has evolved out of the common sense language to which we all are heirs in different degrees depending upon our verbal skills and intelligence. The object of systematic academic disciplines is to replace or to augment common sense constructs with scientific constructs which are defined in a clear and distinct manner. In the natural sciences this means that the concepts have to become "operationally defined," that is, tied to operations which yield exact measurements. In all other disciplines the definitions are arrived at descriptively and they are developed and purified by means of the collaboration of generations of co-workers who constitute a world-wide fellowship of truth seekers.

Over time this fellowship develops a knowledge-producing industry in which the key elements of basic research and training become tied to the social institution of the university. There the knowledge is gathered, published, and packaged in textbooks for presentation to incoming generations. The knowledge specialists, that is, the professionals, act as custodians for this field, and they also certify the preparation of the teachers who go out to teach the young. A "politics of knowledge" is involved.

So here we are in the classroom. The teacher, "armed" with textbooks and references that carry the accumulated knowledge, and capable of employing abstract concepts and of speaking the expert "discipline language," sets out to address the students. He begins to tell the story of the subject matter's evolution. However, this is by no means a one-sided process. It is the beginning of a dialogue because the student has to respond, has to feel challenged enough, or curious enough, to question in his own right if he is to make that subject matter his own.

What does this mean for "the student to make the subject matter his own"? First, it means that the student has to gain access to the field of study; he has to begin to see the concerns of the discipline, and he has to recognize the phenomena or process-events that are talked about in the discipline. He must learn the vocabulary and the meaning of the concepts as they are employed in the particular field of study.

The teacher speaks in a certain way regarding the subject matter; he uses a certain specialist language which is also the language used in the textbooks. There the student can "read-up" on the subject, study the definitions, learn the facts and the interpretive theories that show how to relate these facts. He begins to appropriate the subject matter as the teacher helps or invites him to continue his search in good part through the teacher's own commitment and enthusiasm. This means that the teacher teaches as much through his being as he does through the explicit presentation of the subject matter. A good teacher also makes his material presentable and understandable through the use of illustrations and examples taken from everyday life, that is, that part of social life that both the teacher and the student hold in common. The teacher feels understood or successful when he senses the students' attention, the nodding of their heads, the flick of recognition that dawns as a glint in their eyes. Questions and comments from students also help, and meaningful examinations or papers seemingly establish "for sure," "with certainty," that teaching and learning have taken place.

But can the teacher be sure? Does an "A" test or paper adequately reflect the student's mode of participation in learning? Does it reveal the nature of the learning that has taken place? From the earlier description of the social dimension or social function of teaching and learning we already know that teaching-learning succeeds to the extent that the student comes to take on the discipline as his own, when he appropriates it and incorporates it into his own life, and in this process influences his teachers' understandings.

The Appropriation of Knowledge

How does this process of appropriation work, how is it accomplished, and what exactly must be the role of the teacher in the classroom in order that this central process of the teaching-learning dialogue take place?

Appropriation means: "to make your own"—to own or to possess some thing or some quality. When we say that the student must learn to make the subject matter his own, we suggest that he must learn to perceive, observe, conceptualize and think about the discipline in his own meanings, in terms of his own experience. He can learn by rote from the textbooks, he can repeat all the concepts, definitions and findings but this does not yet constitute appropriation in the full sense of taking on the discipline *as* his own and *on* his own. Appropriation occurs when he can bring his own substance into play, when he can represent and even develop the discipline further in an autonomous manner, beyond the mere repetition of what others before have already said.

In our contemporary situation, when so much knowledge floats around in our media environment, becoming available to people as fractionated bits, the systematic work needed to integrate knowledge into coherent patterns of understanding becomes especially important. Contemporary students know much in terms of isolated fragments of knowledge but often they cannot think systematically about a given field of inquiry. The job in today's classroom, therefore, in part becomes one of helping students to integrate their already available but dissociated stock of knowledge.

But let us look at the psychology of appropriation more closely. When the student comes into the classroom he has a general preacquaintance with the subject matter just by virtue of alert participation in his everyday culture. Let us say that he is signing up for a course in abnormal psychology. We can usually assume that he has some general understanding of Freud. He has heard of "unconscious," and of the "id, ego and super-ego"—concepts that Freud coined as scientific constructs on the basis of his work experience as a psychoanalyst but which by now, sixty years later, have become common place and common sense knowledge.

Nevertheless, though the students may thus have a general acquaintance which they bring into the classroom, they usually have not read Freud himself, and even if they have they still may lack precise and systematic knowledge of the coherence of psychoanalytic theory.

But the students do bring preunderstandings, vague ideas perhaps, perceptions as well as misperceptions, and certainly rather specific personally grounded images and apprehensions. That is what comes into play and what the student must learn to struggle with in order to purify and refine his understanding so that it becomes congruent with that expressed by the author himself. This inner dialectical process of the appropriation of ideas in terms of one's own biographical stock of experience and knowledge is usually left up to the students to accomplish on their own. It is seldom made the object of explicit concern in the classroom, but rather is taken for granted as something that will automatically happen if the student is to learn.

We think that the experiential process of appropriation is the crux of learning, and that teachers ought to be giving more attention to this process. Ways must be developed to assist the student to move toward genuine appropriation of subject matter. We think that personal comprehension has not occurred unless the student is able to perceive and define the relevant concepts and phenomena in terms of his own experience, whatever this might have been. Only if and when the student can examine his own uniquely experienced world and can draw upon it for examples can we speak of personal, existential learning. Only then can he also make a personal contribution by sharing his observations and his own interpretations. Participation, however, should go beyond the mere expression of personal feelings and opinions which too often dominate classroom discussions. If we acknowledge that the student and teacher are co-respondents—by which we mean mutually contributing partners in dialogue—then we have to invent structured ways of classroom participation that will allow students to systematically

relate their own everyday experiences to the concepts and processes discussed within the discipline.

How might this be done? Concepts are usually quite abstract.
They have no specific "here-and-now" references such as uniquely
named events have. For example, when we are discussing a concept such as "society," what are we really talking about? Is it American society, a tremendously large-order concept, or is it society as
my involvement in the institutional life of Duquesne University
this semester of 1973? Looking at this example, we find that there
exist many levels of abstractions ranging from the unique, concrete
event to the most general and abstract concept that transcends all
particulars and that aims at general validity at all times for all
places.

It is through speech and the experience-storing power of language generally—as a social institution—that the achievements of
all of mankind are embodied and accumulated; it is speech that
allows us to participate in reality both perceptually and conceptu-
ally. We actually find that perception and conception inevitably
inform one another. On the one hand, concrete perception contains
elements of a cognition/conception that gave form to it (we see what
we are prepared to see). And on the other hand, conceptual abstraction contains perceptual referents to concrete experiences. These
concrete experiences are primarily in the form of images that fill in
or "flesh out" the concept in such a way that the concept becomes
comprehensible and capable of being appropriated. There are
usually several images associated with a concept that help to constitute its practical meaning. It is important that the teacher address
himself to, or elicit from his students, this level of personal, psychological experience which is a significant part of the process of appropriation. The teacher must find ways to work with this dimension of learning in the classroom. That is, he must help the individual student *find and bespeak the imagery of his biographically
rooted experience-meaning* that is relevant to the subject matter.
Only thus, when biographically experienced meaning becomes
linked with the universally defined abstract conceptual meaning,
has full personal learning been accomplished.

There is another important matter. When we as teachers ask students to become our co-respondents, we also invite them into a new
type of social relationship. Teacher and students have to face each
other on some level as coequals, as coresearchers, as a fellowship in
the search for truth. They must recognize that they both learn from
each other and that each will be changed in the process. They must
learn to confront each other in freedom, willing to alter precon-

ceived notions, each one secure in his own role and status, free of the limiting and inhibitive anxiety, fear, uncertainty, self-criticism that often accompany the traditional experience and reality of the teacher-student relationship. The traditional relationship often is grounded in a subtle power-play or the game of "academic achievement documentation," that is, "how to make the grade."

We feel that a relaxed atmosphere that is more characteristic in a relationship between coequals should prevail in a classroom if participatory learning is to occur. Feelings and imagination must be encouraged to flow freely rather than be suppressed. The prevailing mode of classroom learning is the copying of lecture content in order to learn the material by rote. Even though some classifying and judgmental skills are involved, this method of grasping the materials and of achieving mastery over new ideas must yield to a greater range of cognitive abilities such as creative listening, imaginative association, and the elaboration of personal meanings within one's own biographical flow.

If we want our students to learn to let go and to relax and to inspect and examine their ideas and concepts freely and in peace, without undue pressure, we as teachers must also manifest this open attitude. We must work actively against the expectations of the students themselves insofar as they still contain the old-fashioned cultural stereotypes of "hard work," "no-nonsense," "brain-straining," linear learning. *"Give me subject matter,"* the students silently demand even in their bodily expression; *"Discover the subject matter in your own living"* is a profound rejoinder the teacher embodies in personal conduct and in silent hope.

This is no easy accomplishment. The socially stereotyped conventions of what a teacher and a student ought to be are deeply entrenched. Hence very explicit and specific procedures for furthering relaxation have to be introduced into the classroom in order to alter consciousness to a level where participatory learning can occur. In practice we have found various techniques to be useful. Such techniques are derived from the arts, from autogenic training, from psychosynthesis, and from meditation. It is also useful to distinguish between two conceptual metaphors of psychophysiology, namely the measureable dimensions of a "beta state of consciousness" and an "alpha state." Beta consciousness is typical of problem-solving activities. It is a tense state of awareness that accompanies classifying and judgmental efforts. Beta consciousness is traditionally considered to be the most effective and hence the most desirable state of awareness that should prevail in the classroom.

By contrast we propose that for the type of mental functioning described here as "participatory learning," the "alpha state of consciousness" is more desirable because this state is associated with a more relaxed and absorbent state of being. There are research suggestions that alpha consciousness may be more "effective" in such learning situations as learning a foreign language. Therefore, we have to transform the classroom situation into a setting that is able to produce and sustain "alpha consciousness" for both teacher and students. This, naturally, does not mean that "beta consciousness" is not appropriate for certain kinds or stages of learning and application. However, it should not be the only way insisted upon by fiat or merely by tradition.

The Procedure of Cognitive Mapping

One way of introducing students to participatory learning is via "cognitive mapping." If we ask students in the classroom to discuss a given topic in a dyad or in small groups, we often find that the discussion starts to ramble, to swerve away from the topic. Often the discussion degenerates into what we commonly recognize as the "bull-session." In order to keep the discussion focused, we have developed the following procedure for tuning into and appropriating a concept.

We call this procedure "cognitive mapping," because we are trying to schematize the processes involved in relating a concept as defined by an "expert" to the experience of the student who draws on his everyday life to achieve comprehension. The expert's concept is presented formally in the text, with illustrations, examples, and sometimes even with diagrams. The student, while reading the text or listening to the lecture-presentation, now has the task of relating the concept to his own already constituted biographical experiences, which we call his "stock of knowledge" (Schutz 1962). Much of this stock of knowledge is verbalized, much of it is organized and stored as images (cf. Boulding 1969). There is typically a pattern of relationship, an "arrangement," a diagram or a map implicitly contained in the person's understanding, one that he can be asked to articulate on paper.

A concept, such as "super-ego," is the name for a process, an anchorage point which holds together our understanding. Using another metaphor, we could say that a concept acts as a lens that focuses a complex process. Upon closer examination this process turns out to have an intricate organization or structure, a multiple context of meaning which defines it. For instance, if we take the concept-process "super-ego", what does it signify, or point to, or mean? In attempting to unravel the meaning in a psychological sense, we ask first what it points to in our own experience. Freud may have given us a definition but we must connect this definition with the substance of our own life-experience situations, with our own imagery, emotions, and ideas in order to comprehend and to appropriate its substance. How do we provide such a learning experience in the classroom? Our procedure involves four steps: (1) personal collecting and reflecting, (2) sharing dialogue, (3) group integration, and (4) literature tie-in or scholarly contextualization.

Personal collecting and reflecting. (a) The first step of the procedure is to give the individual time (perhaps fifteen minutes) to collect himself on the chosen topic-concept, for example, "super-ego." "What does this mean to you; how do you understand this? What ideas, particularly what images, emerge as you concentrate and dwell upon this concept? Listen to yourself, watch your own consciousness proceed and unfold; record all that happens on a sheet of paper."

We ask the student explicitly first to concentrate on the topic, that is, the process to which the chosen concept refers in his own understanding. We ask him to dwell on this process by holding his attention steady and to observe what emerges ("personal collecting"). In particular we ask him to notice and then describe and list on paper all the images that come up during the process. We call this "The Student's Imagery Regarding the Concept."

(b) After this we ask the students to reflect individually on what this concept means to them in terms of their own biographical experience ("personal reflection") and to express this meaning in writing. We call this "The Student's Biographical Experience as a Written Text."

(c) Finally we ask him to inventively construct an integrated picture, a "cognitive map" of the concept-process that synthesizes his knowledge and understanding for him. We then ask the student to draw this map on paper so that with appropriate commentary and explanation it becomes communicable to others. We call this "The Cognitive Map of the Process by the Student."

Initially students will need to be encouraged to stay with this process of tuning-in, of collecting, of natural reflection. They have to be reassured that what appears, what surfaces to the level of awareness does not have to make sense at this stage of learning. They do not have to be intelligent or logical. Usually they also have to be told that if they slip into silence it's all right, that silence can be pregnant and creative. Whatever comes up in the process of

**DIAGRAM 1: The Student's Contribution to His
Appropriation of a Concept-Process**

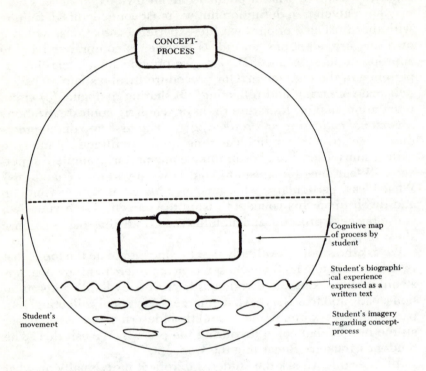

CONCEPT-
PROCESS

Cognitive map
of process by
student

Student's biographi-
cal experience
expressed as a
written text

Student's
movement

Student's imagery
regarding concept-
process

focused collection is valuable because the "self" is becoming ready
for authentic participation, the self is being activated for learning.

Diagram 1 helps to bring these steps of the process of appropriation together in a cognitive map. This map of the process shows the
contribution to the student who wants ultimately to appropriate the
expert's concept by dialoguing it with his already constituted stock
of knowledge.

The following is an example from a student who followed the
procedure outlined above focusing on the concept-process
"super-ego." The example is not unusual in revealing the total
private character of a person's experiential understanding. The
biographical matrix of experience is so unique that it may be difficult for an outsider to see at superficial reading what this has to do
with "super-ego." Nevertheless, the biographical experiential referents and associations that the concept evokes, however unique and
often seemingly autistic, are the necessary starting point for the

experiential learning process. It may turn out, however, that a person's understanding of a concept is already totally conventional and partisan. He may have already appropriated the established definition given by his favorite expert or the one prevalent in his cultural group, and thus really have no original view on the matter. This is also important for him to recognize, and our procedure makes it possible for him to do so.

Before you go on to read the example we invite you to try the procedure yourself. Read the instructions again under (a), (b), and (c), and write your own response where the spaces call for them. You can then enter the next step, "sharing dialogue," by comparing yourself to the student's example and by responding to his expression. Then you can continue by comparing what you did with Freud's expert view.

Turn to the example on pages 158 and 159.

Thus we have collected the material that is initially relevant for *this* student with regard to *his* concept-process, super-ego. What he has listed is rooted in his own biographical stock of experience. His comprehension is limited and partial but it represents his own selective emphasis. It is *his* starting point for further development on the road toward systematic thinking. What we have arrived at in our procedure at this point is not yet fully cognitive; it is not yet highly developed thought. This will become evident as the student moves toward sharing and response with peers and finally as he encounters the systematically developed thinking of the expert.

The task now becomes to help the student to develop his understanding first by sharing with fellow members of the class, his peers ("sharing dialogue"), and finally by studying what the experts in the field (e.g., Freud) have to say about it ("literature tie-in or scholarly contextualization"). The key problem in participant learning is to link up the individual's knowledge with that of the wider scholarly community that deals with a topic of knowledge professionally.

From the point of view of the student this presupposes that he is seriously motivated to "check out" his own idea by comparing it with that of others, notably the specialists. One meaning of becoming educated thus is to learn to transcend the limits of your own point of view by benefiting from the experience of others. It is with this aim in mind that the procedure of cognitive mapping was devised: to assist the serious student to test out the limits of his own cognitive processes and to allow growth to occur.

Sharing dialogue. The next step in the procedure of cognitive mapping, "sharing dialogue," inaugurates a genuine social dis-

(a)

The student's imagery of "super-ego"	Your own imagery regarding super-ego:
"a memory of a medieval town and the priest being the corollary to the super-ego by way of the confessional" "an eagle - a chief of a tribe symbolizing the broad visual extension possible to him" "a group of animals who seemed to be sharing calls for protection, all of different species but each keenly dependent on the others' call, for it covered a complete area of the forest; the calls being the super-ego"	

(b)

The student's biographical experience expressed as a written text:	Your own biographical experience expressed as a written text:
"people who have impressed me at times with the general societal view collected in the idea or concept of super-ego would be ministers and schoolpeople—basically institutions that deal in a concrete problem of humans in a society. The most interesting event was a stay in Western Psychiatric Hospital where I had to learn to literally walk through their reflections of me based on their reflections of generalized 1971-72 humanity. So my speech had to change from mystic poet to sedentary pragmatic quasi-realist with a good standing definition of that which bumped into you or which mattered as reality."	

(c) The student's cognitive map of the concept-process "super-ego":

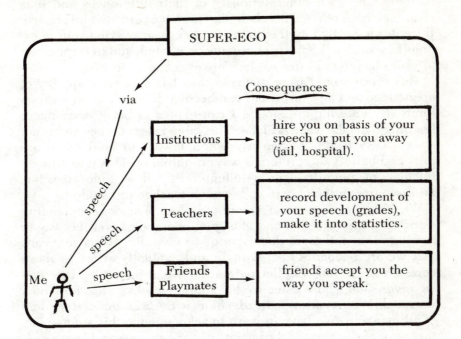

Your own cognitive map regarding "super-ego":

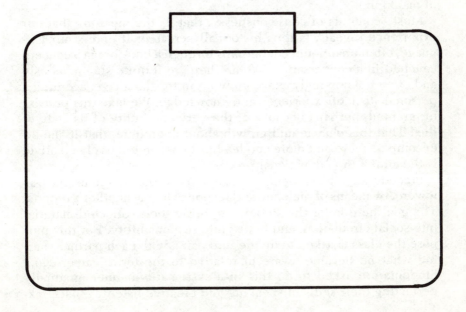

course among partners, a dialogue. In a meaningful dialogue both partners take each other seriously in their differences and thus challenge each other. This challenge promotes growth and change. If I enter honestly into the dialogue, then in answering your questions face to face, I have to clarify my own stand, and in responding to your challenge I must express my own convictions.

This process of sharing dialogue thus has a dynamic quality of openendedness and surprise. I can become liberated from my own limits. By entering a dialogue I can expect to become changed; learning will take place if I let it. This often takes courage and is not always easy to do, particularly when I want to hold on to entrenched beliefs and preferred ways of thinking. This is as true on the level of "peer-dialogue" (students with fellow students) as it is for discourse in the classroom between teacher and students.

We listen and respond to one another, each one becoming clarified in the process, and changing one another on the way to coming more and more deeply into our own. But this also means that we are becoming increasingly and explicitly aware of those corespondents—our intellectual and spiritual ancestors, the men we revere—in whose name we hold and defend an idea, for whom we speak. We are, always already, heirs to the accumulated wisdom of all mankind. We have to learn to acknowledge this strange fact that most of the ideas and concepts of our own personal consciousness are also the accomplishment of an historical author who dedicated his life to bringing this idea or insight into the consciousness of mankind.

Most "contents of consciousness", that is, the meaning that our experience reveals, is thus historically created. It enters our language, often unannounced, perhaps through a book or via a concept couched in a conversation. We are heirs to it quite spontaneously and often unknowingly as we grow up in this language, accruing a personal stock of experience and knowledge. We take this process for granted, perhaps because of the very continuity of its state of flux. That this change and growth should continue, that it should encompass more and more and lead us to become actively creative, is the aim of the educational process.

Procedurally, the students are asked to externalize themselves, as it were, by means of dialogue and response to one another's reports. The goal here is for the students to bring their collected material into social circulation, and hence into responsibility. For this purpose the class is asked to divide into pairs, with each partner sharing what he became aware of relative to the term "super-ego." Students are asked to do this in a systematic manner, gradually perfecting their skills of speaking and creative listening, each taking turns in telling and responding to the other's written recollections and reflections, as well as his maps. Another fifteen minutes of class time may be spent in this fashion.

It is important to emphasize to the students that this sharing dialogue has to be entered into with an attitude of respectful concern for one another's views, images, and productions, whatever they may be. A warning should also be given that sometimes strong feelings are evoked during such a tuning-in process. Students should feel free to stop at a level with which they feel comfortable or at that point when they feel it is right and necessary to do so. Students also have to be encouraged to withhold materials that they feel are too private to be shared. Naturally it makes a great difference whom the partner in dialogue is. With an intimate friend one may feel freer to share a powerful image than with a stranger in class. All this has to be left to the discretion of the participants.

Group integration. After exchanging this personal material the students are ready to integrate the material of the whole group or class. They are asked for verbal contributions, for observations or comments on both the *process* of their tuning-in procedure as well as the *content* of the materials that emerged. It is now dependent upon the skill of the teacher to bring out the relevant dimensions of this selected concept. The class participation after an initial small-group sharing is usually quite lively. It seems that the dyadic dialectic easily extends to class exchange. The varied dimensions of the concept-process are listed and then an attempt is made to gestalt them into a *pattern*, into a "conceptual map." This synthesizing picture is usually quite complex and sophisticated, representing a mixture of personal experience and remembered expert definitions drawn from the individual's stock of experience. We speak of this as the *structure* of the phenomenon under investigation. The concept as the comprehensive name for this process turns out to have a structure, an organization, which reads like an electrical circuitry map referring to a richly complex intertwining of experiences.

Literature tie-in and scholarly contextualization. The last step in the procedure of cognitive mapping is to examine the texts containing opinions or conclusions of the experts, those who professionally represent the discipline or the subject matter under consideration. For instance, in this case, the students may read Freud himself on the topic of "super-ego" and relate Freud's ideas with their personal discoveries and with the group composite. Steps one through three in the classroom procedure prepare the way for a personal appropriation of these expert concepts.

The students are now asked to research and list the definitions of the expert (Freud) and to give a representation of this in a conceptual map of the student's own creation. In our illustration Freud has already done the work of creating a cognitive map for us. We find his famous diagram summarizing his views on the super-ego in relationship to the rest of personality on page seventy-eight of the *New Introductory Lectures*. Thus, Diagram 2 contains our cognitive map of the full process of the appropriation of the concept of "super-ego," representing the point of view and movement of the expert as well as that of the student. In this illustration the student can compare the map he created with that of Freud's own making. Many students already know Freud's map and use it as their own.

DIAGRAM 2: Participation of Both Student and Expert in the Student's Appropriation of the Concept "Super-Ego"

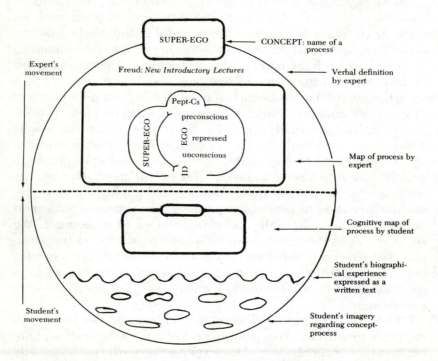

With regard to most psychological processes there are as yet no experts' maps created by the experts themselves, although many theorists use diagrams to summarize their views. Kurt Lewin in particular is well known for his conceptual map in psychology, and many other authors utilize partial diagrams. Wherever the expert himself has not provided us with his own map, we, the students of his work, have to construct such maps from the written text. There is no guarantee that we will all agree on the best solution. There are many ways that concept-processes can be cognitively mapped. Some will be more plausible or elegant solutions than others and will invite agreement. Others will foster controversy, as they contain personal idiosyncratic points of view. Each case, however, is a stimulating basis for discussion regarding the adequacy and relative merit of the created maps. Students become quite involved in their representations as they come to explain the reasons for their own solutions.

We have found that this procedure of cognitive mapping can effectively bridge the gap between personal, biographical experience, and the expert conceptual definitions which are often abstract. What I mean as a student, based on my own knowledge, and what Freud meant in his writing as an expert is brought into close interrelationship through this process of systematic tuning-in and appropriation. Students in this way come to see the subject matter in terms of their own lives. They become engaged in the question: what is this process that we call "super-ego"? Once they can experience this as a question pertinent to their own life-processes, once they can become seriously involved in this *linkage* of different levels of awareness, of consciousness, and of types of knowledge, then effective transmission and *succession* from teacher to student has taken place.

Each person can now understand the concept in the light of his own biographical experience. The sharing of his experience with others through mutual dialogue now creates a new *common* dimension of understanding within the class as well as with the expert who represents a long line of already established knowledge. In other words, co-respondence takes place. Both teachers and students have changed one another's original position. They have moved from a polarity of being distemporaries into being contemporaries, co-respondents, and partners in the process of learning.

The Scholarly Context for Participatory Learning

Whenever we think, speak or write, we are grounded in a context of fellow thinkers who help give us direction in our thinking. We do not create out of a vacuum. It seems appropriate, therefore, to list some of the sources that I find important in my work: Neil Postman and Charles Weingartner: *Teaching as a Subversive Activity*; George B. Leonard: *Education and Ecstasy*; Maria Montessori: *The*

Absorbent Mind; Rudolf Steiner: *The Essentials of Education*; Eugen Rosenstock-Huessy: *Man Must Teach*; John Holt: *The Underachieving School; How Children Fail; Freedom and Beyond*; Carl Rogers: *Freedom to Learn*; Buckminster Fuller: *Utopia or Oblivion*; Marshall McLuhan: *Understanding Media*; Ivan Illich: *Deschooling Society*.

CASE HISTORY: CO-RESPONDENT LEARNING IN A COURSE ON RELIGION IN AMERICAN SOCIETY

The second part of this essay is a description of a practical application of the above theoretical position and procedures in an actual course. There are many ways in which such a course might be organized and different instructors will undoubtedly develop the theory of co-respondence in different ways, applicable to particular subject matters or age groups. Over several years Dr. Chisholm has taught a one-semester college course in sociology entitled "Religion in American Society." This course was specifically designed to develop systematic procedures of participant learning and correspondence from her own interpretation of the approach.

Introduction to the Course

I have found it useful to prepare the student for his role in relation to me, the teacher, by writing him a letter to be given to him at our first meeting. The letter states what work I have done in preparation for this particular course, what I hope or anticipate as its outcome, how inadequate my preparation has been without my knowing him and what he needs or expects from the course, and how a part of my preparation is therefore based only upon my phantasies in regard to him and others in the class. The letter goes on to outline briefly a tentative course procedure with text, readings, assignments, projects, and type of examinations. Finally, the student is invited to withdraw should he not care or be able to participate at this particular time. Should he decide to remain in the course he is asked to reply to the letter informing me of his general reaction to its contents and any suggestions or recommendations he may have for changes in my preplanning. The letter also states that his reply will be shared with other members of the class so that the many divergent or convergent points of view represented here may be recognized and acknowledged as soon as possible.

The "open letter" introduction seems to have some positive

qualities that facilitate the establishment of an atmosphere or climate for cooperative learning among the students themselves as well as between myself and the student because it eliminates the "captive student" syndrome. So far in the courses that I have begun in this fashion a number of students, perhaps a half-dozen or so from a class of thirty or forty, do leave. Usually they answer the letter explaining why. Some typical explanations are that their present course load is too heavy for them to participate fully, or that the course content as outlined seems to duplicate what they have already had, that they are unfamiliar with the method of participant learning and this is an approach they did not expect or that they are not ready to undertake. It seems, however, that an equal or like number of students from other courses transfer into this course because through friends they learned what it will entail and they desire to participate in an active manner.

From the students who choose to take the course and who write their reactions and/or suggestions I get a realistic first insight into the potential of the class as a whole. I am able to sense the level of involvement, of background preparedness, of emotional set (enthusiasm, hostility, indifference), and of curiosity with which this particular group is beginning the course. The typical immediate response has been one of euphoria: a high degree of anticipation and a willingness on the part of the student to commit himself or herself to collaboration. The more deeply motivated individuals, the more creative students, often stand out in this first response; by circulating their letters for the other students to read there is a reinforcement of many students' positive anticipation. A general tone of synergistic possibilities is set.

My next endeavor is to channel this emergent energy before it dissipates and disillusionment sets in. We begin to tell the story of man's religious development and to lay a foundation for a common understanding of the scope of our subject when each student is asked to select one of five religious traditions for his reasearch project. At our first meeting, after the students have read my letter and have had time to write a reply, I list on the blackboard the five religious traditions to be explored and indicate the number of investigators for each that will give a somewhat balanced distribution. Thus, in the usual class of about thirty students, I would request that six students sign up for each religion. I also suggest that they choose, so far as possible, a religion with which they are least familiar. I give them a general outline to be followed in their written research reports which includes: (1) origin and development of the particular tradition; (2) precepts or beliefs; (3) their own reactions or relationship to that religion. Each student is free to develop in more detail any specific aspect of the religion that may strike him as interesting or provocative. For instance, one student developed tree worship as an aspect of primitive religions.

The class does not meet formally for the next two periods so that students have time for their investigation and for writing a paper. I am available to answer questions or to give any help the students may request.

Collecting and Reflecting

The main purpose of this first assignment or procedure is to invite the students to prepare themselves in a serious way for an experience of authentic dialogue, one that can flow quite naturally in the sense that each student will be the "author" of his own contribution. Individual research precedes class discussion or explanations from myself so that each student is to some degree forced to rely upon his own resources: self-selection of his topic or any aspect of it, search for a general survey of source-materials, the writing of his discovery, and an interpretation according to his own meaning. The assignment introduces him to the "collecting and reflecting" phase of the learning process when he may ask himself, "What do I already know and what more should I discover about this topic? What meaning does this information have for me?" It is one way of encouraging the student to come to grips with the course material on his own terms in his own way, and then to share not only the contents of his knowledge but also his own style of acquiring it.

Dyadic Sharing

At our next meeting the students are requested to exchange papers, each person reading three or four different reports during the period. A simple way of exchanging and at the same time becoming better acquainted with one another is to ask the students to seat themselves in a circle or semicircle, and as roll is called, each person will place his paper on a chair or table in the center, taking the one that is already there. Each individual can read three or four reports during a given period. After reading each one, he is asked to write a note to the author expressing his reactions or any comments he feels may be appropriate. In this way the author receives three or four responses as immediate feedback on the paper he has written. Should further clarification be needed, authors and readers have an opportunity for verbal exchange as well.

The "collecting and reflecting" phase thus has now progressed into a dyadic sharing, a personal exchange of information and of reactions among the students on a one-to-one basis. Toward the close of the session I lead a brief discussion on the meaningfulness of this first experience. Volunteers often express their recognition of the quality of work done by other students: the evidences of sincerity, thoroughness, originality, possibly even artistic, poetic, or humorous talent that was expressed through the papers. Because each student has himself been engaged in the same task there is, at this moment, a common bond of empathy in both personal and group accomplishment. On the level of content, the class is now ready for the pooling of individual efforts toward developing a common perspective of the subject-matter which, at this point, will be a general survey of major religious developments as they have occurred within society.

Small Group Presentations

To this end, students are asked to group themselves according to their respective research topics: primitive religions, Hindu, Tao, Jewish, and Christian. During the next two meetings each group prepares a class presentation of its pooled research findings on that particular religion. These class presentations often entail an expenditure of time and energy, of ingenuity that surprises me. The initial rather high level of anxiety in having to write a paper and the worry entailed about its acceptance is now relieved, and a sense of camaraderie appears to develop quickly within the small groups that are now collaborating. The students seem to identify wholeheartedly with the religious tradition they have selected, and they somehow recognize and convey a sense of the sacred or transcendent quality of the subject they are interpreting. The class as a whole is itself made up of persons who represent various religious denominations: Roman and Greek Orthodox Catholics; Orthodox, Conservative, and Reformed Jews; Protestants of many affiliations be they Baptist, Episcopalian, Lutheran, or Presbyterian; Oriental (foreign students or a sprinkling of contemporary searchers and devotees). When Catholic students interpret Jewish traditions and practices mutual astonishment often emerges in discussions that follow. Or when a Baptist student explains the Catholic sacramental system with his own interpretation, the Catholic students begin to see their own taken-for-granted beliefs in a new light. The open dialogue that follows each group presentation has within it immediate corrective and balancing elements because the "lived-world" and the "textbook-world" are simultaneously brought into play.

My first experimentation with such small-group presentations was not wholly satisfactory. With successive presentations I discovered that the time lag between the first and the last one was too great to maintain maximum interest and involvement. The edge of enthusiasm and anticipation had dulled by the time for the last group's turn to present. For them the momentum of active participation was lost. Discussion or feedback after some of the presentations was disappointing because the class as a whole was too large to be reached in a direct manner. A few dominant or more capable students might respond quickly while the more hesitant, timid, or less able students slipped back into passivity, refraining from overt participation. Likewise, the focus of attention then tended to center upon the more entertaining or vividly dramatized presentations, thus blurring the underlying purpose of becoming acquainted with an overall development of religious consciousness in society.

Recently, therefore, we arranged that two or three of the small groups make their presentations to one another in a direct exchange. Within a ninety-minute class period five or six different presentations can be made within two or three small-group exchanges each about thirty minutes in length. All groups are then meeting simultaneously. In the next class period all groups exchange again but in different combinations. This means that each presentation is given two or three times to different small groups and each individual is present for every other group's rendition. The repetition does not seem boring to those who are presenting. On the contrary, they gain in skill and self-confidence with each round. Students who have seldom or never actively volunteered for class participation throughout their college career now find themselves in direct and immediate discussion in a face-to-face situation that is relatively unthreatening.

Depending upon the "spirit" of the particular group, the quality of background preparation, and the degree of self-initiative they have previously been accustomed to, some groups seize with alacrity this opportunity of presenting their combined research in a creative, highly original manner. Students may possess varied talents as amateur artists, dramatists, musicians, poets—all of which they may call into play. Some of these small-group presentations have left lasting impressions upon all of us who participated in the course at that particular time. For instance, I recall that one group invited the rest of the class to share in a simulated experience of a Peruvian Indian religious ceremonial complete with a recorded native chant, drums and other simple instruments, solemn dance around a campfire, and then a final meditation. The factual information about primitive religious meanings came alive that year in a memorable way. At another time one student was well versed in the I-Ching directives and her specialization brought into the classroom an Oriental flavor that books alone fail to convey.

Literature Tie-in and Integration of Theory

During the group presentations there is a light-hearted tone within the class; almost a spirit of playfulness prevails. We are not analytic or critical from a scholarly point of view. However, no unifying sociological framework has yet been introduced into which each religious tradition fits, nor has meaning been demanded beyond that which the individuals or small groups have themselves given. Some of the more alert or thoughtful students begin to express dissatisfaction, even frustration, that they are left with many loose ends, that they are lacking a firm sense of direction in the course because there is no primary focus. There is liable to be an emotional "let-down," and though they have expended their time, energy, and talent effectively in the presentations and have enjoyed the group interaction, we now begin to sense a change of pace and of mood.

This seems to be a time of genuine questioning, of doubts and confusion arising in an area where many students of whatever religious persuasion—and especially of none—begin to see their own traditions or their own religious experience in a different light. For some this is decidedly unsettling and I can now expect some absenteeism. I am not sure that I am meeting this transitional phase with adequate skills or competence. Perhaps some students need to back away from the genuine questions that begin to emerge. As one student said to me, "You know, for all its friendliness among the students, this is a violent course, Dr. Chisholm."

At this time I deliberately "take over" as the teacher, and in lecture-fashion with diagrams and excerpts from recognized writers in the sociology of religion I introduce theoretical dimensions of the course. I here present a basic sociologic framework, to be found in the writings of Rosenstock-Huessy, into which each of the religious traditions with which the students are now familiar can be explained. We discover that each religion we have studied fits into a time-space axis of historical and cultural development. Primitive beliefs may be prehistorical but their counterpart can still be found and experienced even among modern-day men. Hindu religion, or Buddhism, emerged as a counter-balancing force in a predominantly externalized culture; Taoism through Lao-tzu had its origin and roots in a culture that was internal, focused inward, and that gave exaggerated significance to "face" and to ritual. Judaism rests upon tradition, loyalty, and a vivid sense of the past, of the covenant with Yahweh. Christianity introduced the meaning of an everlasting future wherein all cultures, all previous and all future generations can meet, be unified and harmonized in a supertime of an everlasting present.

This transition phase is difficult and I "lose" some students at this point. They may not yet be ready or they may be unwilling to move from the more "student-centered" kind of experience to the "beyond themselves" expert focus of a textbook or to that body of knowledge which we call sociology. For others in the class, this part of the course offers greater security, for it is the more familiar classroom procedure.

Appropriation

The students are now asked to read a text such as *The Sacred Canopy* by Peter Berger, where they must come to grips with what a theoretical sociologist has to offer as an explanation of religious phenomena in any society. Not only are they asked to read what the experts have said but they are likewise asked to translate the expertise, the highly abstract and specifically defined language, into their own terms. They are asked to translate Berger's thoughts into their own words and to invest these thoughts with *their* meanings, which may or may not coincide with the author's meanings. At first such an assignment baffles the student, for he seldom realizes that *his* understanding and interpretation of an author's thoughts may be quite different from the interpretation of his fellow-students, or quite different from what the author himself intended.

One way of introducing and of highlighting these different styles of perception and interpretation, different styles of learning or of appropriation of a text, is through the construction of a "cognitive map." Reading a chapter of Berger's book is tantamount to taking a trip within the mind of the author, discovering what he sees as social reality and how he sees it. When each student draws a partial diagram of the ideas or the relationship of ideas that he encounters in a chapter, then we have a variety of enlarged, often colorful and artistic original interpretations of the chapter or some part of the chapter. Making a cognitive map calls for a reflective, even a contemplative mode of study, and its execution reveals unconscious, imaginative influences as well as the rational use of memory, reason, logic. Again, some students feel confident enough to express their grasp of the text in free-flowing images, in symbols, color, original design. In every class the variety of cognitive maps forms the basis for lively discussion of a chapter and its significant concepts. No two maps are ever alike. Each student retains his own unique style of impression and expression. Yet there is a reinforcement of the main ideas, and I have something very tangible to work with in responding to, amplifying, correcting or channeling the thinking of the students as the contents of each chapter emerge through successive meetings.

I consider this phase the meat of the course, the content that is to be mastered and appropriated by the student. For some students this is likewise the most satisfactory aspect of the course. For others, it is the least satisfactory. To some degree, at least, I find myself being pulled in opposite directions. On the one hand, I am aware of how much more the discipline of sociology or our present body of expert knowledge has to offer the students by way of explanation and clarification of religious phenomena in society. On the other hand, I sense that I may be doing violence to the student, imposing information upon him or eliciting doubts and questions that he is not ready or willing to handle. I find myself asking the questions: "How much and at what precise time is 'hard teaching' needed? When and for how long should the student be left free to discover and to express his own conclusions?" I am aware of this struggle and to a more or less degree the students are also aware of it. The tolerance of such a struggle to teach and to learn, as its own ultimate resolution, seems to call for something beyond the empirical facts of what we are actually doing here together. It seems that the significance of my *intentions*, what I believe and hope can or will happen, becomes the sustaining force of my teaching. This struggle leads me to an appreciation of the underlying spirit by which each of us as teacher and as student can put up with one another, can co-respond to a process for which we are jointly responsible, to which both must *respond* in some fashion if the process is to continue. I may be presenting to the student less than adequate knowledge in a less than adequate fashion. He may be responding in less than adequate ways to sustain my role as teacher. But if at this point we can maintain our trust in one another's *potential to change*, if we can *hope* that we may continue to communicate, to maintain open dialogue, in short, if we can learn to forgive and to genuinely care for one another, then the climate of our classroom becomes such that we can mutually change toward common understanding. But if I lose this faith, and the kind of energy this faith imparts, in the "not-yet-realized" (future) of both myself and my students, then I shall lose the spirit or the enthusiasm of hope also. The possibility of shared differences, that emergence of something new out of the struggle in which we are engaged, will be lost.

During this time of *appropriation* all the traditional arsenal of teaching devices comes into play. Students are expected to read the text chapter by chapter, at times with specific questions to answer. I present lectures of explanation or of amplification of the text, guide discussions in small groups or with the class as a whole, and finally prepare a written examination designed to "test" the students' grasp of the textual material. The students do not, as a rule, take this phase of the course as seriously as I do. Being asked to write a traditional type of essay examination for specific knowledge is a distinct disappointment to some students. For others, it is a re-assurance that they are learning and will be fairly evaluated for a final grade even though the tests are not the only basis of evalua-tion. In my introductory letter I had explained that the final grade would be based upon (1) the quality of class participation (40 per-cent); (2) written reports or papers (30 percent); (3) the results of two tests, a mid-term and a final (30 percent).

Personal Integration and Group Recognition of the Learning Process

After dealing with sociological theory relative to the study of religion in society and its appropriation to a greater or lesser de-gree, followed by traditional "testing" of acquired knowledge, we have covered about two-thirds of the course. The last third (approx-imately five weeks) again concentrates more directly upon the stu-dent, inviting him to trace his own religious experience and its development to the extent that he may be aware of it. The personal aspect of this part of the course may be a wholly private undertaking and the student is always free to share his insights or not, according to his own choice. For this part of the course we turn to another kind of text, one that is not so theoretical but which offers a per-sonal model of a lived religious experience and its unique mean-ings for the author. For example, Michael Novak in *Ascent of the Mountain, Flight of the Dove* chronicles and explains his own re-

ligious journey through early training, skepticism and rejection of
the institutional structure of the church, subsequent social perspective, and tentative conclusions. This text often reads like a novel
and several students quickly identify with Novak's position. Others
are highly critical of the text and express emotional distaste. The
book has served well as a catalyst within the class, giving a clearly
articulated basis for controversy as well as stimulating the student
to take a position in regard to his own beliefs. Furthermore, it gives
a working model for tracing the influences and the range of input
which constitutes the student's own religious life.

While the students are reading, reacting to, and discussing
Novak's text, I likewise introduce a number of psychosynthesis
exercises within the class. Such exercises might include an autobiographical questionnaire which the student may use or not according to its value to him as a vehicle of self-understanding, or
exercises in imagery as an introduction to recognition of his own
peak experiences and religious consciousness, or finally, exercises
in directed meditation such as Ira Prognoff's taped recording, "The
Well and the Cathedral."

When the underlying "spirit" of the class has moved to positive
directions of mutual esteem for one another, and where there now
exists a serious, yet relaxed sharing of insights, this phase of the
course reveals strong contrasts in life-patterns and religious value-
systems among the students in a way that accurately reflects what
"religion in American society" actually is today. During the course
and as an outcome of the group interaction, an ecumenical spirit
emerges within the classroom. We have all been exposed to a vicarious experience of what it means to David and Sharon to be
Jewish and to believe in Judaism; Catholics have discovered that
their Lutheran classmates are just as conscious of the liturgical
season as they are or were; the foreign student who is a devout
Buddhist has shown that his desire for peace is the same as that to
be found in the notion of Christian brotherhood. A few of the students may belong to a Pentecostal prayer group or to a Hare Krisna
community and when they demonstrate their simplicity and kind-
liness, what they stand for begins to make sense on a practical level.
Nobody is expected to change his own beliefs and convictions. But
by expressing them in a variety of ways each person seems to have
become both a contributor and a receiver of deeper understandings
through more personal relationships, and also to have learned or
appropriated a more general theoretical point of view from which
he can articulate his position in a reflective, sensitive manner.

As one of the last assignments, members of the class are asked to visit a church or to attend a religious ceremony different from their own, even though it may be within the same denomination. Many students choose to attend a service of another faith, and when they all report back on the experience an interesting kind of ecumenical awareness is evident, expressed in changed attitudes and appreciation of the many ways in which contemporary religious consciousness is being expressed.

When feasible, I try to have a personal interview with each student toward the close of the course. At this time he can retrace his own learning experience during the semester. If not an interview then I request the student to write an account of his learning experience and to suggest changes or improvements for the next class.

Summary

In this chapter we have presented a view on teaching and participant learning as co-respondence. By this we mean that active dialogue and autobiographical work with ideas pervade the classroom. There is mutual give and take between teacher and students. While the model discussed deals with college students, the same underlying principles are applicable in any teacher-student relationship at whatever age level. Teaching and learning always imply a relationship, a two-way process where both the older and the younger contribute toward the creation of a new social reality. They create a common bond of present understanding through open dialogue. Neither teacher nor student is alone responsible for the process but each must be enabled to co-respond in order that a new, third dimension, which is not wholly predictable nor controllable, may emerge. Teaching and learning go beyond the level of empirical methods and calculated procedures. Faith, hope, and caring for one another are the sustaining forces of education at whatever level it may occur.

We discussed the way in which knowledge is appropriated by the student and we presented the method of "cognitive mapping" as an example of a way in which work with concepts and processes may be used both by individuals and groups within the classroom setting. We also presented a model for the development of a whole course based on the processes of (1) collecting and reflecting, (2) sharing dialogue, (3) literature tie-in and appropriation, and (4) personal integration and group recognition of the learning process.

REFERENCES

Assagioli, R. 1971. *Psychosynthesis*. New York: Viking.

Berger, P. 1967. *The sacred canopy: elements of a sociological theory of religion.* Garden City: Doubleday.

Boulding, K. 1969. *The image: knowledge in life and society.* Ann Arbor: University of Michigan Press.

Freud, S. 1965. *New introductory lectures on psychoanalysis.* New York: Norton.

Fuller, B. 1969. *Utopia or oblivion: the prospects for humanity.* New York: Overlook Press.

Holt, J. 1964. *How children fail.* New York: Pitman.

———. 1969. *The underachieving school.* New York: Pitman.

———. 1972a. *Freedom and beyond.* New York: E. P. Dutton.

———. 1972b. *How children learn.* New York: Pitman.

Illich, I. 1970. *Deschooling society.* New York: Harper and Row.

Jencks, C., Smith, M., Acland, H., Bane, M. J., Cohen, D., Gintis, H., Heyne, B., and Michelson, S. 1972. *Inequality: a reassessment of the effect of family and schooling in America.* New York: Basic Books.

Kohl, H. 1969. *The open classroom: a practical guide to a new way of teaching.* New York: Random House.

Leonard, G. 1968. *Education and ecstasy.* New York: Delacorte Press.

London, H. 1972. Experimental colleges, university without walls: reform or rip-off? *Sat. Rev. Ed.* October: 62–65.

McLuhan, M. 1964. *Understanding media: the extensions of man.* New York: Signet Books.

Montessori, M. 1967. *The absorbent mind.* New York: Holt, Rinehart and Winston.

Novak, M. 1971. *Ascent of the mountain; flight of the dove.* New York: Harper and Row.

Postman, N., and Weingartner, C. 1969. *Teaching as a subversive activity.* New York: Delacorte Press.

———. 1971. *The soft revolution: a student handbook for turning schools around.* New York: Dell.

Progoff, I. n.d. *An experiential religious service.* New York: Dialogue House Library (recorded tape cassette).

Rogers, c. 1969. *Freedom to learn.* Columbus: C. E. Merrill.

Rosenstock-Huessy, E. 1966. *The christian future, or the modern mind outrun.* New York: Harper & Row, chap. 3.

———. 1971. *Man must teach.* Norwick, Vt.: Argo Press.

Schutz, A. On multiple realities. In *Collected papers, vol. I.* The Hague: Nijhoff, 1962.

Steiner, R. 1968. *The essentials of education.* London: privately printed.

Toffler, A. 1973. Future shock in education. *Saturday Evening Post,* May: 245–47.

9.
School Records: Whose and for What?

LEO GOLDMAN

For years and years, schools maintained records of their pupils with hardly a question or complaint from the pupils, their parents, or anyone else. There were occasional minor disputes between counselors on the one hand and teachers and administrators on the other, as to who should have access to the cumulative records. However, on the whole, the schools decided what to include in their records, what tests and other data to collect, what incidents or judgments to record, and who might have access to these recorded data. Pupils and their parents for the most part seemed to know very little about what was on their records, nor did they have much knowledge of the transmission of any of the recorded information to colleges, employers, and others. And for a long time nobody seemed to see any serious problems in the system of pupil records.

In the decade of the 1960s the situation changed drastically: from many quarters there came complaints and demands for change. By the end of the decade schools throughout the country were engaged in studies of their record keeping practices, with major attention being given to such matters as the rights of parents to see the records, confidentiality of records in relation to college applications, and the very basic question of what information should be collected and recorded in the first place.

To understand the motive power for these challenges to a long established and long unchallenged system, consider these few examples of incidents that occur daily in public schools:

• A newspaper reporter phones or visits a school and asks about a former student who has been arrested and accused of committing a crime. What kind of student was he? What was he like personally? Were there any signs of impending trouble? Apparently in many schools someone answers such questions, because newspaper stories frequently report a student's grades, IQ, extracurricular activities, and opinions about his personality and character. Who gave the information? Where did it come from? How did the informant decide whether to tell or not? These questions usually remain unanswered.

• A local merchant telephones the school principal or counselor, saying something like this: "Keith W. has applied to me for a job. Can you tell me something about him? Is he reliable? Is he honest? How did he do in school?" The clerk or counselor or principal who receives the call may hesitate for a moment, may stall briefly while trying to decide how to handle the request, but more times than not probably will select some items from memory or records and tell something about the pupil or former pupil. Usually the informant will benevolently try to find favorable things to say, but if the employer presses hard enough and pumps skillfully enough, some negative things may be revealed also. Are there guidelines in the school so that any employer would receive the same responses, no matter which school staff member he reaches? Do Keith or his parents know what information the school will reveal? Do they in fact know what information is recorded? Does anyone know whether the telephone caller is indeed a prospective employer, or might it be someone who has other motives?

• A woman appears in the guidance office, introducing herself as the mother of Helen G., a junior in the school, and asking for a written statement attesting to the fact that Helen had received counseling in the school and had then followed up the school's referral to an outside agency. The statement, she says, is needed in connection with a complaint that she and her husband have been neglecting the child. The mother feels that the statement from the school will help prove that the parents have been trying to help Helen solve her problems. Should the school provide such a statement? How much of what Helen has revealed to the counselor should be released to the mother? Suppose that Helen had told the counselor that her parents had indeed been neglectful, even brutal? Should this confidence be recorded somewhere? On what basis does the counselor decide whether to reveal the confidence to the mother, or to anyone for that matter?

• A phone call is received from the admissions office of Prestige College. Samuel T., a senior at the high school, has applied for admission to Prestige. He seems to them to be a good prospect, but they got the impression that Samuel might be a little too radical for their campus. What does the school know about him? Has he been involved in protests, demonstrations, or marches? Is he a "troublemaker"? The counselor or administrator who takes the call may well wonder what, if anything, should be revealed. No matter what they decide, they may also well wonder whether Samuel should be informed of the call.

Perhaps in rural areas and small towns such problems do not often arise. But in cities and suburbs and probably in large centralized schools—the schools that enroll most of the pupils of this country—such incidents occur fairly often. And other incidents too: FBI agents do "security checks" and ask whether there is any indication of possible disloyalty to the United States (a vague concept that raises questions about the student's political activities, efforts to avoid being drafted, or just his expressed opinions about almost any controversial matter). Probation officers write or phone or visit on a "routine check" in preparation for a court hearing: "Let me see Susan's records, please." (True, it is for the judge, not the prosecutor, but there is no subpoena based on a specific rationale; the probation officer is on a "fishing expedition" and might turn up something that could be harmful to the girl and that perhaps she has a right to keep secret.)

In most schools it is fruitless to ask for their guidelines for handling requests from credit bureaus, college representatives, prospective employers, even parents, and even pupils themselves. Not only are written guidelines rare, but most schools do not seem to have even a clear *un*written policy to guide those who answer the calls and receive the visitors. And professional probers are usually skillful in catching people off guard and making them feel that it is entirely proper and normal to spill the beans.

But, one might object, there is nothing wrong in any of these situations. The school keeps records for the very reason that legitimate questions will arise. Counselors, psychologists, social workers, and principals use their professional judgment in handling all such requests and will tell only what they think is in the best interests of the child, the school, and the community. However, these sincere professionals do not recognize that this procedure places them in a self-appointed position of guardian, judge, and jury, a position in which they are relatively safe and unchallenged because most of the time neither the pupil nor his parents knows what has been spilled about them and how it may have affected the student's college or job application, a judge's decision, or the family's welfare rights. In fact, in past years, much of the time parents and pupils had never seen the records and so did not know what was in them; they were the *school's* records. Fortunately, this attitude has been changing.

Strangely enough, the change in public and legal attitudes toward school records began with complaints from essentially conservative parents and organizations, and then later and for different reasons from "liberal" and civil liberties sources. Only much later did the education professionals recognize the need for change; their first reactions, sad to say, were defensive and resistant.

THE COMPLAINTS

Some of the first rumblings came from parents and from organizations that joined them in their fight. These parents were concerned that their children were being probed about personal, sexual, and religious matters by means of personality and attitude measures and interviews. Moreover, they were concerned that the results of such probes were on school records that might be available to people inside and out of the school but were unknown to the parents themselves (for details, see Ackley 1972, Killian 1970, and Ware 1964 and 1971). Apparently these parents tended to be conservative people who saw the invasion as coming from the political left. These complaints led to rulings by courts and state departments of education, rulings that on the whole tended to open records and data-collection procedures to the inspection of parents. Armed with this knowledge, parents were in a stronger position to object to both the test or other data-collection procedures and to the records themselves.

Increasingly during the 1960s there was concern from legal and civil liberties groups about threats to privacy (for summaries, see Godwin and Bode 1971, Lister 1970, and Westin 1967). School records were only a part of that concern; greater emphasis was on "bugging" devices, personality inventories used by employers in connection with hiring and promotion, and the increasing use of electronic data banks which potentially could combine information from many sources—credit bureaus, correctional institutions and courts, schools and colleges, FBI and other investigative agencies, income tax agencies, and so on. These posed a serious threat to the individual's privacy and right to withhold information that might be misused or be otherwise damaging or embarrassing. Although schools and colleges were not seen as a threat to the same extent as some of the other agencies, there was still concern about personality ratings, records of counseling regarding personal problems, and records of political activities in which students engaged or were believed to engage.

From this quarter came the second set of pressures on schools to do something about their records—to refrain from collecting or recording such information, to permit students and parents to know what was recorded, and to restrict the release of the information to others. A summary of the rationale for such new policies and a set of suggested guidelines for public schools were published by the Russell Sage Foundation (1970) following a work conference on the problem. A second conference devised similar guidelines for higher education (Russell Sage Foundation 1973).

Still a third main course of criticism of school records came from "disadvantaged" groups—blacks, Chicanos, native Americans, and Puerto Ricans. They too were concerned about labeling of their children in terms of personality characteristics ("belligerent," "uncooperative," "lacks motivation," and so on). But they added an important new emphasis: the self-fulfilling prophecy. Their children, they said, began school with a serious handicap because of the family's poverty and also because the language and customs and values of the home and neighborhood were different from those of the middle-class white school. As a result, their children scored low on tests. This was bad enough, but it was even worse in its effects. Teachers, they felt, accepted the low test scores as fixed indicators of the child's learning limits and did not expect enough of the child. As the result, the expectation was indeed fulfilled: the school set too low levels of expected achievement for those children, let the children be aware of it by class placement, and, aware of the "prophecy," neither teachers nor children tried to achieve at the higher levels.

These parents increasingly demanded to know what the school records contained, and then pushed their demands further: don't even give the tests, let alone record the results, they urged. Give teachers a *minimum* of information about our children, and let them keep trying harder and harder without forming any preconception as to what the child's maximum level of attainment might be.

Naturally, this kind of demand (and practically *all* the demands and complaints) were completely counter to all that teachers and counselors and psychologists and administrators had learned and believed to be good practice. All of them had been taught to keep thorough records, to share information with those involved in the education of the child, and to use their professional judgment in protecting the confidentiality of the information—protecting it even from the pupil and the parents when judged necessary.

Here then was a clash of interests and goals, that persists to this day and that has, as a general rule, not been satisfactorily resolved. Before proceeding to formulate recommendations, we will explore a bit more deeply some of the dynamics of this clash, some of the assumptions and beliefs that guide the parties in these disputes. In general, it will be seen that parents and students on one side have somewhat different assumptions and beliefs from the professional staffs of the public schools on the other.

DYNAMICS

The School's Mandate

Perhaps the most fundamental issue is: what is the mandate given to the public schools? The public in general and their elected representatives tend to see a more restricted range than do the education professionals. The average parent sees a mainly cognitive purpose in schools—knowledge, understanding, and skills. Most parents probably also want the school to teach certain common values and attitudes.

But schools are also under pressure from many special interest groups to perform other functions—to provide diagnostic and therapeutic services in the mental health area, to check children's medical and dental needs, to give special attention to the gifted or the slow learners or to some other group. Schools seem to have found it difficult to resist any of these pressures and have in fact been all too ready to take care of the "whole child," although usually without sufficient resources to take care of even the limited cognitive functions.

Counselors, psychologists, and other pupil personnel workers have also jumped on the "whole child" bandwagon, usually encouraged by books and articles and professors in graduate courses.

One of the results of this dedication is a readiness to probe into children's personal lives—their feelings, family relations, and their religious, sexual, and financial situations, attitudes, and problems. Understandably, a few parents over the years became concerned about these incursions into what they saw as nonschool aspects of the child's life. These concerns led to the legal actions, mentioned previously, directed to courts and state education authorities, aimed at restricting the scope of probing and intervention into the personal lives of students.

The Russell Sage *Guidelines* (1970) takes the more conservative position on this issue—that the general mandate given the schools is to develop the cognitive lives of children, not the "whole child." Beyond that restricted area, any probing or recording or disseminating of information about pupils should be done only with the specific informed consent of the parents; the school serves as an extension of parental guidance, not as an independent institution. These recommendations will be discussed more fully in a later section.

The School Knows Best

Related to the question of mandate is that of who knows better what is good for the child—the school or the family. School people tend to think that they know better; it is this belief that has led them to collect all kinds of personal information without ever seeking parental permission—questionnaires about family matters, personality inventories, problem checklists, and so on. This belief has also led counselors and psychologists and others to engage in counseling and therapeutic activities with children and youth, sometimes without informing the parents, and almost always without bothering to seek parental permission. The result has sometimes been a situation in which several people in the school (including fellow students in the case of counseling groups) might know things about a student that his parents know nothing about—important things such as his involvement in drugs or sex or criminal activities.

This patronizing kind of attitude on the part of school staff members seems to be more prevalent in the case of poor and uneducated parents than with those whose socioeconomic and educational levels more nearly approach (or exceed) those of the school professionals. Perhaps the greatest infringement upon parental prerogatives occurs in the case of poor people of color and of foreign language; it appears that they are viewed as unable to understand what is happening or perhaps as unconcerned.

Whatever the reasoning of the school staff, for me the principle seems clear: no matter whom the parents are, no matter what their educational level, and no matter what anybody thinks of their competence to make decisions regarding their children, parents are morally and legally the ones who must decide what services their children are to receive beyond the mandated educational scope of the schools. Professional intervention on the part of school personnel in more personal areas is usually done with the best of intentions, but the goodness of the intentions does not change one whit the basic principle that parents are responsible for the well-being of their children. It is they who by law and custom must decide when the children need help and where to seek the help. Even poorly educated parents have the right to select their child's helper—whether counselor, social worker, psychologist, psychiatrist, or even astrologer.

The school's professionals surely have the right, indeed the responsibility, to help parents understand the child's needs as they see them, and to try to persuade the parents that the child should be studied through tests and interviews and through exchange of information with other helping agencies that may have been in touch with the pupil or family. The family members become informed participants in such discussion, with the final decision being theirs; only a court order should be permitted to countermand that prerogative. And courts, it has been found, are extremely loathe to interfere with that prerogative. When the parent says stop, the school should stop, just as would any outside agency or private practitioner.

Public Schools, Therefore Open Records

A third kind of assumption that seems to have prevailed is that, because the schools are public, and education is compulsory, therefore the *records* of public schools are public records. Perhaps they are not regarded as being open in the sense that records of real estate transactions are open to the public, but at least they are assumed to be freely open to other public agencies, such as police, probation, and welfare departments. They are open also, though perhaps not quite so freely, to colleges, employers, credit investigators, newspaper reporters, and other nonpublic agencies and organizations.

The logic of this assumption is a bit obscure. There are, after all, other public agencies whose records are kept quite confidential— hospitals and clinics for one, and social work and psychological agencies for another. In these instances, perhaps the important factor seems to be that the agencies work within strong professional traditions that include the professional's right and responsibility to keep information confidential even though he or she works in a public agency. Most school counselors were classroom teachers before they were counselors and therefore lack that kind of tradition and that source of support from a strongly organized profession. If anything, logic should persuade that the public schools should be even more protective of its records than private institutions. Specifically, pupils have little choice; they *must* attend the public school (or an equivalent private school, an alternative that is not appealing or financially or geographically feasible for most). They are therefore a captive audience and can easily be taken advantage of. School people tend not to realize their power as officers of a large public agency, with the power of government and the courts behind them to enforce compulsory attendance, and the threat of poor grades and the ensuing difficulty in gaining admission to college. Even parents who have a personal sense of power, those who know their rights and can speak up are often reluctant to antagonize teachers, counselors, and principals for fear that their children might suffer.

This is in no way to suggest that school staff do consciously abuse their power; to the contrary, most of them have little sense of power. But the fact is that they do control some of the important goodies that parents and pupils value. Perhaps even more important: the parents and pupils *perceive* the school as having that control and that power.

The Student as "Client"

One source of conflict between parent and school arises from the helper's attitude that the student is the "client" and that the helper therefore need not reveal even to parents what has been told in confidence by the student. In most such cases, the student personnel worker seems to have extrapolated into the school situation a conception of the student-as-client that is neither indigenous to the school nor congruous with the worker's role in the school. Frequently the helper picked up this conception in graduate courses and especially in practicum experiences on a university campus where those being helped were indeed voluntary (young adult) clients.

But most students in elementary and secondary schools who talk with counselors are not clients in the sense of coming voluntarily to seek help with a problem. Further, the notion of client includes the assumption that the person seeking help has the judgment and competence to decide that he or she has a certain kind of problem and that the counselor or psychologist in the school is the most appropriate person to help with that problem. And still further, the concept of client implies that the person being helped is in a position to decide what to reveal to the helper.

Surely all would agree that a six year old in the first grade does not satisfy the criteria for being a client. But at what point can one assume that these criteria *are* met—sixth grade, ninth grade, twelfth grade? Perhaps at the high school senior level, when the students are reaching the age of eighteen, one can make a case for their having attained the necessary level of judgment, competence, and independence from their parents. But surely below that level we are dealing with minors and with less-than-fully-mature beings. Neither legally nor morally nor in wisdom are they ready to take their emotional lives fully in their own hands. Therefore, with the possible exception of the high school senior, the student cannot be regarded as client, and the helper cannot maintain that kind of one-to-one relationship. Instead these helpers should come to see themselves as facilitators and adjuncts, as people who work in collaboration with school and family and who continually check to be certain that they are not making the error of placing themselves in the position of a private practitioner or independent agency to whom a parent has voluntarily brought a child and to whom the parent has given authority to deal with the child, even sometimes to the extent of in loco parentis.

From this point of view, the notion of confidentiality takes on a different perspective. It is not the pupil personnel worker, or even the student to the exclusion of parents, who owns the confidence and the recorded or unrecorded information that has been conveyed. The family and school administration have the right, indeed the responsibility, to set limits as to what information pupil personnel workers may collect, what they may record, and what they may do with what they record. Once such delimited information is gathered, then the parents and school can work together to include the child as an informed participant in the ensuing discussion.

It simply is not enough to reply that the professionals will use their good judgment in deciding where to probe and what to reveal (pregnancy, drug taking, criminal offenses, suicidal thoughts, and so on). That is playing God, and it means that the pupil personnel services (pps) have taken unto themselves a kind of power that almost no professional helpers outside the school would dream of taking into their own hands, except perhaps those in penal and psychiatric institutions.

The Many Faces of PPS

Another major distinction between school pps workers (and the school in general, in fact) and a private practitioner or a community agency is that everyone on a school staff has certain institutional and societal obligations that affect the kinds of relationships they can develop with students and the ways in which records will be used. The failure to recognize this distinction has played its part, along with the previously mentioned factors, in confusing the issues.

A private practitioner or an independent community agency or clinic can with almost complete assurance say to a prospective client: "Tell me whatever you wish; I will record what I feel is necessary in order to help you, but I will never reveal anything to anyone else except if you direct me to do so." In the case of a child, the parents can be given this assurance. But no school staff member can give such assurance. At some time in the future a pps worker might be asked to advise a teacher or administrator who has problems in teaching or disciplining a child. No matter how careful the pps workers are, they cannot help but let their advice be influenced by all that they know about the child, even if they refuse to reveal anything of what was told them in confidence.

Similarly, pps workers, especially counselors, cannot help but be influenced by information obtained in confidence when asked months or years later for an assessment of the student on a college application or for an evaluation to a prospective employer, or asked to testify in a court hearing regarding suspension of the student from school. Whether one answers from memory or with the aid of records, the fact remains that one is in a double-agent position, in effect, and cannot possibly follow through on a promise of full confidentiality. The counselor's already precarious position in this connection is further confounded by the court ruling, in the Bates College case, that the college had to reveal the high school's "confidential" statement to the parents of a rejected applicant (Graham 1969). This precedent-setting case, added to Noland's (1971) findings that many high school counselors would reveal confidential matters to college admissions officials, should put students, parents, and school counselors all on notice to be most wary in discussing personal matters that might have harmful consequences.

There probably are a few schools where counselors or

psychologists or social workers are hired almost as private practitioners-in-the-school and are not expected to have any function save that of helping students directly through counseling. But except for those few schools, pps workers in public schools, like all other staff members of the school, have responsibilities to the school and to the community that must be taken into account when defining the kinds of records that should be maintained, how they should be maintained, and how information should be released.

RECOMMENDATIONS

Principles

In simplest form, three principles comprise the essence of the recommendations that follow:

1. First, because the school staff cannot truly guarantee any degree of confidentiality for information it has collected, it should be strictly limited in the kinds of information it is permitted to collect from pupils without explicit informed parental consent.

2. Because inevitably the school is privy to quite a bit of information about its students (after all, it has the student for two hundred six-hour days each year for a total of twelve or thirteen years), very stringent, explicit written rules should be formulated that would define the ways in which that information is recorded.

3. The student and parents should be regarded as coowners of all information recorded in the school. With rare exceptions, one pervasive operating principle should be that no information is leased without explicit informed parental consent (or the student's consent if he or she has reached a predetermined "age of consent").

The Russell Sage *Guidelines* (1970, 1973) contain detailed recommendations for an entire system of information collection, maintenance, and dissemination, and may very well serve as a model for beginning consideration by school systems. Also, the federal Congress has continued to refine the "Buckley Amendment," which mandates privacy as well as student and parental access to school records. No effort will be made here to go into the detailed recommendations of the *Guidelines* or the amendment; rather a few guiding principles will be emphasized.

Collaborative Guidelines

It would probably be a serious error for a school system to adopt a ready-made set of rules and procedures, such as the Russell Sage *Guidelines*. What will serve well for a rural district may not serve well for an urban district; what makes sense in a stable small town district may not in a high-turnover city neighborhood; what will meet the needs of an affluent suburb may be entirely unsuitable for an impoverished area.

Secondly, it is essential that any set of guidelines be drawn up collaboratively by representatives of all relevant groups—teachers, administrators, pupil personnel workers, pupils, parents, and some of the agencies and institutions that would be affected. It is tempting to take the easy route of drawing up a set of guidelines entirely within the school staff and then try to "sell" it to the others, or perhaps to bring in token representatives of the outside groups and ask them in effect to rubber-stamp the finished product. In the long run, the guidelines themselves will probably be more viable and the entire system more successful if all those who will be affected by the plan engage fully in its development. It may make life a bit more difficult for the school staff if the planning group includes representatives of less articulate or even hostile parents, pupils, and others, but it is better to work out a plan that will receive acceptance from all than to find later that the finished product does not work in practice.

Records Restricted to Educational Development

As mentioned earlier, some of the pupil personnel workers bring a strong tradition of confidentiality from their respective professional specialties—medicine, social work, psychology, nursing, and so on. These traditions certainly should be fed into the process of developing a set of guidelines. But it would be a mistake merely to import a foreign code bodily. Yet this happens sometimes when one or another of these specialists operates what in effect is a self-contained clinic within the school; such operations tend not to feed into the essential processes of the school and might as well be located (and supported) outside of the school.

What makes more sense is for the planning committee to begin with an examination of the most important informational needs of the school, in relation to its main purposes. It might be interesting to know this or that about a pupil or his family, but if it will not clearly help the school to accomplish its specific objectives, or if the information might in some instances do more harm than good, then it might better be omitted. Some examples may help.

1. Personality ratings by teachers have been traditionally included on cumulative record forms. Most of the rating scales on examination turn out to be badly flawed in that they often contain vague undefined terms such as "self-control" or "responsibility" or ask for ratings such as "satisfactory" or "superior" without providing any norms or training to insure that all raters use a common scale.

   Perhaps even more telling is the fact—at least it is a fact in my experience—that little if anything is done with the information. It may be reassuring to a counselor or other person to find a collection of such ratings on the card, but it is doubtful that the information makes any significant contribution to the school's understanding of the child or the school's educational activities on behalf of the child. And there is more than a little chance that a teacher may become biased against a child by the ratings of previous teachers; some very good teachers have in fact said that they never look at any such material until after they have obtained their own impressions of the child, and that, by then, the previous ratings make little if any difference.

2. It has been customary in some schools to include such items as father's and mother's birthplace somewhere on a cumulative record form or folder. Presumably this information helps teachers and others to understand better the problems that a child from a bilingual home or a foreign cultural background may be facing. But black, Chicano, and other minority groups complain sometimes that this kind of information leads the school to stereotype the child's learning potential and therefore to expect too little of him. Could not this information better be collected, if and when needed, at the time that there is a clearly defined need for it?

3. Medical kinds of information are often found on record cards. In some communities it may still make sense to check in order to be certain that the child's family is aware of possible health problems, but in most areas this may be an unquestioned carryover from another era. Even when health data are needed, the question should be raised as to whether the information obtained through a teacher's or nurse's cursory observation is such as to warrant permanent recording.

These are merely a few examples of the kinds of information that are sometimes included either out of tradition or because one particular agency or person—usually not the teacher—might occasionally find it helpful. The chances are that it would be more useful for that agency or person to collect fresh information at the time it is needed. *The record should serve mainly to facilitate the educational development of the child.* Every suggested addition should be challenged and should finally be included only if it can be shown that that kind of information is truly necessary, will indeed be used to serve the major functions of the school, and is not a threat to the family's privacy or freedom of opportunity.

Necessity for Supervision and Training

The completion of a carefully prepared system of record keeping is only a beginning. The system will probably never operate at full effectiveness, and may even break down, if the teachers and others are not given continuing inservice education in its use. Also, as the Russell Sage *Guidelines* recommend, someone in the school should be designated as the one responsible for maintenance of and access to the records, and for the smooth functioning of a system for review and challenge. Without these procedures and adequate staff to monitor them, the best plan in the world will soon lose whatever potential value it had.

CONCLUSION

Perhaps this entire paper has dwelt too exclusively on the negative aspects of pupil records. To attain a better balance, it should be said that good records, well kept, can help teachers and pupil personnel workers and others both in and out of the school to be effective practitioners of their respective specialties. But, at least in this one observer's experiences, records rarely are utilized in the ways in which textbooks say they should be. Poor practices creep in and are usually not removed. Rarely do teachers or counselors take the time, or have the clerical and other assistance necessary, to record carefully and thoroughly, let alone to develop and revise the record system itself.

Ladd has neatly summarized the dilemma: "The more one person knows about another, the better he can serve the other. This commonplace is generally true. But it is also true that the more one person knows about another, the better he can injure him" (Ladd 1971, p. 262).

With due attention to the positive values of good records, our past experience suggests that we would do well to lean in the direction of (1) keeping to a minimum the information that is collected; (2) insisting on informed parental consent for all information beyond the absolute minimum (identification and achievement) that is necessary for the school to accomplish its announced goals; (3) keeping parents and students well informed as to the information that is in the school's possession; and (4) releasing no information to anyone, outside of those on the school staff who have a valid need for it, without written consent of the parents or of the pupil when he or she reaches the designated age for consent.

No school can be said to be taking care of its responsibilities in this area until it has distributed a written statement that spells out in detail the rationale and guidelines for the collection, maintenance, and dissemination of information about pupils and their families.

REFERENCES

Ackley, S. 1972. Individual rights and professional ethics. *Professional Psychol.* 3:209–16.

Godwin, W. F., and Bode, K. A. 1971. Privacy and the new technology. *Personnel and Guidance J.* 50:298–304.

Graham, J. G. 1969. Legal problems surrounding recommendations of students. *J. Nation. Assoc. College Admissions Counselors* 14:20–24.

Killian, J. D. 1970. The law, the counselor, and student records. *Personnel and Guidance J.* 48:423–32.

Ladd, E. T. 1971. Counselors, confidences, and the civil liberties of clients. *Personnel and Guidance J.* 50:261–68.

Lister, C. 1970. Privacy and large-scale data systems. *Personnel and Guidance J.* 49:207–11.

Noland, R. L. Damaging information and the college application. *Personnel and Guidance J.* 49:544–54.

Russell Sage Foundation. 1970. *Guidelines for the collection, maintenance, and dissemination of pupil records.* New York: Russell Sage.

Russell Sage Foundation. 1973. *Student records in higher education.* New York: Russell Sage.

Ware, M. L. 1964. *Law of counseling and guidance.* Cincinnati: W. H. Anderson.

———. 1971. The law and counselor ethics. *Personnel and Guidance J.* 50:305–10.

Westin, A. F. 1967. *Privacy and freedom.* New York: Atheneum.

10.

Informed Participation in Industrial Consultation

LESLIE H. KRIEGER

A young man sits in my office. He's good-looking, presentable, probably bright. He's definitely upset. He's been refused a position in a bank's management training program. The bank's personnel officer will tell him only that the refusal is based on the report of the industrial psychologist who assessed him. A call to the psychologist's office is equally uninformative: the testing was paid for by the bank, and it now owns the data!

The young man wants to enter banking and would like to know in what way he must change in order to qualify for the management training program. He allowed himself to be examined by a psychologist, but now he can learn nothing from this experience— nothing except a deep distrust of psychologists, personnel men, and the whole employment selection system.

UNILATERAL DECISION MAKING

Hidden beneath the refusals to allow this man access to information about himself are several assumptions. The first assumption is that one person or organization can buy and therefore "own" data about an individual. These data have been ordered and paid for like any other service or product and therefore belong to the company.

193

The person about whom so much is known must remain ignorant of his own psychological profile.

A second assumption operating in this situation is an extension of industry's frequent paternalism: the company knows what is best for its employees, and therefore they need not have access to the data on which decisions about them are made. As long as a person is loyal to the company and consents to all the decisions made about him, that person's need satisfactions are assured. Even if the employee has access to all the relevant data about himself, he cannot further his own interests as effectively as the company can take care of them for him.

The refusal of access to information rests also on a third assumption, the belief that only the professional can understand the data and use it in an appropriate way. In fact, one job of the professional appears to be to protect the individual from the harm that might result if he learned too much about himself. By not sharing the data, the professional reserves the option of controlling the person and making decisions on his behalf. The professional also protects himself from the discovery of error in his own decision making.

The validity of these assumptions of ownership, paternalism, and expertise should be found in the ultimate benefits of the consulting practices which stem from them. If the assumptions are valid, all parties to the industrial consulting relationship—the client company, the psychologist, and the individual—should be better off when a person is denied access to data about himself.

But who really benefits in the situation where a person cannot learn why he was turned down? The client company? Not in the long run. With the current shortage of skilled and motivated managerial manpower the company cannot afford to lose a single potential employee. If the job applicant had knowledge of the areas in which he fell short of the company's expectations, he might take constructive steps to improve his skills or change his style to make himself suitable for employment sometime in the future. Without this feedback the applicant can do nothing that will help the company fill its manpower needs. In fact, he may actually caution other prospective applicants to avoid such an impersonal and inconsiderate organization.

Does the psychologist benefit in this situation? Not really. The person's inability to get feedback after allowing himself to be examined generates fear, distrust, anger, and serious ethical questions about the practice of psychology. In the absence of his own feedback from the person, the psychologist's practices and assumptions cannot be questioned or corrected. The psychologist appears as a cynical manipulator of men's lives rather than as a constructive contributor to rational decision making. The applicant may share these unflattering views of psychological practice with friends, and his negative feelings may surface as resistance to future personnel testing. These unkind views of psychology also generate objections to any attempt by psychologists to expand their professional role in nonindustrial settings such as schools, mental health centers, and hospitals.

And the individual himself certainly does not benefit. He leaves the situation ignorant, frustrated, and filled with self-doubt. He wonders what secret shortcomings the psychologist uncovered, and wishes he knew how better to prepare himself for appropriate employment. He is hostile toward both the company and the psychologist, for he feels he has been taken advantage of. He has revealed himself in considerable depth and detail and received nothing in return.

Obviously no one, not the client company, nor the psychologist nor the individual, really benefits from the consulting practices generated by the assumptions of ownership, paternalism, and expertise. All three of these assumptions lead to opportunities for manipulation and control of employees, opportunities directly opposed to industry's increasing emphasis upon individual responsibility and decision making. Clearly, the foundations of the industrial psychologist's consulting relationships must be made more consistent with this growing respect for man's self-determining abilities. Each person must have the opportunity to share in the generation and interpretation of his own psychological data.

INFORMAL PARTICIPATION PRACTICES

Therefore, the practicing industrial psychologist should replace the assumptions of ownership, paternalism, and expertise with a respect for each individual and his right to informed participation in the consulting process. Whenever possible the psychologist should include opportunities for co-generation of data, feedback, and discussion of the meaning of findings with all who will be influenced by them. Every consulting function performed by the psychologist can and should be made more responsive to the person's right to informed participation. The justification for this shift in emphasis should be found in increased benefits for the client company, the psychologist, and the individual.

The goal of informed participation in industrial psychology is not utopian. Three consulting procedures currently in use in our office demonstrate the practicality of the approach. These procedures are management assessment, group attitude survey, and career planning.

Management Assessment

The first procedure, management assessment, is one of the industrial psychologist's most frequent assignments. The case cited at the beginning of this paper is an example of the traditional approach to this task: a job applicant is exposed to a battery of tests and interviews. The psychologist reviews the scores and makes recommendations to the client company about the person's suitability for employment. At no time in the procedure is the applicant given an opportunity to share in the construction of the evaluative process or to receive feedback about his own test performance or employment potential.

The alternative approach to management assessment invites the participation of the individual from the very beginning of the evaluation procedure. When the job candidate comes in for a day-long assessment, he fills out a personal data blank and then is introduced to the consulting psychologist. The psychologist asks him what prior testing experience he has had and what expectations he has about the assessment procedure. Together they discuss the role of an assessment from the viewpoint of both the client company and the person being evaluated. When the applicant is told that the day's testing will end with a feedback session in which he can find out how well he performed, the entire procedure takes on a new perspective. Here is an opportunity for the individual to learn in one day facts about himself that otherwise he might take years to discover. The assessment can be just as valuable a source of information for the job candidate as it is for the client company.

The psychologist continues the orientation by explaining the role of the various types of tests—general ability, special aptitude, and personality—that make up an assessment. He next opens a discussion of test-wiseness and test anxiety and, when necessary, offers suggestions on strategies for successful test taking. Finally, the concept of norm group is introduced, and the applicant is asked to place himself according to his age, education and occupational group.

Although the design of an appropriate test battery is ultimately the responsibility of the psychologist, the individual has provided many inputs which influence choice of tests, level of difficulty, and sequence of presentation. Frequently these decision-making processes are shared with the person, and often the battery is changed in midstream if it is obvious from the first few test scores that the applicant is not getting the opportunity for the fairest possible evaluation. Throughout the day the psychologist checks on the applicant, his feelings, and his performance. Sometimes the purpose of a particular test is explained, at other times the individual's feelings of frustration or discomfort are discussed. At all times the psychologist, the psychometrist, and the entire staff do everything they can to help the person through the day as pleasantly as possible.

By midafternoon the testing is completed and an hour-long interview is begun. The psychologist talks about the purpose of the interview: it's easier to know a person by being with him than by learning about him only through the intermediary of test scores. The interview is informal, and the applicant is encouraged to talk about his personal history in general and his work experience in particular. The interest and involvement of the psychologist in the interview are genuine; the more an industrial psychologist knows about the perspectives people bring to the world of work, the better he can perform his consulting functions. The interview can become a growth experience for the applicant as well. Sensing the psychologist's real interest in the dialogue, the person may explore his own history and feeling with considerable depth and insight.

The final step in the assessment procedure is the feedback session in which the psychologist shares the test results and interpretations with the candidate. Test scores are not infallible; they require the experiential confirmation of the person who generated them. So the psychologist seeks the involvement of the individual through a candid discussion of the test results and their probable interpretations. The resulting profile is a cooperative product couched in shared everyday language; it should make sense to both the psychologist and the applicant.

If the feedback is successful, the individual leaves the assessment with a clearer picture of his strengths and weaknesses as well as an outline of his personal style. He also has a pretty good idea of how he compares to other people of similar age, education, and work experience. Although the applicant may not like or agree with every interpretation, he has some guidelines for recognizing and sometimes remedying problems that have given him trouble in the past. And his areas of greatest potential growth have been brought into sharp focus. In short, if the applicant has been at all receptive to the feedback process, he can leave with considerable insight into his employability.

Needless to say, the psychologist ordinarily cannot tell the person if he is to be hired for the particular position which initiated the assessment. The hire-no hire decision is made by the client company, and the psychologist's description of the applicant is just one of many inputs to the organization's selection apparatus. But whether he is hired for the position or not, there is a good chance that the individual will view the assessment procedure as a worthwhile investment of his time. He has come away from the psychologist's office with some valuable knowledge about his employment potential.

Group Attitude Survey

A second procedure which often is assigned to the consulting industrial psychologist is the administration of an employee attitude survey. Such a survey is used to gather information relevant to company decisions, rather than to assess performances of individual employees. Again it is valuable to contrast the traditional approach toward survey administration with the more participatory procedures used by our office. The standard practice for conducting an attitude survey is simple, fast, inexpensive, and of little value to the participants. Usually the psychologist presents employees with a booklet of attitude items to be scaled. The scaled scores are tallied by computer, and the psychologist returns the tally along with an interpretation of the findings to the company's top management. The employees who participated in the study hear little or nothing of the results; they wonder if top management really cares how they feel or was just going through the motions for public relations purposes.

This traditional attitude survey procedure affords the participants little opportunity to learn how their attitudes compared with others and no chance at all to participate in attempts to interpret the data or implement change based on the findings. No wonder that many employees view attitude surveys as a farce and go out of their way to sabotage them by distorting responses or making entries designed to disrupt the computer analysis of the data.

In our more participatory approach the psychologist brings small groups of employees together and discusses their involvement in the survey prior to the administration of the attitude items themselves. Procedures relating to sample selection and protection of anonymity are explained. The need for creation of a subsample of the surveyed group for in-depth interviews is also outlined, and participants are encouraged to write in their survey booklets topics and problems which they feel should be explored through the interviews. Finally the participants are assured that the data will be fed back accurately to the employees and that it is really in everyone's best interest to respond as honestly as possible.

The written survey is then followed up by hour-long individual interviews with the subsample. The interviews are built around the comments which employees wrote on the questionnaire. These participant-generated topics yield far more meaningful discussion and ultimate utility than do interview themes proposed by the psychologist or management. Employees appreciate the opportunity to discuss their work problems with a concerned professional, and most make the comment that management must really care about them or it would not spend the time and money required for all these individual interviews.

The computerized data analysis which is the end point of the traditional survey procedure is just the prelude to further employee involvement in our praticipative approach. In a survey recently completed for a large banking organization the feedback included five distinct steps. First was the traditional written report to the bank's management team. This report was followed with a verbal presentation by the psychologists in charge of the survey. The second step was a series of private meetings between each department head and a psychologist. The psychologist discussed the survey results relevant to each man's area and elicited his reactions to these findings.

In the third step, twenty-five middle managers were chosen to be trained as feedback discussion leaders. These men were selected on the basis of their interpersonal skills and relationships with employees in their departments. They were excused from their regular assignments to attend a two-day seminar in feedback leader training. In the training sessions the psychologists went over the survey findings item by item. Results were presented for the bank as a whole, the bank compared to other banks, and each department compared to the bank as a whole. Each trainee was given the opportunity to practice feeding back material to the rest of his class with the psychologists role-playing as troublesome, questioning employees.

In step four the newly trained feedback discussion leaders met with small groups of employees throughout the bank. Every employee was included in a group, but no employee was in a group with his own supervisor as either a participant or a discussion leader. Survey results relevant to each group were explained, and the leaders elicited reactions to the findings as well as suggestions for follow up. Each group elected a recorder who kept track of the members' ideas and feelings and submitted the transcript to the discussion leader at the end of the meeting.

The fifth step involved the sorting and content analysis of the employee reactions to the feedback sessions. Ultimately each department head received a report of both survey findings for his area and his employees' responses in the feedback discussions. Through this multistep procedure all members of the banking organization had an opportunity to react to current problems and to participate in the formulation of constructive responses to their own needs. The periodic reconvening of these feedback discussion groups will provide a continuing vehicle for employee participation in organizational problem-finding and solution.

Career Planning

A third industrial consulting procedure, employee career planning, is built entirely around the participation of the individual and is probably unique to our office. The program was developed for a hardware buying organization that wanted to give its employees every opportunity for individual growth and development. The career planning procedure is offered as a benefit to everyone employed by the company for more than one year. The program is unusual in that it gives the employee complete control over the generation and use of his own psychological data.

When an employee signs up for career planning, he is mailed a personal data blank and some interest inventories. When the inventories have been returned and scored, the employee is scheduled for an initial interview and a day of testing. The format of the interview and testing procedure is similar to that used for individual career planning in our office. The unique aspect of this program is that the company not only pays for the procedure but also gives the employee full salary for the time he must take off to complete it.

The initial interview centers on the employee's past history, current position, and plans for future growth. He is encouraged to ask questions about himself and the directions his career might take. Each test battery is individually constructed to provide data to help answer these questions as well as to offer information about career alternatives the employee may not have thought of on his own.

Usually within two weeks of the date of testing the employee meets with the psychologist for a counseling session. In this meeting test scores are fed back and explained, and the person is helped to develop a picture of his current abilities and limitations. Then, with the guidance of the psychologist, the employee is encouraged to combine the psychometric description of himself with all the real-world factors operating in his career development decisions. Family demands, availability of appropriate schooling, actual job opportunities, the advantages of staying with the hardware organization compared to those of leaving it, financial and personal needs—all must be considered. The result of these deliberations is usually a list of two or three possible plans for individual growth and development. The psychologist helps in ordering these plans according to their reality and probability of success and also provides information about such things as school programs, training requirements for specific jobs, and sources of career information.

Next the psychologist organizes the results of the counseling session into a written report which is mailed directly to the employee's home. The man then has a number of options available to him. The first is to read the report, put it in his dresser drawer, and forget it. A second is to read the report and decide on some course of self-improvement. Neither of these options involves the company in any way. The employee, not the company, has the report, and he is free to do with it what he will. However, if the report indicates the potential to benefit from schooling and/or to move to a better position within the hardware organization, the employee might choose the third option of showing the findings to the company's personnel officer. Sharing the report with the company entitles the individual to full tuition for recommended schooling and priority consideration for appropriate promotion.

Early indications are that the hardware organization's employees like the program and appreciate the opportunities for self-determination and growth which it offers. During the first five months in which the career planning was available, 247 of the company's 411 employees, about 60 percent, participated. They ranged in educational level from fifth grade through graduate school and in job position from hourly warehouse workers, maintenance personnel, and clerks to the very top line and staff levels. About 47 percent of the employees who received reports released them voluntarily to the company, and the number of people receiving tuition benefits has more than doubled in less than a year. Some people already have taken advantage of the program's opportunity for an additional check up session with the psychologist, and many employees have asked that the career planning service be made available to spouses and children as soon as possible.

BENEFITS OF INFORMED PARTICIPATION

The three nontraditional consulting procedures just described vary in the extent to which they offer opportunities for informed participation, but all three are based firmly on a belief in the individual's ability and right to share in the generation, interpretation, and use of his own psychological data. If this belief is sound, the practices which it generates should lead to far greater benefits to all parties in the consulting relationship than did the no-access procedures based on the assumptions of ownership, paternalism, and expertise.

The benefits of informed participation are most obvious for the individual. In the management assessment procedure he helps to shape the testing and norms by which he will be evaluated. He shares in the data interpretation and hopefully gains considerable knowledge about himself and his employability. He has the information he needs to formulate plans that will optimize his career development.

In the attitude survey the individual knows how his perceptions compare with those of other employees. He also knows that top management has seen and digested the survey responses. But most important the employee now has the opportunity to engage in a continuing problem-finding and problem-solving procedure through which he participates in the control of his own working environment.

Employee career planning provides the individual with both considerable psychological data about himself and the ability to control the use of that data in the employment situation. This procedure could become a model for informed participation personnel data banks in which the employee not only helps to create his own file, but also is given options which govern its use within the organization.

The client company receives many benefits from the use of an informed participation procedure. First, the data are bound to be both more honest and more accurate when the individuals involved share in its generation, interpretation, and control. The company stands a better chance of learning what it needs to know by respecting its employees' personal rights and decision-making abilities.

Secondary benefits to the company come through changed employee attitudes. As individuals realize that the organization has some respect for them and their abilities, they are less likely to engage in nonproductive activities and to interfere with or distort valuable information sources. Morale and production may improve and there may also be an increasing employee identification with company goals and values.

Finally, informed participation procedures help the company find, keep, and develop the employees it needs to function optimally. Job candidates who are told in an assessment feedback how they measure up to company expectations may take constructive steps to make themselves more suitable. Employees who know that their attitudes really matter will offer valuable suggestions on how to keep the organization a good place to work. And individuals who participate in employee career planning may accept the opportunity to develop themselves and grow with the organization.

The psychologist, too, benefits when he uses more participatory consulting procedures. His oft-stated goals of interpersonal openness and authenticity are reinforced by sharing interpretations with the client. The psychologist's expertise is enhanced, not diminished, as the individual receives feedback about himself and can dialogue about the incredible complexity of his own behavior. And the psychologist's work is made easier by the individual's willingness to participate in a procedure in which his personhood will be respected.

The psychologist also will benefit as client companies see the increased effectiveness of the more participatory procedures. The psychologist will become a more welcome and more trusted member of the industrial consulting group. As he is invited to participate in a variety of projects within each company, his familiarity with its organization and people will expand, and he will have even greater opportunities to share his human values and perspectives.

The psychologist's public image may change, too. As he becomes increasingly open in his consulting practices, he is perceived less as a manipulator and more as a trusted and valued professional. His advice and expertise will be sought on a broadening range of community problems and his inputs given their proper respect alongside those of other more established professionals. In fact, increasing the individual's involvement in data generation, interpretation, and control may be the most synergistic thing the industrial psychologist can do. His professional credibility rests on this move toward interpersonal authenticity.

11.

The Subject as a Person in Psychological Research

ROBERT J. SARDELLO

THE PRESENT SITUATION IN EXPERIMENTAL PSYCHOLOGY

Situation A

A young sophomore college student, Greg Anderson, is enrolled in an introductory psychology course. Last Tuesday the professor announced that all the students enrolled in the course would be required to participate in a psychology experiment in order to receive credit for the course. Greg signed up for 11:00 A.M. Tuesday morning.

Greg arrives at the psychology laboratory at the appointed time. He hesitates before entering the small, white-walled cubicle with its cement floor and laboratory smell. There is a large mirror on one of the walls and a slide projector is sitting on the table. The experimenter glances up from his desk and asks Greg to enter the room.

Experimenter: Hello. My name is Dr. Welch. I am conducting an experiment in verbal learning. I am trying to find out how people go about learning certain lists of verbal materials. Thank you for volunteering to help us in our work. Now, I am going to show you a

series of nonsense words—words that have no meaning—on this screen. When you see a single nonsense word you are to guess what other word goes with the nonsense word. Then, in a few seconds you will see the nonsense word paired with the correct response.
Subject: How do I know what to guess when I have never seen the words before?
Experimenter: You won't know the first time. You just guess. But, let me give you all the instructions first and then you can ask any questions you might have.

After you see the two words paired together you will then see another single nonsense word. Once again you are to try to guess the word that goes with it. We will continue in this fashion until we complete the list. We will then begin again and continue going over the list until you have all the responses correct.

Do you have any questions now?
Subject: No, I guess not. Is this an intelligence test or something?
Experimenter: No. We are just trying to find out how people learn.
Subject: O.K. I guess I'm ready to give it a try.
   . . . Click . . .
   X V E —
Subject: X V E — uh, blue
   . . . Click . . .
   X V E — pipe
   . . . Click . . .
   M O Z —
Subject: M O Z — uh, smoke
   . . . Click . . .
   M O Z — stove

This little description of an experimental research situation of a contemporary psychologist contains many implicit questions concerning the meaning of the discipline of psychology, and the meaning of method in psychology.

Let us contemplate this situation for a moment. First, this situation is experimenter oriented. This means that the experimenter takes the responsibility for defining the structure of the situation within which the exploration of a psychological phenomenon proceeds. The experimenter orientation of this situation is also a method-centeredness. The experimenter has defined the problem to be investigated. He has constructed a hypothesis. He has determined the independent and the dependent variables. He has decided what controls must be employed to preserve the purity of the experiment. The result of this method-centeredness is that the experiment is outside of the context of the day-to-day life of the subject. This procedure is necessary, for the psychologist is interested only in how the subject performs in the laboratory situation.

The experimental psychologist has a tremendous investment in the procedures of the scientific method. B. J. Underwood indicates the strength of this faith:

> Now you may ask: "why this fixation or fetish on the application of the scientific method to psychological problems?" The answer is that no one has conceived of a better way of demonstrating and understanding the lawfulness of nature. I therefore, believe that we should promote with all our vigor the appropriate use of these powerful tools of understanding [Underwood 1957, p. 3].

The key word in this quotation is the word *nature*. We see that the method-centeredness of the experimental psychologist presupposes a certain understanding of the subject matter of investigation. B. J. Underwood tells us that he is interested in understanding the lawfulness of nature. He does not say human nature. We must, therefore, assume that for him there is no difference between human nature and physical nature and that the former is reduced to the latter. Suppose that I am a geologist and that I find an interesting rock in the road. I want to know more about it. I pulverize it, analyze it, and relate what I discover to what I know about other rocks. In this whole procedure it is of the utmost importance that I remain removed from my procedures of understanding. I remain objective in the determination of the rock's constituents. Objectivity here is taken in a narrow sense and means that the experimenter's methods presuppose a total independence between the observer and the observed. For example, the experimenter does not allow his perception of the beauty of the rock to interfere with his analysis of its composition. The geologist will not avoid breaking off a piece of the rock that is particularly beautiful.

The experimental psychologist in our first description observes and records the correct and incorrect responses of his subject. He simply collects data. He cannot allow the subject to enter the experiment as a person. The subject is, after all, a person with a history, with feelings, with perceptions and thoughts about the situation that he finds himself in with the experimenter. All of this "surplus" meaning would contaminate the experiment conceived within the rubric of ideal objectivity. When we say that the person is not allowed to enter into the experiment, we mean that the methodology of experimental psychology cannot recognize the subject as a person who lives a life of even minimal self-awareness. Even though experimental psychologists themselves investigate such phenomena as cognition, recognition and even self-awareness, the responses of the subject are never understood as expressive of a person's experience. They are understood as "verbal data."

This description of experimentation is not a criticism. We must clarify the framework within which experimental psychology operates in order to avoid demanding things of experimental psychology that the very approach cannot incorporate.

Notice that the subject in our description was not informed in any way of his performance in the task or of its meaning for him. Such an expectation is an unreasonable demand. First, to expect the subject to be informed of the meaning of the experiment would be to expect the experimental psychologist to violate his own fundamental presupposition that the subject is part of nature. The geophysical chemist does not talk with his rocks. To expect the experimental psychologist to talk with his subjects about the meaning of his work for them would be to ask the psychologist to simultaneously see his subject as an object of nature and as an understanding, meaning-giving, meaning-receiving being.

A second reason why it is unreasonable to expect experimental psychologists to inform their subjects of the meaning and outcome of an experiment is that such information would have no meaning for the subject. Learning of nonsense syllables, for example, does not relate to the life of the person. At most, the subject would learn some information about his performance in that situation. Since the subject is assumed to be an ahistorical entity by the experimental psychologist, his performance cannot relate to his life as a historical individual with a personal history who is taking up his history in the process of becoming.

The experimental psychologist is first of all interested in his science—the development of a systematic explanation of some dimension of human behavior. He cannot directly care whether or not he is helping someone to attain self-understanding, neither should he be expected to care. He does often care indirectly, and usually hopes that his findings are put to good use.

Later in this chapter it will be argued that the person who agrees to take part in the kind of experiment just described should have the right to be informed that upon entering the experiment he will no longer be considered a person and that for the purposes of the investigation he will be considered an object.

Situation B

Jannie Hawley is a sophomore college student enrolled in a psychology course. Jannie describes the course as "most enjoyable." She says that this is the first time she has been in a class where she has felt free to speak openly and be listened to by the instructor. She has grown to feel that her opinions are valuable. One day after class Jannie's professor asked her if she would be willing to come by his office and work with him on a project. Jannie agreed to come the next morning.

Experimenter: Hi, Jannie! How are you? So nice to see you. Please come in and sit down. Isn't it a beautiful day?

Subject: Oh, yes. I just love spring on our campus. The flowers are blooming all along the mall.

Experimenter: Jannie, I am working on a research project. I am trying to learn more about how people experience themselves. You know, we have talked a lot in class about the notion of self. You know that as a teacher I am interested in the power of self. Well, I have worked out sort of a hypothesis. I think that people who can freely admit to themselves that they are interested and desirous of power are people who are more respectful of others. People who are not able to admit that they have power needs close in on themselves and become removed from others.

Jannie: That makes a lot of sense to me, Dr. Sandor. That speaks to my experience.

Experimenter: Well, thank you Jannie. Now, I want to try to be more systematic and to clarify this notion. I have made up a questionnaire. I would like you to answer this questionnaire. Then you can ask me questions about it if you like. In fact, I really think what you have to say is important, and I will make that part of my research. So, if you don't mind, we shall talk together about your responses to this questionnaire.

This is a second description of an experimental situation of another contemporary psychologist. You may find it hard to believe that both of our researchers call themselves experimental psychologists. They appear to be worlds apart. Actually, they are very close together. If we followed our second researcher through the entire experiment, we would see that he also has a hypothesis. His questionnaire probably is oriented toward certain variables. He will quantify his results. But he is in opposition to the tradition of experimental psychology depicted in our first description.

Psychology is in a state of transition, a state characterized by an initial opposition to the status quo. Documentation of the dissatisfaction with the methodology of experimental psychology is not hard to find. Koch (1969) forcefully argues that psychology cannot be a coherent discipline. Schultz (1969) concluded a historical outline of the subject's role in experimentation by proposing an alternative way of studying man: "Perhaps, then, the best way of investigating the nature of man is to ask him" (Schultz 1969, p. 227). This suggestion opposes the whole tradition of experimental psychology in its presupposition of man as a natural object. Kelman (1967) has argued that the nature of research in psychology entails deception of subjects and that new techniques of research are needed which entirely do away with the need for deception. Such new approaches, he states, will call for a radically different set of assumptions about the role of the subject in the experiment. Kagan (1967) cites the end of what he terms "authoritarian psychology" or one that is outer-directed, absolutistic, and intolerant of ambiguity. He foresees that the decades ahead may nurture a discipline that is relativistic, oriented toward internal processes, and accepting of the idea that behavior is necessarily ambiguous. Lyons (1970) forcefully argues that the personhood of both the subject and the experimenter are hidden in the traditional laboratory experiment, but each enters the situation as a person in a covert manner where a dialogue goes on between the experimenter-person and the subject-person.

This sort of documentation could be continued at length. The dissatisfaction is widespread enough to conclude that psychology is indeed in transition.

What happens when the paradigm which is set up to ensure objectivity begins to be seen as faulty? What happens if, in fact, it is possible to understand the situation of our experimenter and subject in the first description *as a social interaction*? One thing that such a view would mean is that the power and influence in the experimental situation is *not* simply unidirectional—from experimenter to subject—but a *mutual* interaction of power and influence. The problems generated by such questions is the subject of research in contemporary psychology. The meaning of such questions varies depending on whether the question is asked by a psychologist committed to traditional psychology, to transitional psychology, or to visionary psychology.

THE APPROACH OF TRADITIONAL PSYCHOLOGY

Traditional psychology is beginning to understand that both the experimenter and the subject of a psychological experiment can be understood as persons and not objects. For example, Masling (1960), working in the area of projective testing, has shown that the relationship between the experimenter and the subject could influence the outcome of a projective test. McGuigan (1963) pointed out that many studies in psychology employed more than one data collector, and that this "experimenter variable" was never taken into account. Binder and his associates (1957) describe an experiment in which two experimenters performed the same experiment, each experimenter with a different group of subjects. These experimenters were described as follows:

> The first—was—an attractive soft-spoken, reserved young lady—5′½″ in height, and 90 pounds in weight. The—second—was very masculine, 6′5″ tall, 220 pounds in weight, and had many of the unrestrained personality characteristics which might be expected of a former marine captain—perhaps more important than their actual age difference of about 12 years was the difference in their age appearance: the young lady could have passed for a high school sophomore while the male experimenter was often mistaken for a faculty member (Binder et al., 1957, p. 309).

Wouldn't you act quite differently in an experiment if the experimenter was a blue-eyed young woman instead of a marine captain? A rock would not.

Robert Rosenthal of Harvard University is chiefly responsible for instigation of sustained systematic research into the relationship between the experimenter and the subject in psychological experimentation. His substantial contribution has been to provide evidence that experimenters transmit (unknowingly, of course) expectancies to subjects concerning the outcome of experiments. A basic paradigm for Rosenthal's studies involves the creation of two or more groups of experimenters with different hypotheses about the effects they might obtain in an experiment. For example, Rosenthal and Fode (1960) randomly divided a single group of rats into a group they arbitrarily labeled "maze-bright" rats and into another group they arbitrarily labeled "maze-dull" rats. Naive experimenters ran these rats through maze-learning experiments with the result that although in actual fact all the rats were randomly selected from a single group, those rats labeled "maze-bright" performed significantly better in the task than those rats labeled "maze-dull." The "effect" has become known as the experimenter bias effect, and further research indicates that this effect also occurs when the subjects are persons rather than rats.

Rosenthal's work has further demonstrated that different experimenters can obtain significantly different data from comparable subjects. He calls this the "experimenter personal attributes effects." This effect is similar to that described in the quotation concerning the young woman and the marine captain.

John Jung (1971) presents a reflective work which compiles and systematizes the major concerns resulting from research into psychological research. The major questions posed by such research can be summarized as follows:

1. What effect does experimentation have on subjects?

2. Can experimenters unintentionally prejudice outcomes of experiments?

3. Do other factors besides the experimenters' expectancies prejudice the outcome of experiments—factors such as sex, age, race, status, friendliness, and anxiety of the experimenter?

Notice that all of these questions presuppose a unidirectional "interaction"; that is, the model of ideal objectivity is guiding the questions. The way in which the questions are posed indicates the direction of the answer. What must be answered is how can ways be devised to stop the interference of the experimenter in the collection of data. The question of this research as viewed by the experimental psychologist is how can the status quo be maintained? This question has great merit because it does not attempt to make traditional experimentation do something it is not capable of doing. The question helps traditional psychologists recognize that there are limitations to their methods:

> The attitude toward experimentation presented in the following pages is critical, if not negative. In a sense, this commentary will be seen as antiexperimental. Yet, the writer is an experimental psychologist and believes that the scientific approach is *a*, not *the* method of great value for studying psychology. Perhaps my critical tone is assumed in order to counteract the attitude that many experimentalists have that their method is the only one. My goal is not to reject the experimental method but rather to call attention to some of the limitations of both the method and the manner in which it is commonly employed in research (Jung 1971, p. 1).

That our analysis is correct can be seen by the fact that Rosenthal

(1966) proposes several methods of executing "purer" experiments. One way of insuring the separation between experimenter and subject would be to have some measure of experimenter expectancy effects. Experiments could employ expectancy control groups in which expectancy effects are maximized. This group could then be compared with the normal experimental and control groups to provide an index of the effects of expectancy occurring in an experiment. Another way of controlling expectancy effects would be to employ a random sample of experimenters instead of a single experimenter. This procedure would eliminate bias in any one particular direction. Finally, Rosenthal proposes that the effects could be circumvented entirely by the use of automated data collection.

One other way in which traditional experimental psychology approaches the problems raised by research on the interaction between experimenter and subject is to attempt to dispel the research as insignificant. Such psychologists appear to fear a revolution in psychology. Levy, for example, states:

> For without such a taxonomy and the sampling of situations it would permit, it is impossible to make any generalizations about the seriousness of the experimenter bias effect as an epistemological threat to psychology on the basis of successes or failures in demonstrating it in particular instances. . . . Further, by far the most rewarding stance toward the experimenter bias effect is likely to be as an exemplar of some theoretically important class of phenomena [Levy 1969, p. 276].

Barber and Silver even more strongly deny the importance of this research:

> It is our opinion that approximately 19 of the 31 pertinent studies that were available for critical analysis as of early 1967 did not clearly demonstrate an experimenter bias effect [Barber and Silver 1968a, p. 2].

> Although there is some suggestive evidence in 2 of 31 extant studies, the investigations in this area are not as yet sufficient to conclude that a revolution is imperative in psychological research [Barber and Silver 1968b, pp. 61–62].

THE APPROACH OF TRANSITIONAL PSYCHOLOGY

I wish to define transitional psychology within the bounds of the problem of this paper—the meaning of the interaction between

experimenter and subject in psychological research. Within the
scope of this problem, transitional experimental psychology attempts to preserve the structure of a psychological experiment
while moving to interpret that structure as a social interaction in
which the interaction is bidirectional. That is, *both* the experimenter and the subject are viewed as active, as experiencing meaning in the situation of the experiment. Such psychologists tend to
be revolutionary; that is, they move to revolve psychology, to op-
pose the status quo. Yet these same psychologists often do not have
an alternative vision of psychology. In that sense, they are revolutionary rather than rebels. The rebel opposes, not merely to over-
throw, but because he has an alternative and truer vision (May
1972).

Neil Friedman, in *The Social Nature of Psychological Research*,
strongly calls for viewing the psychological experiment as a trans-
ient dyadic relationship. If this situation is realized, he sees far
reaching implications for the scientific status of psychology:

> Psychologists have accepted a normative definition of the
> "clean" psychological experiment, rather than an operational
> definition based on what is observed to go on in the psycho-
> logical experiment.
>
> Now, after looking instead of legislating, we are beginning to
> have some evidence as to what does go on in a psychological
> experiment as opposed to what is supposed to go on. The
> difference is anything but indescribable. It is systematically
> and intricately related to the fact that the psychological exper-
> iment is a social interaction [Friedman 1968, p. 159].

This quotation shows us that a shift in attitude is occurring. This
shift can be understood as a drawing together of the everyday life
situation and the experimental situation. Suppose a psychologist
wants to do an experiment in verbal learning. He has already
worked out the experiment on paper. The first thing that he has to
do is to enlist the help of others by asking them to be subjects in
this experiment. This little gesture is extremely significant. A
physicist does not do this. A chemist does not do this. A biologist
rarely has to do this. The psychologist who *recognizes* that inherently he has to do this construes an experiment as a specialized
contractual situation. The implicit contract of the traditional psychology experiment is that the subject will be treated as an object
and he will, insofar as possible, act like an object. To be treated as
an object means that the subject is not considered to have a past or

to be oriented toward a future. Again, there is nothing ethically wrong with such a contract *if* the subject is informed of the agreement. We have learned much about the objectlike dimensions of man through such an attitude of experimentation. In the quotation above, however, the nature of the contract has changed. The contract proposed by Friedman presupposes that two persons are involved in an experiment and that the experiment involves a human relation between the person called the Experimenter and the person called the Subject.

The psychological experiment as a social interaction means that two people come together for a specified purpose. There are *two people*, neither a person and an object, nor a person and a physiological organism, nor a person and a machine, but precisely two persons. Persons have a history. Persons experience meaning. Persons are future oriented. What holds for the experimenter as a person must hold for the subject as a person. Then, the occurrences *between* the experimenter and the subject are of fundamental importance.

I am moving too rapidly here, and going beyond what Friedman actually states. Friedman does not recognize that a shift in attitude means a shift in the very meaning of experimentation. In spite of the fact that Friedman strongly criticizes the current view of the philosophy of psychological experimentation, it is very strange that the methodological suggestions offered by Friedman are within the attitude of traditional experimental psychology. That is why we have to understand his contribution as transitional. He does not know where to take his own understanding. He has no explicit vision. Thus, he suggests having representatively sampled data collectors, or filming data collection to tap the social interaction, or use of post-hoc methods of controlling the interaction. These suggestions are nearly identical with those of Rosenthal. Friedman has one foot in tradition and one foot in the future, but has no clear vision of that future.

Let us look at the deeper probings of another transitional psychologist. Sidney Jourard (1968) recognizes the bidirectionality of interaction in an experiment. He has tried to ask how the subject is active in the experiment. He argues that the subject sees the experimenter as the person with the power, often a trickster and a manipulator. The subject often handles this dehumanization by lying or by responding at random in an experiment. This sort of subject is concerned about the meaning of the experiment for him. He wants to learn something about his life. He would also like to know the experimenter as a person. He would like to be able to trust the experimenter. He would disclose himself if the experimenter would do the same. Jourard has worked intensively with this understanding:

> And I knew that many subjects falsified their performances in psychological experiments. And so the hypothesis occurred to me that, perhaps all of published psychology is grounded on the false disclosure of people who are treating the researcher the way he treats them—behavior evokes its own kind [Jourard 1971, p. 196].

This approach to psychology could be called revolutionary in that it overthrows the limitations of the former psychology by undertaking a different attitude toward research. This attitude is subject centered rather than just experimenter centered. However, it denies the power of the experimenter in its attempt to equalize the experimenter and the subject.

The procedure of many of Jourard's studies involves an initial interview session with the subject. This interview consists of a mutually revealing dialogue concerning certain personal issues such as aspects of sexual experience. Then the subjects participate in an experiment of self-disclosure among themselves. One of Jourard's coworkers describes the effect of such a procedure:

> The type of relationship established between the experimenter and subject is an important situational determinant of the subject's self-disclosing behavior, as reported in questionnaires and in actual dialogue. When the experimenter was transparent with subjects, subjects tended to trust her more. Reported themselves to be more willing to be ... open on intimate topics at a deeply personal level with her and with other subjects, than did subjects when the experimenter remained an impersonal interviewer, or an anonymous "other" [quoted in Jourard 1971, p. 111].

The self-disclosure approach to experimentation has the appearance of full participation of experimenter and subject. Both people are seen as people with a "world." That is, the experimental situation is not temporally isolated from the ongoing lives of the participants. However, what this approach does not recognize is that the "world" of the experimenter is not the same as the "world" of the subject. The experimenter brings the specialized world of his discipline to the experiment. He has read and thought a lot about some aspect of psychology. He has formulated a hypothesis. The subject brings a less specialized world of meaning to the experiment. These two "worlds" of meaning cannot be equalized without the subject being subtly manipulated by the unrecognized deception. He is manipulated unknowingly because the power of the experimenter is formally denied but actually executed under the guise of nutrient power (May 1972). The experimenter denies that he is the powerful person in the situation, or if he admits his power he implies that the subject will learn about his life from the experiment. For this reason, the approach of self-disclosure is a transitional stage in the meaning of investigation in psychology. The direction of this particular transitional approach often confuses therapeutic, humanistic aims with the project of understanding man in a systematic manner.

A VISIONARY APPROACH: HUMAN PSYCHOLOGY

What I wish to do in this section of the paper is to begin to explicate the direction of a human psychology, focusing on the meaning of research for such an approach to psychology. This explication is not merely a matter of speculation. We can point to the actual beginnings of such a research psychology.

An approach to psychology as a human science begins with a ground clearing, a reexamination of the familiar ground of psychology and of science in order to make explicit the presuppositions which found and provide direction for traditional psychology. This ground clearing helps in the understanding of the merits and the limitations of psychology as a natural science. For example, Merleau-Ponty (1963) examined the meaning of behavior as understood within the tradition of reflex psychology and was able to show that a reflex notion of behavior limits the understanding of behavior either to being a thing or to being an idea. Rather, when a person is behaving or is present to behaving it is more appropriate to speak of behavior as a form. A human psychology must learn to deal with form. Giorgi (1971a) made explicit the fact that since the inception of psychology as a science there has been a current of psychology as a natural science and a current of psychology as a human science. The former has dominated but the latter has persisted so that the approach to psychology fostered by such people as Brentano, McDougall, and Stern prefigured the development of a systematic human science psychology. Van Kaam (1966) examined the foundations of science as a human activity and, within that framework, has suggested a definition of psychology and the possible direction of its development.

Simultaneously with the redefinition of the ground of psychology much work has concentrated on methodological limitations of traditional psychology. Traditional psychologists themselves are extremely active in these critiques. I have traced the meaning of these critiques in an earlier article (Sardello 1971). The difficulty with methodological critiques stemming from the natural science tradition of psychology is that these critiques are *only* methodological. They do not bring to the question of method an understanding of the importance of foundational questions of the nature asked, for example, by Merleau-Ponty, Giorgi, and Van Kaam referred to above, but rather seek to alter method without understanding that method flows from approach. While the following considerations are also methodological they flow from an immersion in basic foundational questions. The following considerations are not meant to suggest an alteration in methodology for methodology's sake. Rather, these considerations of method concretize a research stance necessary when one confronts the image of man as a person rather than as a natural object.

The image of man as a person begins with a very situated, concrete presence to a person. This presence is given as a fundamental intuition, an awakening of the imagination in which a person is revealed as a center of life. This awakening occurs through a concrete bodily presence to another person in which I realize that the other as a center of life participates in the same kind of life as mine. In this fundamental intuition the inexhaustibility of personhood is presented. A mastery of such a mystery is impossible. This is not a conclusion or a deduction but is given in the very presence to personhood. The discipline of a human science psychology begins with the care and fostering of this imagination. The discipline of human science psychology demands that we keep close to the "soul" of things. Method, then, is primarily a disciplining of the imagination so that the images of the person given through the various dimensions of behaving such as speaking, thinking, sensing, and so on, can be given a sustained systematic conceptualization. The movement toward conceptualization is not an abstract theorizing but rather is an analogical presentation of the image. By analogy I mean that the systematic work of articulating a human psychology must participate in the original intuition or presence to persons while moving to conceptual clarity. The achievement of this kind of speaking in psychology requires great talent. The psychologist must be close enough to phenomena to be a participant-observer and at the same time he must be able to stand far enough from the phenomenon to avoid being engulfed. As a concrete example of the kind of speaking we are considering here, examine this short understanding of the behavior of laughing:

> Laughing breaks out of the body, erupts, takes over and infects. Any attempt to control is fruitless. The body doubles up, straightens, the head goes back sharply, or forward just as sharply. It moves as it pleases, out of control. Tears fall as the sound of laughter gush forth from the body. It seems to make no sense.
>
> We become sense-less in laughing. Perspective disappears, lights dim and brighten at will, there is no horizon. We lose balance, taste, touch, and smell. Time just does not exist for the laughing person. There is no weight, no burden, no hunger, no fear, no past, and no future. There is only the laughing. This is the full and complete abandonment to laughter.
>
> It has beckoned and teased us into its grips and there to wring from us the conflicts of our embodiment. As human beings we are embodied and simultaneously have a body. In laughing we give up the awareness of that paradox.
>
> Only in the rhythm of the laughing is any control possible. It is a rhythm inherent in the laughter itself. It rises and falls, moves from one person to another and back again. The body grabs a breath before it can return. It is in this moment that we grasp a quick sight of an absurd vision in fantasy or an absurd vision of another person and quickly the laughter recaptures us. Our bodies give up their strength to feed the laughing. They pour and pour until we are weak and sore, until we have completely lost our posture. The laughter is in complete control (Brown 1973, pp. 5–6).

The phenomenological imagination guides this understanding—phenomenological because the understanding moves from within the life of the phenomenon itself and does not seek to explain the phenomenon in terms of controllable variables.

The description above also illustrates what we mean when we say that in human science psychology a disciplining of the imagination is demanded. Otherwise, this approach to psychology becomes esthetical and impressionistic. Strasser speaks well to this difficulty:

> The phenomenologist who has lost his theoretical bearings is

exposed also to the temptation of taking refuge in the esthetical. To a certain extent it is easy to see why. The experiences which this phenomenologist describes in an impressionistic fashion are fortuitous snatches of reality. If he were to express them in dry and prosaic terms, their insignificant character would show itself glaringly [Strasser 1963, pp. 298–99].

Method can provide the proper disciplining of the imagination as long as it does not become an end in itself as has become the case in traditional psychology (Romanyshyn 1971). Method in traditional psychology is usually communicated in the following form: (1) statement of the problem; (2) statement of the hypothesis; (3) procedure; (4) results; (5) discussion. How would this form be altered if method becomes seen as a disciplining of the imagination?

From problem to wonder. Traditional research in psychology begins with a statement of a problem. Psychology as a human science does not arise so much out of the context of *logical* problems situated within paradigmatic topical areas with the demand of a solution. Rather, human science psychology arises out of simple wonder in the face of the phenomena of the lived world. Jaspers speaks of this originary intuition:

> Alternatively, we can stay close to the "soul of things": their psychic quality. No interpretations are made but we open our sense to living experience, to the perception of the inward element in things. Goethe's "pure reflective gaze" accompanies a contemplation of form which does not know but sees, and this vision of the inward life of things forms the substance of our union with the world. This union may be of unlimited depth; it comes as a gift with every step we take and cannot be methodically developed; it remains bound up with everything that reveals itself to a receptive attitude and an unfeigned preparedness to accept [Jaspers 1913, p. 256].

Jaspers does not mean to say that the task of human scientific observation ends in intuition, but it is the point at which it begins, as we have already stressed. Instead of beginning with definitions, we begin in wonder, and this wonder pervades and influences the research tasks of psychology. For example, Giorgi (1971b) and Colazzi (1971) begin within the stance of traditional research in the psychology of verbal learning, and employ research procedures which focus on the meaning of learning for the persons engaged as subjects in such learning. Stevick began her research on the phenomenon of anger not by assuming an understanding of anger and then asking how certain variables relate to anger, but questions from within:

> Since it is in his everyday living that man experiences anger, psychological experimentation should turn to the lived-world to investigate how anger is experienced and distinguished, the kinds of situations out of which it arises, its distinguishing behavioral and experiential constituents. This paper proposes to find a description of the experience of anger which will encompass the phenomenon and to answer the questions: 1) What does it mean to experience anger? 2) What is anger? [Stevick 1971, p. 135].

Similarly, C. Fischer (1971) breaks through the current arguments for and against the maintenance of the value of privacy as it relates to the profession of psychology by beginning her research in the following form:

> Our answer to the question "what is privacy?" will not be a simple one; it must specify that matrix of human intertwinings with circumstances. That is, our description of privacy must take the form of: privacy is, when: (such-and-such a matrix exists). From this we can then point to both its desirable and undesirable aspects [C. Fischer 1971, p. 149].

All of these researches share the common origin point of slowing down to engage in a contemplative presence to the phenomenon in question in order to begin proper research questioning with a listening, a hearing, and an understanding.

From hypothesis to meaning. A research in psychology traditionally moves from the statement of the problem to the statement of a hypothesis. Fraisse speaks of the establishment of hypotheses in a manner which implicitly recognizes the human action of the researcher:

> Hypothesization is the creative phase of experimental reasoning in which the worker imagines the relation which could exist between two facts. The setting up of the hypothesis is the work of thought. It differs from the phases of active observation or of experimentation in that the worker is apparently doing nothing, but it is this moment which gives his work its original value [Fraisse 1968, p. 108].

The formation of an hypothesis is too selective for research in human science psychology. Rather than select one possible relation given with an image and form it into an if . . . then relation, human science research allows all the possible meanings inherent in the image to begin to reveal their meaning. For example, there is a great deal of experimental work in traditional psychology of perception relating to the Mueller-Lyer figure, the perceptual figure which consists of two metrically equal horizontal lines, one line between "arrowheads" and the other between "wings." All traditional research assumes this figure to have one meaning, that of a perceptual illusion. Investigators then utilize this assumed singular meaning to explore a wide variety of variables. Alapack countered this trend in a fundamental manner. He began his research within the stance of wonder spoken of above, seeking to understand the various meanings such a figure could have for persons, and discovered that the Mueller-Lyer figure provides multiple possible meanings which each person resolves in a thematic meaning for him. One possibility is that metrically equal lines are perceived as unequal. But the figure was also thematized in many other ways by the persons in the experiment. For example, when asked to "Describe what you are seeing," one person stated the following:

> It looks like arrows pointing in two different directions. They also look like some type of road sign. The bottom is just the opposite of the top. It looks like a floor and wall where it meets. A child, a small child drawing a dog or some sort of animal without a head [Alapack 1971, p. 35].

The task of the researcher working within a human science stance is to allow all possible meanings to reveal themselves, irrespective of whether they might at first appear to be contrary to one another. The investigator operates on the basis of a fundamental faith that a unity of meaning will eventually unfold.

From procedure to unfolding of form. In traditional psychological research, procedure involves the specification of the experimental design, the statement of independent and dependent variables, and the statements of controls. Within the context of wonder embodied in a specific dimension through imagination, the procedure with subjects as persons is no longer oriented toward removing the experimental situation from the ongoing life of the participant. Instead, the research participant is invited to thematize the ongoing form of his life along a certain dimension, a form in relation to the researcher's imaginative questioning. For example, Stevick

(1971) in her investigation of anger proceeded by asking her participants the following question: "Try to remember one of the last times you were angry and tell me about the situation, how you felt and acted, and what you said" (p. 135).

What must be understood is that in answering such a question the whole life of the person is involved, coalescing in that moment in the form of a dimension of anger. It is more appropriate to think of this research as a research into the meaning of being angry than a study of anger. The use of nouns to describe psychological reality conveys the impression of a reified entity rather than the unfolding character of life that the psychologist seeks to begin to understand.

From data analysis to qualitative synthetic explication. Traditional research in psychology which employs numerical statistical analyses not only provides a proof of the hypothesis but also convinces and persuades the community of psychological researchers that the researcher in question has some insight. The rhetoric of human science psychology, because it focuses on the lived meaning of psychological phenomena, must be qualitative rather than quantitative (Giorgi, 1971a). This qualitative rhetoric takes the form of staying with the wholeness of the qualitative data and carefully explicating, drawing out the meaning of the behavior-experience, remaining always true to the protocol report of the participant. Additional examples of this kind of explication can be found in research on decision making by Cloonan (1971), in an understanding of anxiety by W. Fischer (1970), and in a research into human learning by Giorgi (1975).

ETHICAL IMPLICATIONS

We can now provide a clearer understanding of the ethics involved in psychological research.

Where research removes a person from his on-going life situation and places him in a presumably "valueless" situation, ethical issues are an especially important question. Ethics here requires that measures be taken to ensure that the experimental situation, in its removal of the person from his life-context where he is capable of his own decisions and responsibilities, does not violate the fundamental humanity of the person. Traditional psychological researchers should be obliged, at a minimum, to protect the personhood of a subject by forewarning him that he is about to be treated as a natural object.

Transitional psychology raises even more complex ethical issues than traditional psychological research. In this approach to psychology there is an ideological commitment to humanity, but the procedures of research are usually bound to a natural science methodology. The researchers within this approach might feel that they are quite humane while the quasi-therapeutic atmosphere generated by their ideological concerns merely conceals the same basic fact that we find in traditional research—the subject is treated as a natural object. Thus, here again, the ethical experimenter should inform the research participant that he will expose himself to naturalistic manipulation.

These ethical problems evaporate with the approach to research we have termed human science psychology. A radical human psychology is simultaneously a *fundamental* ethical stance toward man. There is no need for an ethical imperative that these participants be informed about the manipulative dangers in the research they submit to because this approach begins with the dictum that the participant's experience is the subject matter of the research. To ask a person to describe a situation in which he has participated is to recognize his being a person—a historical, meaning-giving, meaning-receiving, becoming, value-oriented, individual. The participant's life is "in-formed" in that he is asked to share his lived experience which, with the respectful presence of the researcher, provides the opportunity and the freedom for the participant to contemplate the meaning of one of the dimensions of his life. A violation of the person here would be a contamination of the research.

REFERENCES

Alapack, R. J. 1971. The physiognomy of the Mueller-Lyer figure. *J. Phenomenol. Psychol.* 2:27–49.

Barber, T. X. and Silver, M. J. 1968a. Fact, fiction, and the experimenter bias effect. *Psychol. Bullet. Monograph*, 70:1–29.

———. 1968b. Pitfalls in data analysis and interpretation: a reply to Rosenthal. *Psychol. Bullet. Monograph* 70:48–62.

Binder, A., McConnell, D., and Sjoholm, N. A. 1957. Verbal conditioning as a function of experimenter characteristics. *J. Abnormal and Soc. Psychol.* 55:309–14.

Brown, R. F. 1973. The phenomenon is laughing. Unpublished manuscript. University of Dallas.

Cloonan, T. F. 1971. Experiential and behavioral aspects of decision making. In *Duquesne studies in phenomenological psychology* vol. 1, ed. A. Giorgi, W. F. Fischer, and R. von Eckartsberg. Pittsburgh: Duquesne University Press.

Colaizzi, P. F. Analysis of the learner's perception of learning material at various phases of a learning process. *Duquesne studies in phenomenological psychology*, vol. 1, ed. A. Giorgi, W. F. Fischer, and R. von Eckartsberg. Pittsburgh: Duquesne University Press.

Fischer, C. T. 1971. Toward the structure of privacy: implications for psychological assessment. In *Duquesne studies in phenomenological psychology*, vol. 1, ed. A. Giorgi, W. F. Fischer, and R. von Eckartsberg. Pittsburgh: Duquesne University Press.

Fischer, W. F. 1970. The faces of anxiety. *J. Phenomenol. Psychol.* 1:31–49.

Fraisse, P. 1968. *Experimental psychology: History and method.* New York: Basic Books.

Friedman, N. 1968. *The social nature of psychological research.* New York: Basic Books.

Giorgi, A. 1971a. *Psychology as a human science.* New York: Harper and Row.

———. 1971b. A phenomenonological approach to the problem of meaning and serial learning. In *Duquesne studies in phenomenological psychology*, vol. 1, ed. A. Girogi, W. F. Fischer, R. von Eckartsberg. Pittsburg: Duquesne University Press.

———. 1975. An application of phenomenological method in psychology. In *Duquesne studies in phenomenological psychology*, vol. 2, ed. A. Giorgi, C. T. Fischer, and E. L. Murray. Pittsburgh: Duquesne University Press.

Jaspers, K. 1913. *General psychopathology.* Chicago: University of Chicago Press.

Jourard, S. 1968. *Disclosing man to himself.* New York: Van Nostrand Reinhold.

———. 1971. *Research in self-disclosure.* New York: Wiley.

Jung, J. 1971. *The experimenter's dilemma.* New York: Harper and Row.

Kagan, J. 1967. On the need for relativism. *Am. Psychologist* 22:131–42.

Kelman, H. C. 1967. Human use of human subjects: the problem of deception in social psychological experiments. *Psychological Bullet.* 67:1–11.

Koch, S. 1969. Psychology cannot be a coherent science. *Psychology Today* (September) 3:14.

Levy, L. 1969. On experimenter bias fact and fiction. *Psychol. Bullet.* 71:276.

Lyons, J. 1970. The hidden dialogue in experimental research. *J. Phenomenol. Psychol.* 1:19–31.

Masling, J. 1960. The effects of warm and cold interaction of the interpretation of a projective protocol. *J. Projective Techniques* 21:377–83.

May, R. 1972. Power and innocence. New York: W. W. Norton.

McGuigan, F. J. 1963. The experimenter: a neglected stimulus object. *Psychol. Bullet.* 60:421–28.

Merleau-Ponty, M. 1963. *The structure of behavior.* Boston: Beacon Press.

Romanyshyn, R. 1971. Method and meaning in psychology: the method has been the message. *J. Phenomenol. Psychol.* 2:93–115.

Rosenthal, R. 1966. *Experimenter effects in behavioral research.* New York: Appleton-Century-Crofts.

Rosenthal, R. and Fode, K. 1960. The effect of experimenter bias on the performance of the albino rat. Unpublished manuscript. University of North Dakota.

Sardello, R. J. 1971. The role of direct experience in contemporary psychology—a critical review. In *Duquesne studies in phenomenological psychology*, vol. 1, ed. A. Giorgi, W. F. Fischer, and R. von Eckartsberg. Pittsburgh: Duquesne University Press.

Schultz, D. P. 1969. The human subject in psychological research. *Psychol. Bullet.* 71:214–27.

Stevick, E. L. 1971. An empirical investigation of the experience of anger. *Duquesne studies in phenomenological psychology*, vol. 1, ed. A. Giorgi, W. F. Fischer, and R. von Eckartsberg. Pittsburgh: Duquesne University Press.

Strasser, S. 1963. *Phenomenology and the human sciences.* Pittsburgh: Duquesne University Press.

Underwood, B. J. 1957. *Psychological research.* New York: Appleton-Century-Crofts.

Van Kaam, A. 1966. *Existential foundations of psychology.* Pittsburgh: Duquesne University Press.

12.

On the Way from Olympus: Questions and Responses

CONSTANCE T. FISCHER
and STANLEY L. BRODSKY

QUESTION: *Isn't it harmful to some clients to be told everything?* For example, suppose a man were turned down for promotion because his supervisees rated him as power-oriented and insensitive to their situation?—wouldn't he function still less well if he were confronted with those actual judgements?

RESPONSE: We certainly agree that confrontation is not part of the Prometheus principle. We also agree that the human service agent must address himself to the clients' own understandings; the client is not truly informed nor can he or she fully participate in decision making unless he and his collaborator are speaking the same language. In this case, the adjectives "power oriented" and "insensitive," to be helpful to the personnel officer or to the employee, would have to be presented first through concrete instances. These could be shared with the employee easily enough, along with the information that these instances have been experienced by some of his supervisees as insensitive to their situation and even as evidence of his or her caring more for personal power than for their welfare.

QUESTION: *But what if this employee weren't ready to handle even that sort of discussion?* Isn't the professional obliged to decide how much the client can deal with?

RESPONSE: Yes, the professional indeed is obliged to consider the probable significance of "information" to his client, and he must provide adequate preparation, timing, and appropriate wording. He also must be prepared to explore with the client constructive, concrete, viable avenues out of his current difficulty. However, clients just are not as fragile as professional helpers often assume. Clients' strength depends in part on knowing the criteria of success—the rules and score of the game—which the professional should be able to clarify. Moreover, if we continue to treat people as fragile and needy of external direction, they are more likely to live out that self-fulfilling prophecy.

QUESTION: *But what if the client denies the validity of your information?* Suppose a psychiatric patient insists that contrary to his activities report he *has* been on time to his laundry assignment and he has *not* been disruptive in education therapy?

RESPONSE: Right. Sharing your information with this patient allows him to correct false records. If it turns out not to be a mistake, but a difference of opinion between the patient and the therapeutic activities workers, then you can clarify for the patient just what criteria are being employed as well as that ward staff are in serious communication with other staff. Concomitantly, the workers become more careful and reflective in their observations and reports.

QUESTION: Doesn't all this sharing of information and opportunities for rebuttal open the door to challenging the particular human service program itself? The psychiatric patient in the above example could challenge the usefulness of "therapeutic" activities. He could charge that the hospital's criteria of improvement are in fact signs of submission to authority, of loss of initiative and individuality. In short, *doesn't the principle of informed participation risk a disruption of the human services delivery system* whenever you run into a client who is in bad faith—defensive, paranoid, militant, or whatever?

RESPONSE: A critical function of the Prometheus principle is to allow systems to be questioned. Whether or not he is precise in his challenge, it is the "wearer of the shoe who eventually knows when it doesn't fit." If systems are to be accountable, criticisms by clients should be taken very seriously, although not always literally. Moreover, if the client is to take a program seriously himself, he must ask his questions and know that they are truly considered. Collaboration—laboring together—requires mutual trust especially in the face of uncertain outcome. This position, however, does not imply that the human services worker allows the client to push him around. At some point, he may simply specify what options are available at the moment, what the probable outcomes are, and so on. He can be honest about the imperfections of his service while still offering to do what he can within the given contingencies.

QUESTION: Ah ha! Isn't that the kicker in this principle of informed participation? That with the impossibility of absolute prescriptions for how to do it, *there's always the potential copout* of "But my own hands are tied," "I only work here," and so on.
RESPONSE: Yes! The collaborative approach to human services is indeed "laborious." Prometheans must repeatedly ask themselves whether they are carrying out the *spirit* of the principle or only parading in its trappings. But at least as the principle of "the client as collaborator" becomes increasingly better known, each practitioner will have an additional conscience/consciousness in his colleagues.

QUESTION: About the chapters in this book: *aren't some of them one-sided in their criticisms of traditional practices?*
RESPONSE: Probably. Even the authors don't agree with one another about all of the critiques or all of the specific suggestions. But disagreements themselves have served as rallying points for discussion of basic issues and for reaching consensual conclusions. Also, even where an author hasn't presented the "other side," his criticisms may be valid.

QUESTION: *Isn't it true that in most cases a client's files are too technical for him to understand* even if he did have access to them—for example, the records of a mental retardate or a child, or a psychological assessment?
RESPONSE: Right now, that's certainly the case. So the practice of opening files to the individual client necessitates changes in the ways records are kept. Educational, psychological, psychiatric, and institutional reports should describe actual incidents and contexts rather than merely make judgmental notations. Wherever possible, only everyday language should be used. Where portions of technical terms cannot be avoided, as in medical charts, then someone should be readily available to the client to explore the record's meanings and implications. These principles should hold even in

those cases where the client is unable to read or fully understand any kind of report; his relatives, guardian, or other advocate are then the ones who require genuine access to records for the client's sake.

QUESTION: *Doesn't traditional practice oblige a professional to keep a colleague's documents on a client confidential between the two professionals?* For example, wouldn't it be unethical for a college registrar to show an applicant a negative letter of "recommendation" written by his high school counselor?

RESPONSE: The counselor should be informed in advance that the student has right of access to his file, including the letter of recommendation. Until the Prometheus principle becomes broadly practiced, evaluation forms or other requests for information should contain printed advisement about the client's right of access to the document. Actually, both state and federal courts are now upholding this right regardless of the author's or recipient's original understanding.

QUESTION: *But if a human service professional knows that the client may see what he writes, isn't he likely to tone down his report—so as not to offend, or risk being sued?* Isn't it possible that a parole officer, social worker, or teacher, for example, in writing a letter of recommendation would state only established fact and not hazard his negative opinions? *Wouldn't reports thus be compromised, perhaps even becoming useless?*

RESPONSE: Perhaps. Even now we all occasionally read such noncommital, timorous evaluations written by our colleagues. In the end, the success of informed participation depends on the integrity and courage of the individual practitioner. In this case, however, we see decreased information as preferable to unchallenged judgements. Moreover, if clients are to profit from evaluations, they must know what impressions they are making so as to begin correction of missteps. And in discussion of the evaluation a more refined, contextualized understanding is often achieved, which is still more helpful for planning. For example, discussion may reveal that a client is "unmotivated" *only* when he feels that authorities are trying to set his goals for him. At any rate, an evaluator will be fair if he shares his impressions with the client and amends his report to include the latter's reactions. In so doing, he also demonstrates responsible action, and eliminates grounds for legal suit. Perhaps equally important is the evaluator's chance to correct and develop his particular skills as he receives feedback on his judgments. For example, the client might report: "Well, maybe I wasn't very 'industrious' in your course, but frankly you didn't seem very excited about the content either"; or "It certainly wasn't your fault that I didn't stick with that job—your firmness helped me to last as long as I did."

QUESTION: *But won't the professional's evaluation carry more weight with his colleagues than the client's rebuttal?* Also, won't many human service workers just go through the motions of respecting the client's opinions in their addenda?

RESPONSE: No doubt that often will continue to be the case. Again, the old unilateral power structure remains wherever the full *spirit* of the Prometheus principle is lacking. Still, in many instances just "going through the motions" affords greater client advisement and participation than before. As for self-protective professional versions of the client's modifications of a report: as always, readers will judge the author's orientation, competence, and biases in order to come to their own conclusions about the client. The ideal form of client collaboration in written reports, however, is never that of prosecutor-defendant. Instead, the professional's addendum should note that he now agrees with specified client modifications of his initial write-up, and they have agreed to disagree about such-and-such. In many instances, the client himself is the best person to write this second stage of the document. In our experience, in the course of such collaboration, numerous disagreements dissolve as the participants come to identify their respective assumptions and perspectives.

QUESTION: *What if your supervisor won't allow clients to be collaborators in the human service program?*

RESPONSE: Surely you should neither rise up in sudden revolt nor excuse yourself from pursuing Promethean interests. In our experience the most reasonable and effective approach has been to try out informed participation in safe increments until one's professional peers and superiors know firsthand that the procedures really are rather commonsensical and harmless. For example, one office, without setting a longrange plan, in fact first agreed to tell clients whenever they could not write a favorable recommendation for job training. Then they found themselves discussing their reasons with the client. Later, they were discussing with all clients what they planned to write, making some revisions on the spot. Finally, all these procedures came to be routinely concluded by the clients' initialing on the final report.

Where a critical incident arises and there's no time for gradualism, as in the case of a medical patient whose doctor has not supplied him with full information about the dangers of an immanent operation, then knowledge of legal precedents can be quite persuasive to job superiors. Federal and state judicial decisions as well as legislation have built a substantial case for informed participation in diverse areas: college admissions folders, medical patients' "right to know," psychological reports on juveniles accused of delinquency, psychological and educational records of mental retardates, public school records, credit bureau dossiers, and presentence court reports. Clients in many areas have a good chance of winning civil suits for access to information that is used in making decisions about them.

QUESTION: *Then informed participation isn't just another passing fad?*
RESPONSE: No, it certainly is not. As outlined in the "Why Now?" chapter, it is a deep and widespread grassroots as well as professional response to our permanently technologized society. Although this book will be historically dated by its particular examples, we believe that its principle is both inevitable and necessary. Naming that principle (variously as Promethean, as informed participation, and as client collaboration) serves to promote implementation.

QUESTION: *Isn't it dangerous to throw off older traditions? And how do you know that a particular effort to assure client participation will work?*
RESPONSE: Agreed. We do not advocate merely "doing one's own thing." The human service agent is responsible not just to the client, but to agency, self, and the larger society. He must respect the traditions of all if he is to be constructive. We say this not only in a spirit of cooperation, but in the knowledge that traditions develop over time and represent as much accumulated wisdom as they do errors and vested interest. We might also point out that according to Greek mythology Prometheus' brother, Epimetheus (meaning "hindsight") was assigned to share with him the task of creating the earthly world.

Much was learned through Epimetheus's acknowledgement of his mistakes, especially those arising from impetuosity. But such knowledge went nowhere without Prometheus's daring forethought and innovation. In short, as we try out new ways of assuring genuine client participation, we must continually evaluate the efforts and revise where necessary; but we must also seek a creative future.

QUESTION: The practice of informed participation seems to be based on a lot of common sense, use of everyday language, giving up of the power of privileged professionalism, and so on. *Doesn't the Prometheus principle threaten the existence of the established professions?*
RESPONSE: Yes and no. "Yes," in that human service professionals can no longer wield unilateral power. As they collaborate with clients, the latter will learn more quickly that the professionals' opinions are not beyond question. Specialists' credentials will not be overvalued into surrounding areas of life. And demonstrated competence will count more than academic degree. Those who are afraid of these developments are indeed threatened.

But "no," the practice of informed participation does not threaten the existence of the human service professions themselves. Daring to be ordinary in one's relations with clients does not supplant rigorous training in skills, knowledge, and theory. While disciplinary boundaries need not be the self-protective barriers often raised in the past, there is an inescapable necessity for persons who accumulate, ponder, disseminate and utilize various segments of ever-increasing information. In short, we continue to need well-trained specialists. The professions will, however, somewhat redefine their research, theories, and service roles as they enter into greater dialogue with their clients.

QUESTION: *Isn't it true that there are only certain kinds of clients that can actually be brought into informed participation procedures?* Surely a regressed schizophrenic, a brain-damaged patient, a child, or even some severely depressed or anxious persons would be incapable of responsible collaboration. And aren't there certain settings, like prisons, where you would be foolish to trust the clients' remarks? In other words, wasn't the Prometheus principle really formulated for college counselors, personnel workers, and other agents working with essentially normal adults?
RESPONSE: No. Informed participation is a guiding principle for *all* service relations with fellow humans. To whatever degree you assume *beforehand* that your client cannot participate actively in directing his own life, you are perpetuating his dehumanization. Your obligation is to tax yourself to the fullest to create ways of maximizing the client's understanding and independent cooperation. Yes, of course it's a heck of a lot easier with certain clients. But success

at increasing a client's self-reliance and informed participation beyond what it was before you met is not only possible but greatly rewarding at all levels of client involvement.

QUESTION: *Doesn't the professional often honestly know better than the client what is best for him?* After all, the professional has the advantages of objective distance, experience with many similar instances, special training, and so on. How can the client actually participate in such aspects as program decisions and evaluation of the agency's helpfulness?

RESPONSE: Certainly the human service agent has critical skills, background, and information to offer the client. The Prometheus principle simply asserts that the agent should share, in terms relevant to the client, the information, goals, chances, options, and so on involved in decision making. If the client is to experience himself as, and concommitantly act as, "healthy," as able to utilize resources effectively and actively, then he must in fact become engaged in these activities. The human service agent is a knowledgable, caring consultant and advisor, but never strictly an autocrat or caretaker. Besides, it is the client who knows whether various proposals appear to him as viable and desirable. Without that basic point of agreement, which requires collaborative exploration, the client is less likely to be helped or helpful.

QUESTION: *Doesn't the principle of informed participation fit only certain theoretical orientations* such as humanistic or existential ones, or perhaps just plain pragmatism?

RESPONSE: Some of us feel that "third force" psychology holds the best promise of a comprehensive understanding of man, an understanding that allows for scientific observation of regularity and yet takes into account that people are not like other objects of science; that is, people act purposively and in a context of personal meanings. However, in fact the authors and editors of this book differ widely in theoretical orientation. What we agree on is that we must start with the client in his given situation, refer our understanding of that to our theoretical conceptions when necessary, but then return to the concrete level of the client and his daily concerns. Theories and professionalism must not take precedence over effective communication and collaboration at the level of the client's personal understandings. Whatever our other beliefs we all share a commitment to maximizing the individual's possibilities for active participation in determining his own and his community's future.

QUESTION: *Don't some clients expect and even want you to make their decisions for them?*
RESPONSE: Yes. And of course there also are emergencies when a parent, doctor or policeman, for example, does have to make instant unilateral decisions. But the principle of informed participation posits not only the client's right to participate if he wishes, but the necessity of his participation if he is to grow. Whatever a person's age or condition, he should be consistently encouraged to take on increasing responsibility for actively and cooperatively guiding his own life.

QUESTION: *But how can there be a science, or criteria for validity, if each individual client or research subject is the judge of what's true for him?*
RESPONSE: This book has dealt primarily with human services practices, and hence has stressed that to be effective the professional must deal with the perceptions and goals in accordance with which his client acts. However, this personal reality is not more real than the behavioral observations made from the external perspective of researchers and helpers. On the other hand, scientific knowledge, which is based on the regularities that are found across various populations, cannot guide practitioners unless it specifies how situated individual variations make up its generalized knowledge. Both personal and scientific truth are truths-from-a-perspective. Neither is absolute; each qualifies the other.

QUESTION: All of this is well and good in principle, but *doesn't the actual practice of informed client participation take too much time to be practical?*
RESPONSE: The client's engagement in the evaluation and decision processes can be said to take too much time only by "specialists" functioning as lab technicians in bureaucratically isolated way stations. True, as individual practitioners we often find ourselves assigned to a "way station," without official authority to concern ourselves with the whole client; then Promethean endeavors do require more time than our caseloads allow. In such instances, as professionals we are obliged to instigate reforms that will assure us that even where "lab work" is necessary, the client is assured that very shortly someone with the "big picture" will be discussing all its parts with him. Efficient office management has not attained its original goal if the client is not served to help himself.

From the administrative overview, it will be seen that total professional manhours per client are reduced through client collaboration. Specifically, overlap of professional assignments is diminished (for example, intake, referral, testing, case conference, and assignment to therapist are accomplished by fewer persons working more intensively with the client). Often the client himself takes on a greater share of the "treatment" responsibilities. And whether they be trying out life options, seeking information, or whatever, client supervision becomes less frequent and shorter. Recidivism is reduced when the client has been working in an informed manner toward his own goals. Finally, professionals work with greater zest and efficiency when their efforts are experienced as reasonable, concerned, and humane.

QUESTION: If test scores, technical jargon, diagnostic categories, and so on do become second class data in comparison to everyday language, *isn't there a danger that the human service professions might become antitheoretical?*
RESPONSE: American practitioners are already notoriously atheoretical. That is, we tend not to be aware or care that our language and practices, no matter what they are, always perpetuate particular philosophical assumptions. Hopefully, the effort to focus on actual events will help us to realize that theories should not be taken for granted, and above all that theories and constructs are not more real than observed events. Then we would no longer run into such recurring anomolies as the "B" student in vocational school being transferred into special education because the "IQ test says he is retarded." Nevertheless, there does indeed seem to be a danger that practitioners may increasingly adopt as their "theory" an only presumably nonassumptive "common sense." Our hope is that instead theories will be evolved that regard everyday events as their starting points and as their points of return, both for applied practices and for tests of their conceptions.

QUESTION: *How can I know the right way to begin?* I have not been trained in the practice of informed participation, and there is no accumulated tradition to fall back on. There are no established codes, no step-by-step guidelines.
RESPONSE: There are in fact exemplars whom we can consider as we set our own goals. They are the few auto mechanics, doctors, teachers, salesmen, whom we've all gratefully experienced as not only technically competent but also as frank, open, sensitive, and dedicated—capable of serving us as individuals as well as servicing our things. But the moment that we technologize ways of fulfilling

the Prometheus principle, then we have lost its spirit; frankness, openness, sensitivity, and dedication cannot successfully be technologized.

We have found that whenever a human service agent is quietly sincere in his desire to include his client in evaluation and decision making, once he tries himself out, he finds it surprisingly easy to follow his humane, common sense inclination. Continuing reflection on outcomes of sharing, accompanied by dialogue with colleagues, is an adequate safeguard for responsibility. In short, the right way to begin is to begin now!

Contributors

DONALD N. BERSOFF, Ph.D., is an assistant professor of law at the University of Maryland, School of Law and professor of psychology at Johns Hopkins University. He serves as an associate editor of the *Journal of School Psychology*, and as a member of the task force to revise the American Psychological Association's code of ethics. He is coauthor of *Learning to Teach*.

DOUGLAS BIKLEN, Ph.D., is coordinator for legal advocacy at the Center on Human Policy, Syracuse University. He has also taught courses in law and special education. He has published analyses of state institutional programs for "retarded" and "emotionally disturbed" children. He has published *Let Our Children Go: An Organizing Manual for Parents and Advocates*. Currently he is coediting a social textbook in special education, to be called *The Monolith and the Promise*.

STANLEY L. BRODSKY, Ph.D., is an associate professor of psychology at the University of Alabama. He also has served as chief psychologist of the United States Disciplinary Barracks at Fort Leavenworth, and has taught at Southern Illinois University in the Department of Psychology and the Center for the Study of Crime, Delinquency, and Corrections. He is coeditor of *The Military Prison: Theory, Research and Practice*, and author of *Psychologists in the Criminal Justice System*.

MARY R. CHISHOLM, Ph.D., is a professor of sociology at Duquesne University. She has published in the areas of group dynamics and communications. In addition to advising high school educators, she is an industrial consultant in learning dynamics to Neubert Associates.

CONSTANCE T. FISCHER, Ph.D., is an associate professor of psychology at Duquesne University. She has worked in VA neuropsychiatric facilities and is currently a consultant to Somerset State Hospital in Pennsylvania. Many of her publications deal with implementation of human-science psychology in the human services. She has coedited volume two of *Duquesne Studies in Phenomenological Psychology*, and is writing a textbook on human-science psychological assessment.

LEO GOLDMAN, Ph.D., is a professor at City University of New York, affiliated with the Guidance Laboratory. He served on the panel that produced the *Russell Sage Guidelines for the Collection, Maintenance and Dissemination of Pupil Records*. He was editor of the *Personnel and Guidance Journal* from 1969 to 1975 and is author of *Using Tests in Counseling*.

ERNEST KEEN, Ph.D., is a professor of psychology at Bucknell University. His clinical sites have included VA hospitals in Boston and Albany, the Capital District Psychiatric Center in Albany, and the Federal Penitentiary at Lewisburg. His books include *Three Faces of Being: Toward an Existential Clinical Psychology; Psychology and The New Consciousness*; and *A Primer in Phenomenological Psychology*.

LESLIE H. KRIEGER, Ph.D., is an associate professor in the Psychology Department of the University of North Florida. He has also taught at Point Park College, Duquesne University, and Rutgers University. Through his interests in industrial psychology, he has also been affiliated with Newark College of Engineering, Stevens Institute of Technology, and Psychological Consultants to Industry in Pittsburgh. He is a regular book reviewer for *Personnel Psychology*.

ROSEMARIE R. PARSE, Ph.D., R.N., is professor of nursing at Duquesne University School of Nursing. She serves as curriculum consultant to several schools of nursing, is a consultant on client-centered nursing practice with a general city hospital, and is on the Executive Committee of the Western Pennsylvania Regional Medical Program. She is author of *Nursing Fundamentals*.

ROBERT J. SARDELLO, Ph.D., is an associate professor and

chairman of the Department of Psychology at the University of Dallas, where he also directs the graduate psychology program in the Institute of Philosophic Studies. He has published human learning studies as well as articles on foundational issues in psychology, and on the psychology of imagination, death, and mythic-symbolic language.

ROLF VON ECKARTSBERG, Ph.D., is an associate professor of psychology at Duquesne University. He has served as codirector with Mary Chisholm of an experimental master's program in ecological sociology. He has published in the areas of methodology of experiential research, methods of cognitive mapping, experiential social psychology and the experience of technology. He is a past consulting editor of the *Journal of Phenomenological Psychology*, and is coeditor of *Duquesne Studies in Phenomenological Psychology*, volume one.

Index

243